The Last Caudillo

Viewpoints/Puntos de Vista
Themes and Interpretations in Latin American History

Series editor: Jürgen Buchenau

The books in this series will introduce students to the most significant themes and topics in Latin American history. They represent a novel approach to designing supplementary texts for this growing market. Intended as supplementary textbooks, the books will also discuss the ways in which historians have interpreted these themes and topics, thus demonstrating to students that our understanding of our past is constantly changing, through the emergence of new sources, methodologies, and historical theories. Unlike monographs, the books in this series will be broad in scope and written in a style accessible to undergraduates.

Published

A History of the Cuban Revolution
Aviva Chomsky

Bartolomé de las Casas and the Conquest of the Americas
Lawrence A. Clayton

Beyond Borders: A History of Mexican Migration to the United States
Timothy J. Henderson

The Last Caudillo: Alvaro Obregón and the Mexican Revolution
Jürgen Buchenau

In preparation

Creoles vs. Peninsulars in Colonial Spanish America
Mark Burkholder

Dictatorship in South America
Jerry Davila

Mexico Since 1940: The Unscripted Revolution
Stephen E. Lewis

The Haitian Revolution, 1791–1804
Jeremy Popkin

The Last Caudillo

Alvaro Obregón
and the Mexican Revolution

Jürgen Buchenau

WILEY-BLACKWELL

A John Wiley & Sons, Ltd., Publication

This edition first published 2011
© 2011 Jürgen Buchenau

Blackwell Publishing was acquired by John Wiley & Sons in February 2007. Blackwell's publishing program has been merged with Wiley's global Scientific, Technical, and Medical business to form Wiley-Blackwell.

Registered Office
John Wiley & Sons Ltd, The Atrium, Southern Gate, Chichester, West Sussex, PO19 8SQ, United Kingdom

Editorial Offices
350 Main Street, Malden, MA 02148-5020, USA
9600 Garsington Road, Oxford, OX4 2DQ, UK
The Atrium, Southern Gate, Chichester, West Sussex, PO19 8SQ, UK

For details of our global editorial offices, for customer services, and for information about how to apply for permission to reuse the copyright material in this book please see our website at www.wiley.com/wiley-blackwell.

The right of Jürgen Buchenau to be identified as the author of this work has been asserted in accordance with the UK Copyright, Designs and Patents Act 1988.

Library of Congress Cataloging-in-Publication Data is available for this title
ISBN 9781405199025 (hardback)
ISBN 9781405199032 (paperback)

A catalogue record for this book is available from the British Library.

This book is published in the following electronic formats:
ePDFs [ISBN 9781444397178]; Wiley Online Library [ISBN 9781444397192];
ePub [ISBN 9781444397185]

Set in 10/12.5 pt Minion by Toppan Best-set Premedia Limited
Printed in Malaysia by Ho Printing (M) Sdn Bhd

1 2011

To my mother, Sabine Prange

Rosamaria Toffetti

Table of Contents

List of Illustrations

Maps

Figures

Preface

Each book in the "Viewpoints/Puntos de Vista" series introduces students to a significant theme or topic in Latin American history. In an age in which student and faculty interest in the Global South increasingly challenges the old focus on the history of Europe and North America, Latin American history has assumed an increasingly prominent position in undergraduate curricula.

Some of these books discuss the ways in which historians have interpreted these themes and topics, thus demonstrating that our understanding of our past is constantly changing, through the emergence of new sources, methodologies, and historical theories. Others offer an introduction to a particular theme by means of a case study or biography in a manner easily understood by the contemporary, non-specialist reader. Yet others give an overview of a major theme that might serve as the foundation of an upper-level course.

What is common to all of these books is their goal of historical synthesis. They draw on the insights of generations of scholarship on the most enduring and fascinating issues in Latin American history, while also making use of primary sources as appropriate. Each book is written by a specialist in Latin American history who is concerned with undergraduate teaching, yet has also made his or her mark as a first-rate scholar.

The books in this series can be used in a variety of ways, recognizing the differences in teaching conditions at small liberal arts colleges, large public universities, and research-oriented institutions with doctoral programs. Faculty have particular needs depending on whether they teach large lectures with discussion sections, small lecture or discussion-oriented classes, or large lectures with no discussion sections, and whether they teach on a semester or trimester system. The format adopted for this series fits all of these different parameters.

In this fourth volume in the "Viewpoints/Puntos de Vista" series, I analyze the Mexican Revolution (1910–1940) through the lens of one of its protagonists: General Alvaro Obregón Salido, one of the greatest military leaders in the history of Latin America. The Mexican Revolution is of global historical significance because it was the first great revolution with an agrarian and social basis, and its successes and failures helped inform more radical social revolutions in Russia, China, and Cuba.

Obregón was the "undefeated caudillo of the Mexican Revolution" whose military genius and political acumen always put him on the winning side. His alliance of middle-class landowners from the northern border state of Sonora directed the destinies of Mexico between 1920 and 1935, a period that featured the formation of many of the institutions and political practices of modern Mexico. The life of Obregón therefore offers an ideal vantage point from which to appreciate the causes, process, and outcome of the Mexican Revolution. It also affords an opportunity to study political leadership, authoritarianism, and political culture in Latin America more generally.

Jürgen Buchenau
University of North Carolina, Charlotte

Acknowledgments

The idea for this book was born in 1998 during a Latin American Studies Association meeting at a bar at the Chicago Hilton, when Colin MacLachlan suggested that I write a biography of Obregón. At the time, I resisted the idea, as I knew and admired Linda Hall's *Alvaro Obregón: Power and Revolution in Mexico, 1911–1920*, the only extant English-language biography of Obregón and a meticulously researched work focusing on his role in the violent phase of the revolution in the 1910s. Instead, I wrote a life and times of Obregón's most significant political ally, Plutarco Elías Calles, a leader among the primary architects of the country's modern political institutions. But Colin's suggestion never completely left my mind, and my examination of Calles raised fresh questions about the nature of leadership in the revolution and Obregón's role, specifically. Almost twelve years later, at the centennial of the revolution, I have finally written the book that Colin suggested, as part of a larger research agenda on the Sonoran Dynasty in Mexico.

I appreciate the assistance of the National Endowment for the Humanities, which provided a year-long fellowship that gave me the time to write this book. Financial support from UNC Charlotte, and particularly a Faculty Research Grant and an award from the Small Grants Program of the College of Liberal Arts and Sciences, allowed me to undertake the necessary research. I appreciate the permission of the University of New Mexico Press to republish, in shortened and revised form, my book chapter "The Arm and Body of a Revolution: Remembering

Mexico's Last Caudillo, Alvaro Obregón," from Lyman Johnson, ed., *Death, Dismemberment, and Memory: Body Politics in Latin America* (2004).

I could not have written this book without the assistance of the superbly competent staff at the Fideicomiso Archivos Plutarco Elías Calles y Fernando Torreblanca, probably the finest private archive in all of Mexico. In addition, I appreciate the help of my research assistant, Xenia Wirth. Xenia spent six weeks in Mexico City working through thousands of files in the Fideicomiso, and the research for the manuscript would have taken much longer to complete without her help.

At Wiley-Blackwell, I particularly thank my editor, Peter Coveney, for supporting both the general idea for the Viewpoints/Puntos de Vista series and, specifically, the idea for a book that examines the Mexican Revolution through the lens of studying a single individual. Galen Smith was instrumental in keeping me on track and in guiding the manuscript through the production process. At UNC Charlotte, my fellow Latin Americanist historians Lyman Johnson, Jerry Dávila, and Tom Rogers contributed valuable suggestions. Among my professional colleagues at other institutions, Greg Crider, Bill Beezley, Daniela Spenser, Doug Richmond, Tim Henderson, and Linda Hall helped me sharpen and focus my ideas regarding Obregón's career.

Finally, a word of thanks to my family: Anabel, Nicolas, and Julia. Writing this book was a time consuming exercise, which was even more taxing on all of them at a time when I also assumed administrative responsibilities at my university. I know that they are as glad that this book is completed as I am.

Introduction

> He who fights with monsters should look to it that he himself does not
> become a monster. And when you gaze long into an abyss, the abyss also
> gazes into you.
>
> Friedrich Nietzsche, *Beyond Good and Evil* (p. 102)

On November 16, 1989, descendants of General Alvaro Obregón
Salido gathered to cremate his arm. He had lost the limb on June
3, 1915 during a battle that pitted his troops against the legendary
"División del Norte" (Division of the North) commanded by General
Pancho Villa. While Obregón lost his arm, Villa lost the decisive battle
of the Mexican Revolution. The arm was all that was left of the general,
assassinated in 1928 and buried in his hometown of Huatabampo in the
northwestern state of Sonora. Preserved in a formaldehyde solution,
since 1943, it had been displayed in a jar in the Mexico City monument
to Obregón. Located at the exact spot of the assassination, the monument was an impressive testimonial, even featuring the holes in the floor
left by the assassin's bullets. Its role was to remind Mexicans of the sacrifice that the leaders of their revolution had made for their nation—a
message useful to a ruling party that claimed its legitimacy from the
revolution itself: the Partido Revolucionario Institucional (PRI, or
Institutional Revolutionary Party). At the time of the cremation, which

The Last Caudillo: Alvaro Obregón and the Mexican Revolution. Jürgen Buchenau
© 2011 Jürgen Buchenau

occurred exactly one week after the fall of the Berlin Wall, the PRI and its predecessors had ruled Mexico for sixty years. By 1989, the PRI's leadership had given up on most of the goals that identified "the revolution" in the eyes of the public: democracy, national sovereignty, and social justice. The arm eerily resembled this ruling party in that the decades had taken their toll. A ghastly white color, it had swollen to the point that the fingers had acquired the shape of tomatoes. Frayed tendons issued from its severed end. The limb had run its course, both physically and symbolically.

The fact that a severed arm had been on display for so long was a testament to its owner's great stature in history as the "undefeated caudillo of the Mexican Revolution".[1] A farmer who had worked hard to achieve a modest prosperity, Obregón did not participate in the first phase of the revolution, which began on November 20, 1910 as a movement to overthrow dictator Porfirio Díaz. Under Díaz's long tenure (1876–1880 and 1884–1911), a small clique had dominated politics in a primarily rural nation. Large haciendas and foreign-owned mining corporations controlled most of the land and mineral resources. In the spring of 1912, after the triumph of that movement had installed democratic rule, Obregón joined the fighting as the head of an impromptu military force to help defend his state from rebels trying to overthrow the newly elected government. Victorious, he returned to the battlefield in March 1913 following the coup d'état of General Victoriano Huerta, and his army made decisive contributions to Huerta's defeat in July 1914. The war against Huerta mobilized hundreds of thousands of *campesinos* (poor rural dwellers) and workers. Success in this conflict required leaders like Obregón to broaden their aims to include reforms that would benefit campesinos, workers, and an increasingly beleaguered middle class. Relying on different regional and social bases in a far-flung and diverse nation, the winners could not agree on common goals beyond the removal of two dictators, and they turned to fighting among themselves in an all-out war. In this conflict, Obregón combined an appeal to campesinos and workers with a commitment to reestablish political legitimacy. After his army had defeated Villa's División del Norte, Obregón emerged as the nation's preeminent political figure. In 1920, he became president and embarked upon a rebuilding program based on the new, revolutionary Constitution, which promised democracy,

Mexican ownership of resources, land for campesinos, a wholly secular society, and improved working conditions.

Once in power, however, Obregón disappointed those who had hoped for fundamental social reform along the lines of this constitution, and he ended up resorting to some of the same authoritarian tactics that he had opposed during the decade of fighting. He became a representative of personalist leadership—a style of rule in which a strongman becomes the arbiter of social and political conflict. In 1924, he imposed a fellow Sonoran, General Plutarco Elías Calles, as his successor, despite a civil war that turned much of the military against him. Obregón continued to wield considerable influence during Calles's presidency and asserted that influence to assure his return to power. His allies in Congress pushed through a constitutional amendment to allow him to run for a second term in the 1928 elections, and in the fall of 1927, the government executed both of his major rivals. Ironically, two weeks after his election, the bullets of an assassin cut short Obregón's own life on July 17, 1928, at the age of forty-eight.

Obregón's career elicited comparisons to Napoleon Bonaparte, who had emerged from the French Revolution by surviving each of its twists and turns. Napoleon became the most successful general of modern Europe, and his empire controlled most of the continent at the height of his power in 1812. Not by coincidence, Obregón's supporters called their leader the "Napoleon of the West."[2] His detractors, on the other hand, pointed out the parallels between Napoleon's violent seizure of power and Obregón's ambition and cruelty, especially with regard to his effort to dominate the political scene in the 1920s.[3]

As the comparisons to Napoleon demonstrate, Mexicans have held ambivalent views about Obregón ever since his time in power. Through a school curriculum that features both towering heroes and evil villains, Mexican children know Obregón as a hero. But he does not figure among the seven greatest popular idols. That list contains Aztec Emperor Cuauhtémoc, independence heroes Miguel Hidalgo and José María Morelos, Benito Juárez (the only indigenous Mexican to ever occupy the presidency), three important revolutionary leaders—Madero, Emiliano Zapata, and Villa—and twentieth-century president Lázaro Cárdenas. Except Juárez and Cárdenas, those leaders died violent deaths before they could accomplish their goals. Nor can Obregón be found among the "black sheep" of Mexican historiography, which include, among others, Spanish conquistador Hernán Cortés, Austrian-born Emperor Maximilian, and dictator Díaz, whose long rule from 1876 to 1911 precipitated the revolution. Instead, Obregón inhabits an ambiguous space in the historical memory of a nation that continues to struggle with poverty, violence, and social inequality at the centennial of its revolution. To most historians, the man who emerged triumphant deserves credit for many of the accomplishments of the revolution, but also part of the blame for its shortcomings.[4]

As this biography will demonstrate, this ambivalence reflects Obregón's progression from young revolutionary to repressive strongman. Helped by his military genius, prodigious memory, and ability to relate to ordinary people, Obregón rose to power as a unifying force and, at least by rhetoric, a champion of social reform. Once installed in the presidency, however—and even more so in his effort to return to power despite constitutional provisions barring the reelection of presidents following Díaz's long rule—he abused his power. Over time, his strong-arm tactics came to destabilize the political system that he had helped create. Meanwhile, many of his erstwhile supporters from among the agrarian and workers' movements became representatives in Congress, cabinet secretaries, and members of the bourgeoisie.

Because Obregón therefore symbolized the promise of the revolution to his supporters, the "longevity" of his arm illustrated the performative aspects of the efforts of the Mexican state to capitalize on his personality cult. The notion of performativity originated with the 1940s work of the British linguistic philosopher John L. Austin. Austin posited that messages were not always true or false; rather, they could contain an emotion or intention such as a promise or a prohibition. For example, when a groom says "I do" to his bride, he states his intention to marry her and, in so doing, enters into matrimony. Transferring this idea to social science, the gender theory philosopher Judith Butler defined performative messages as the "reiterative power of discourse to produce the phenomena that it regulates and constrains."[5] A performative message can therefore define reality rather than describe it. In this case, the public display of the arm represented a form of political speech that highlighted the Mexican state's devotion to one of its heroes and held up his sacrifice as a model for citizens to follow. In the narrative of the monument,

Obregón's arm represented both the revolution and the nation for which the leader had sacrificed it in battle. Like a Catholic relic, the arm established a link to a past constructed as heroic. The fact that the monument stood at the precise location of Obregón's assassination further impressed upon visitors the drama associated with the general's dual sacrifice. In the official rhetoric of a government that derived its legitimacy from the revolution, the severed limb served as a fetishistic embodiment of national sovereignty.[6]

Other examples from history reveal the same dynamic; for instance, the arm of General Thomas "Stonewall" Jackson, along with Robert E. Lee one of the two preeminent military leaders of the Confederate States of America during the US Civil War (1861–1865). Each year, thousands of Civil War aficionados travel to Orange County, Virginia, to visit the burial site of Jackson's left arm, lost to friendly fire on May 2, 1863 during the Battle of Chancellorsville. Eight days later, Jackson died from the complications of pneumonia, which set in following the loss of the arm. Just like Obregón's arm, Jackson's was buried separately from the body. Adorned by a simple marker, the arm reposes near the battle site. The body lies in an impressive grave site at Stonewall Jackson Memorial Cemetery 124 miles west in Lexington. And just like Obregón's arm symbolized victory in the Mexican Revolution to those who visited the monument, Jackson's arm represented the struggle and defeat of the Confederacy. As today's supporters of the Confederacy see it, Jackson's injury and death doomed the Southern cause. Lee certainly understood the symbolic significance of his friend's dismemberment and death. Upon hearing of Jackson's impending death, he penned a note of farewell, pointing out that "you have lost your left arm but I my right."[7] Thus, a severed limb of someone famous reveals insights about the culture of leadership.

This biography of Obregón examines the culture of leadership more generally. Obregón's political abilities characterized "charismatic leadership" as defined by German sociologist Max Weber in the 1920s: "a certain quality of an individual personality, by virtue of which one is … treated as endowed with supernatural, superhuman, or at least specifically exceptional powers or qualities. These as such are not accessible to the ordinary person, but are regarded as divine in origin or as exemplary, and on the basis of them the individual concerned is treated as a leader."[8] Complementing this definition with regard to prophets as representatives of religious authority, French sociologist Pierre Bourdieu has pointed out that charisma must be understood in relational and socially grounded terms. In other words, charismatic leaders embody exemplary conduct as measured against the traditions and customs of their context, including the social inequalities that characterize that context. In order to displace social conflict, they deliver symbolic capital for the consumption of their followers. Unlike real capital, symbolic capital cannot be used to feed the hungry or provide shelter for the homeless.[9] Rather, symbolic capital can hold a palliative effect, no matter whether it pertains to religion (Karl Marx's "opium of the masses"), nationalism, or personal devotion to a leader. As the discussion of the discourse of the arm's "sacrifice" has shown, Bourdieu's concepts work well with regard to Obregón's charismatic leadership.

Obregón's life and career offer insights into a particular type of charismatic leader: the "caudillo." Historian John Chasteen has characterized a caudillo as someone "capable of inspiring intense devotion among a loyal personal following independent of any formal institution, leaders who became generals *after* acquiring an army of followers rather than the other way around."[10] Crucial elements in caudillo rule include a macho personality cult; heroism in war; and a large number of followers who felt intense personal loyalty to the caudillo. Leading impromptu armies, caudillos filled the void left by the collapse of the Spanish colonial government during the Wars of Independence, and they dominated many of the newly emergent nations until the 1850s.[11] After that decade, in most of Latin America, modernization erased the conditions that had allowed the rise of caudillos. By the 1890s, the caudillos on horseback were "no longer a match for government armies, now equipped with Mauser rifles and Krupp artillery, coordinated by telegraph and transported by rail …"[12] This infrastructure extended the reach of the central government. Imbued with greater power, the leadership of Latin American nations became institutional rather than personal, creating bureaucracies that administered stronger state apparatuses.

In Mexico, however, modernization under Porfirio Díaz did not bring about the definitive eclipse of the caudillo. Due to its rugged geography and vast regional diversity, the nation experienced political centralization later than other major Spanish American countries. Díaz himself came to power as a caudillo, and his imprint on the era in which he ruled led to its popular label as the "Porfiriato." His government could not break the sway of many powerful regional clans, let alone control the countryside. The waves of violence that swept Mexico beginning in 1910 destroyed the central state and the army that had enforced stability under the Díaz regime, re-creating some of the conditions that had permitted the rise of caudillos a century before. However, this twentieth-century upheaval also produced movements and leaders who desired to redeem the aspirations of campesinos and workers: for example, Emiliano Zapata and Pancho Villa. Zapata fought for the return of campesino land appropriated by large agricultural estates in the areas south and east of Mexico City. Cowardly assassinated by his political enemies in 1919, Zapata enjoyed a long posthumous career, focused on his iconic image among the dispossessed; for example, the 1994 campesino uprising in the southern state of Chiapas titled itself the Zapatista Front of National Liberation. He emerged as the primary popular hero of the revolution, representing the struggle of the poor for a better life.[13] Likewise, Villa led an army of *rancheros*, day-laborers, and sharecroppers from northern Mexico. Many of the Villistas fought to resist the encroachment of modernization on their land, their lifestyle, and their autonomy. Had Villa's troops won, rather than lost, the war between the factions in the revolution, he might well have emerged as a caudillo in his own right. In 1923, Villa, too, fell victim to assassination.[14]

Separated from nineteenth-century caudillos by seven decades, Obregón therefore fundamentally differed from his predecessors. His leadership style blended that of the traditional caudillo with the ability to relate to modern popular movements. Unlike the old-style caudillos, many of whom paid homage to traditional Catholicism and oppressed those who did not, Obregón was not a believer, considering religion a private rather than a public matter. Nor, however, did he share the rabid anticlericalism of Calles and some of his other Sonoran associates. As he believed, quite correctly, efforts to destroy the Church in deeply Catholic Mexico would be futile and undermine attempts to centralize political authority.[15]

Nonetheless, the caudillo label aptly describes Obregón's position in 1920s Mexico. His contemporaries used the term, uniquely, to refer to this leader, and especially when he was preparing to return to the presidency. By the time of his death, "*el caudillo*" had become synonymous with Obregón.[16] If not for his murder, he would likely have remained his nation's preeminent political personality for many years, and his death hence marked a watershed moment. On September 1, 1928—only six weeks after the caudillo's death—Calles announced during his final presidential address that his country had entered the transition from a "country of one man" to a "nation of institutions and laws."[17] And indeed, even as Calles himself would come to play a powerful behind-the-scenes role, no one else commanded as many loyalties as the dead caudillo; and no one else came close to matching Obregón's military resumé. Fittingly, Calles—though a general himself—would be known as *el jefe máximo*, or Supreme Chief, and not as *el caudillo*.

Because of its association with military leadership, caudillo rule also entails an important economic component, and especially in the Mexican case, where caudillismo endured until the twentieth century. According to Marxist historians such as Ramón Eduardo Ruiz, military leaders in the revolution served as the handmaidens of foreign corporations, who desired to protect their lands, mines, and other significant economic interests. However, as U.S. economist Mancur Olson has demonstrated with reference to a different historical context, military leaders, or "roving bandits," took advantage of political chaos by creating property and property rights for themselves until they gained enough power that they became "stationary bandits." Once entrenched in power as "stationary bandits," these leaders defended existing property rights in order to foster political stability at the national level. This is not to say that military leaders did not protect U.S. and European economic interests in the revolution—indeed, many of them did. Instead, this study emphasizes their own ambitions for a new economic order in which they replaced a large part of the property-owning class of the Old Regime.[18]

As political and economic ambitions became intertwined, Obregón maneuvered a patron-client system of rewards doled out to his followers in return for their support in his quest for political power. Patron-client systems exist in virtually all political systems. In modern democracies, corporations and influential individuals fund the campaigns of political candidates in order to receive favorable treatment in return. In authoritarian societies, clients curry favor with representatives of the regime at the national, regional, or local levels. In the Díaz regime, *camarillas*, or personal networks, played a crucial role; and such camarillas returned after the revolution.[19] A highly fluid version of a patron-client system structures political and military relations in war-torn areas in which the central government exerts little or no effective control, such as Mexico in the 1910s. This version features rapidly shifting alliances to balance the highly contingent personal interests of the participants. Obregón's expert management of these patron-client relationships—as well as his ability to collaborate with the emergent agrarian and worker's movements—played a major role in his political survival and success.

This book follows the biographical method of studying history by means of examining an individual life in chronological order. In line with the "great man" approach to history, biography traditionally celebrates individual achievement among the rich and famous. It is one of the oldest forms of written history. Traditional historical biographies look outward to examine a leader's impact: consider, for example, the numerous studies of the lives of European royalty, US presidents, or infamous dictators. Such a form of biography is a great exercise in storytelling, but it overly celebrates powerful individuals, and usually men. As the German author Bertolt Brecht sarcastically asked in reference to historical writing centered on great men: "Young Alexander conquered India. He alone? Julius Caesar defeated the Gauls. Did he not even have a cook with him?"[20] In the last sixty years, anthropologists and historians have crafted another form of biography: the micro-study of an ordinary individual or of ordinary families. For example, Oscar Lewis's 1964 biography of a campesino sought to understand what the author called the "culture of poverty."[21] Similarly, *Translated Woman*, the autobiography of a Mexican street peddler, follows a biographical method in narrating the life of its protagonist.[22]

This biography differs from these precedents in important ways. Rather than delivering a fully-fledged account of Obregón's life and times, it focuses on its larger meaning for the turbulent history of Mexico between the late nineteenth century and the Great Depression. Conscious of the shortcomings of the "great man" approach, it examines one person in the context of his time more so than as a shaper of national destinies. Among many other sources, the book relies on the holdings of the Fideicomiso Archivos Plutarco Elías Calles y Fernando Torreblanca in Mexico City, which houses the papers of several members of Obregón's group that came to dominate Mexican politics between 1920 and 1935.

This is the second book in a series of works that endeavor to understand that group.[23]

This book tells the life and times of Obregón in seven chapters. As context, Chapter 1 discusses personalist leadership in nineteenth-century Mexico as well as Obregón's Sonoran background. Chapter 2 examines Obregón's early career as a farmer and small-town political leader during the Porfiriato, as well as his belated involvement in the revolution. Chapter 3 traces his emergence as the nation's most powerful military leader. Chapter 4 evaluates his influence in the shaping of the 1917 constitution, his role in the economic development of southern Sonora and northern Sinaloa, and his rise to power in 1920. Chapter 5 analyzes Obregón's presidency, a period of rebuilding a state from the ashes of a decade of violence, but also an era when the protagonist increasingly showed his ruthless and unforgiving side. Chapter 6 covers the years 1924-1928, when Obregón attained caudillo status and played an increasingly important role during the Calles presidency. Finally, chapter 7 brings the story full circle by returning to the legacy and posthumous significance of Obregón, as represented in the political spectacle of the Monumento Obregón, and particularly the famous limb that it displayed for so many years

1

The Background
of the Last Caudillo

Mexico is not a republic, but a military Díazpotism.

Charles Flandrau (1908)

Obregón's career developed in two different contexts, and both of these contexts are important in understanding his role in the Mexican Revolution. In the first place, Obregón grew up in a somewhat contradictory political context—a system marked by both authoritarian political practices and the inability of governments at the national and state levels to enforce their decisions on a recalcitrant and diverse population. Second, his upbringing in distant Sonora, an arid state that borders the United States, instilled in him the political culture of the northwest. This culture and society differed in crucial ways from those of central and southern Mexico.

Since the beginning of recorded time, the area we know today as "Mexico" has featured struggles between strong central rulers and regional chieftains with considerable autonomy. The rugged, mountainous terrain has always made political centralization difficult. Such was the case in the Mexica Empire under Emperor Moctezuma; and likewise, the authoritarian methods of the Spanish Crown, in what it called the Viceroyalty of New Spain, faced stiff local resistance. The political system of the viceroyalty imposed centralizing features that would survive all the way to Obregón's era: a top-down pattern in all levels of governance;

The Last Caudillo: Alvaro Obregón and the Mexican Revolution. Jürgen Buchenau
© 2011 Jürgen Buchenau

no clear separation of powers; and the appointment rather than democratic election of many regional and local leaders. The king appointed a Spanish-born viceroy to rule in his stead, held in check by a group, the *audiencia*, with executive, legislative, and judicial powers. At the regional and local levels, the viceroy named *corregidores* (regents) although larger towns featured elected *cabildos* (town councils). After the Bourbon Reforms of the late 1700s, the king also sent intendants as a means of enforcing his power. In practice, strong regional loyalties and chiefs remained throughout the colonial period, and subalterns often did not carry out the orders coming from their superiors. Throughout the colonial period, the Spanish authorities struggled to subdue local and regional rebellions, and they never controlled the vast northwestern frontier—including present-day Sonora—much at all.[1]

By the Wars of Independence (1810–1821), France's Napoleon Bonaparte provided a new blueprint for central rule not only for Europe, but also for Latin America. Napoleon's armies overran a checkerboard of local sovereignties in central Europe by means of a brilliant military strategy and a dedicated volunteer army devoted to service of the French nation. Not surprisingly, contemporary artists represented the Venezuelan Simón Bolívar, the Argentine José de San Martín, and the Mexican Agustín de Iturbide as citizens-emperors, scions of Napoleon. In many ways, these liberators constituted the first wave of caudillos in Latin America: self-anointed military heroes who commanded by virtue of their network of clients.[2]

Of these leaders, Iturbide established the most direct bridge to Napoleon by means of his coronation as Agustín I, Constitutional Emperor of Mexico, on July 21, 1822. Unlike the other Spanish American independence leaders, who established republican forms of government, Iturbide became a monarch, just like Napoleon. However, this monarchy was short-lived. Iturbide's empire was vast, stretching from California east to the Louisiana border and south to Costa Rica. Moreover, Iturbide's sudden exaltation went to his head. He ennobled members of his immediate family and ordered their birthdays to be celebrated as national holidays. Petitioners who wished to see him needed to kneel before him and kiss his hand. Thus, an uprising ousted Iturbide in March 1823. After a year in exile, he returned home, only to be arrested and executed by firing squad just two years after his proclamation as emperor.[3]

From Santa Anna to Díaz

Iturbide's brief reign highlighted several important characteristics that would endure until Obregón's days. Most importantly, his dissolution of parliament indicated the supremacy of the executive branch over the legislative one, as well as the arbitrary use of power. Iturbide's self-aggrandizement pointed the way to the forging of personality cults that would prove a crucial aspect of authoritarian political rule. Finally, his fall at the hands of his former lieutenants set a pattern for violent changes of government. Until 1920, the year of Obregón's election, most presidents would come to power via a coup d'état. Two leaders in particular—Antonio López de Santa Anna and Porfirio Díaz—left important legacies for Obregón's career.

Santa Anna belonged to a new generation that came to power in the chaotic decades following the wars of independence. Historian John Lynch calls this group "primitive caudillos:" leaders who ruled over unstable nations with stagnating economies by personal fiat.[4] This generation also comprised other classical cases of caudillo rule such as Argentina's Juan Manuel de Rosas and Venezuela's José Antonio Páez. These leaders had entered the wars as rank-and-file but worked themselves up to important positions by the time the conflicts ended. Hence, they were next in line when the original independence heroes fell from grace. Rosas helped spread the purview of the independence movement beyond the capital region of Buenos Aires by organizing a regiment of the famed cowboys, the *gauchos*. As a champion of the gauchos, he remained the dominant figure of the region until his fall in 1853. Páez joined Bolívar's 1810 insurrection at the age of twenty. He commanded the pro-independence army in Venezuela while Bolívar was helping spearhead the liberation of Peru; and in 1830, he declared Venezuela's independence from Gran Colombia. Páez and Rosas represented themselves as the embodiment of their nations, yet they depended on personal alliances with hacienda owners, the military, the high clergy, and indigenous leaders. Their power remained limited by the absence of political stability, the persistence of local and regional challenges to central authority, and the existence of a minimal national government without the means to make its authority respected.[5]

Mexico's quintessential caudillo, Santa Anna was born in Jalapa, Veracruz, in 1794 into a middle-class creole family. He was a master at sensing the shifting of political winds. After entering the army at the age of sixteen, he served with the Crown's forces until 1821, distinguishing himself by his ruthless persecution of the pro-independence guerrilla. When he sensed that the tide had turned in favor of independence, he proclaimed his adherence to Iturbide's Plan of Iguala. As opposition against Iturbide mounted, Santa Anna declared the "Plan de Casa Mata," the successful call for the emperor's overthrow. Thereafter, he became the most important military figure of the early republic, and the master of an extensive patron-client network centered on his home base in Veracruz. He took center stage in the most important military confrontations of the first thirty years of independent Mexico, which featured wars with Spain, France, and the United States and the formation of two rival political blocs: the Centralists and the Federalists. Sometimes, he helped the nation pull together; at other times, his ambitions constituted a singularly disruptive force. In 1829, he led a successful campaign against Spain's attempt to reconquer its former colony. In 1832, he helped the Federalists to power, and he served a brief first stint as president from May 16 to June 3, 1833. Within a few months, Santa Anna regretted his alliance and helped the Centralists regain power under his second presidency. However, he enjoyed his role as a savior who rode in on his horse whenever the nation appeared in need, more so than he relished the authority vested in the presidential chair. In 1836, another such opportunity came when Santa Anna led Mexican troops to fight the effort of Texas settlers to obtain their independence from Mexico. However, the following year, the Texans dealt him a devastating defeat at San Jacinto.[6]

Soon thereafter, Santa Anna bounced back, thanks in part to a lost limb that became a political spectacle just as Obregón's would a century later. In 1838, a French fleet blockaded the port of Veracruz in order to exact payment of claims held by French citizens. On November 27, at his hacienda near the city, Santa Anna heard the distant rumblings of cannon that accompanied the French attack on the fortress of San Juan de Ulúa. He mounted his white horse to meet the invaders. As the Mexican armies forced the French to return to their ships, a cannonball severed his left leg below the knee. The mutilated caudillo again became a national hero, and he sought to exploit his sacrifice. On September 27, 1842, he gave his leg a state burial, complete with an urn, a mausoleum, and a twelve-gun salute.[7]

However, such a spectacle could not instill lasting allegiance to a caudillo. Upon a successful coup d'état against Santa Anna in 1844, the victorious rebels removed the leg from its mausoleum and waved it around during their procession. In Santa Anna's own words: "A member of my body, lost in the service to my country, dragged from the funeral urn, broken into bits to be made sport of in such a barbaric manner. ... In that moment of grief and frenzy, I decided to leave my native country ... for all time."[8] Of course, within a short time, the caudillo returned despite this nefarious mistreatment of his leg. He weaved in and out of power throughout the next nine years, which included defeat in the US-Mexican War (1846–1848). The traumatic defeat formalized the US annexation of Texas and the transfer of a total of one-half of the Mexican territory to the United States. Santa Anna played an unsavory role in the Gadsden Purchase of 1853, which transferred southern Sonora to the United States. According to some sources, 600,000 dollars ended up in his own pocket.[9] This transaction earned him the moniker of *vendepatria*, or seller of the fatherland. Not surprisingly, official Mexican historical memory has treated Santa Anna as a villain.

It was no coincidence that another caudillo, Juan N. Alvarez, spearheaded the rebellion that finally toppled Santa Anna for good. Just as Santa Anna took advantage of his regional base on the Gulf Coast, so Alvarez enjoyed a privileged position as the commander of the Pacific port of Acapulco. By the time his supporters pronounced the Plan of Ayutla on March 1, 1854, Alvarez had dominated southern Mexico for more than three decades. The program called for Santa Anna's removal due to his corruption, referencing in particular the dastardly act of selling off a part of the nation. The new caudillo found the presidency unappealing and returned to his hacienda after a few months in office. Alvarez's parting words would later find a prominent imitator in Obregón, both in their emphasis on his humble origins and in their denigration of political office: "I entered the presidency as a poor man, and I leave it as a poor man, with the satisfaction that I do not have to bear the censure of the public because I was dedicated from an early age to personal labor, to work the plow to support my family, without the need for public offices where others enrich themselves by outrages to those in misery."[10]

Alvarez's brief tenure paved the way for the ascendancy of the Liberal party and its most famous exponent, Benito Juárez, an attorney of Zapotec origins from the southern state of Oaxaca. Led by Juárez, the Liberals opposed caudillo politics and favored the installation of a genuine representative democracy. They also called for an end to all privileges enjoyed by the Catholic Church, the aristocracy, and the army, groups that enjoyed the protection of special courts. They viewed the Church, especially, as an obstacle to progress and advocated lay education, civil marriages, and the expropriation of its wealth, which included more than half of the nation's arable land. The Liberals wished to turn Mexico into a nation of yeoman farmers who produced enough food to export it to the burgeoning populations of western Europe. In 1857, Juárez became president, and the Liberals codified these ideas in a constitution that remained the law of the land until 1917.[11]

Juárez's government could not establish effective control, however, before encountering stiff resistance from the Church and the Conservative Party. The Conservatives used the Liberal campaign against the Church as a rallying cry that resonated particularly with deeply religious indigenous communities. They could also count on the support of ranchers and hacendados who stood to lose by a reorganization of agricultural land. And, of course, they knew that they could depend on the allegiance of many of the Santannista strongmen, as well as other local leaders dissatisfied with the central government. In 1858, the Conservatives ousted Juárez. The Liberals triumphed following three years of war, only to be driven from power again in 1862 by French invasion forces sent by Emperor Napoleon III. The emperor harbored the dream of establishing a Caribbean dominion. In 1864, he installed the Habsburg prince Maximilian on the throne of a restored Mexican empire.

Maximilian's style of leadership differed from that of a caudillo as much as anyone could imagine. The Austrian fashioned himself as a kind-hearted conciliator who could heal old divisions and solve Mexico's problems in a few short years. He surrounded himself with a circle of educated advisors, the so-called *imperialistas*, to aid him in the formulation of policy.[12] The emperor attempted to endear himself to the Liberals by refusing to roll back the Reform Laws; unfortunately, that step alienated the Conservatives without winning him any Liberal friends. Similarly, he made history by decreeing the end of debt peonage, only to find out that he had added the landowners to his already considerable list of enemies. Therefore, the goal of reconciliation eluded an emperor who served as a pawn of Napoleon's ambitions, and who owed his throne to French arms. Worse yet, the blond, blue-eyed Austrian aristocrat who had grown up in the palaces of Europe remained an utter outsider. Finally, Maximilian held deeply romantic visions of indigenous Mexicans. In his view, he alone was destined to save that population from ruin and exploitation. Consider the following quote of a French military officer: "When ... the burden of his job seemed too heavy, His Majesty would go on a little trip. Amidst the ovations of the poor, morose Indians, he found relief and pleasure, as he considered himself adored by his subjects."[13] Maximilian's failures gave the Liberals a chance to reinvent themselves as patriots, and they went on the offensive. Faced with this threat, the emperor panicked and swore the Liberals a war to the death. As the Liberals waged a guerrilla campaign, a fateful decree promised death to all rebel officers captured by the government.

Not surprisingly, the decree angered the Liberals, who first chased out the French and then returned to power in June 1867. They gave the emperor a dose of his own medicine, executing him and two of his closest Mexican allies. When Juárez returned to the presidency, he knew that his faction had triumphed through military conquest rather than the superiority of the Liberal program. He also embraced repressive tactics in order to deal with rebellions and banditry. For example, he established a roving police force, the *rurales*, a corps made up primarily of former bandits that enjoyed free rein in imposing order in the countryside.[14]

Therefore, the so-called "Restored Republic" already contained the seeds of a new form of dictatorship: the rule of General Porfirio Díaz. With the exception of a brief interregnum in the early 1880s, Díaz controlled the destinies of the nation between 1876 and 1911. The regime known as the "Porfiriato" holds direct relevance for Obregón as a revolutionary caudillo. The members of Obregón's generation were themselves products of the Porfiriato and often held minor political offices during its last years. According to historian John Lynch, Díaz was the archetype of the "modernizing" or "oligarchic dictator."[15] These leaders combined the political style of a caudillo with command over an extensive state apparatus that could enforce central rule with the help of railroads, modern standing armies, and growing tax revenues deriving from booming export economies. But Díaz was one of a kind: no other Latin American nation produced a leader so identified with his era that it bears his first name. Of the leaders of major Latin American nations, only Brazilian Emperor Pedro II and Cuban dictator Fidel Castro exceeded his political longevity.

A poor mestizo, Díaz, like Juárez, hailed from the state of Oaxaca. Born in 1830, he enjoyed a formal education in a seminary, but left before taking his vows. He also passed his fourth-year law examinations, yet did not finish his legal training either. Díaz earned his first military rank during the War of Reform. On May 5, 1862, the brigadier general helped lead his troops to a short-lived victory over the French at the first Battle of Puebla—an event that is still commemorated today as the Cinco de Mayo. Five years later, he directed the army that triumphantly occupied Mexico City and thus put an end to Maximilian's reign. Díaz felt that his military exploits had earned him the right to his own term as president. Thus, he rose up against Juárez in 1871, and a year later, following Juárez's death, he opposed the accession of Sebastián Lerdo de Tejada, chief justice of the Supreme Court. Following Lerdo's reelection in 1876, Díaz led a successful coup under the motto "effective suffrage, no reelection"; a battle cry that would come to haunt him after thirty years in the presidential chair.[16]

Once Díaz was invested with presidential authority, he transformed his persona from that of a rough-and-tumble caudillo into a cosmopolitan leader. Over time, his image transitioned to a European leadership style with heavy borrowings from France, the nation that most Latin American leaders desired to emulate. Díaz's transformation mirrored the nation's modernization during the 1880s and 1890s, when British, French, and US investments poured in to build up an infrastructure that would allow capitalists to exploit the nation's mineral riches and agricultural potential. Within just twenty years, railroads crisscrossed the nation; agribusinesses and mines produced sugar, silver, copper, and many other export commodities; port facilities saw significant upgrades; and an urban middle class of professionals and white-collar workers emerged in the growing cities and towns (see Map 1.1).

Ironically, Díaz's style bore resemblance to that of Napoleon III, the French emperor who had ordered the occupation of Mexico. One key

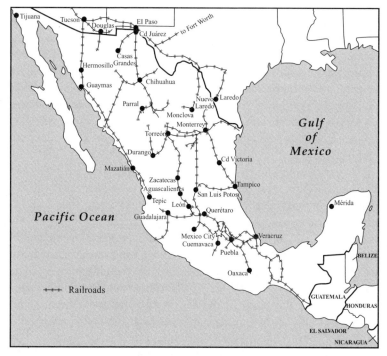

Map 1.1   Mexico in 1910.

to this image was don Porfirio's marriage to his English tutor, Carmen Romero Rubio. Thirty-four years younger than her husband, doña Carmelita belonged to a wealthy and highly educated creole family from the capital. Díaz's association with an elite clan from the capital made him socially acceptable to the other ruling families. Porfirian rituals of rule further demonstrated the shift in Díaz's public persona. One important aspect of a caudillo was his claim to be an ordinary citizen close to the people. However, following the renovation of the National Palace in the 1890s, the rituals surrounding presidential audiences created distance between don Porfirio and his people. Petitioners could only see the president on Mondays, Wednesdays, and Friday afternoons. They first inscribed their names on a list before noon and awaited notification that they were selected to wait for hours in a crowded anteroom known as "hell." Eventually, some of them, often the wealthier among the crowd, won admission into a better furnished room known as "purgatory." After waiting in that room, a number of petitioners made it into a final, lavishly appointed anteroom that visitors referred to as "limbo," in part because admission into that room did not guarantee a personal audience. Díaz only saw ten petitioners per afternoon. Don Porfirio invited important visitors to his personal residence later that evening, and cabinet secretaries and diplomats enjoyed special access to the president via a separate entrance.[17]

These rituals promoted the political motto most associated with the Porfiriato: order and progress. Order and progress signified the Porfirians' quest for political order (i.e. a powerful central state that could make its influence felt in Mexico's most distant regions) paired with economic progress, defined as modernization in infrastructure and technological terms. The Díaz regime was not the only Latin American government to use this term to define its program. Indeed, the contemporary Brazilian flag still carries the words *ordem e progresso* on a band around the equator of the globe in the center of the flag. What is most significant about this motto is its lack of emphasis on democracy and participatory political rule. Thus, modernization did not end the authoritarianism that had plagued Mexico throughout the nineteenth century. Instead, the Porfirians showed that they wanted practical solutions rather than wage and win the political debate necessary to arrive at a solution broadly supported in public opinion.

To help build this authoritarian system with a focus on material progress, Díaz employed the assistance of a new circle of political leaders made up of technocrats with a formal education, a positivist persuasion, and international business connections. The origins of the Mexican technocrat date to Maximilian's *imperialistas*, intellectuals influenced by French positivism. Positivism established the supremacy over the human mind over divine providence; and it explained the technological and economic superiority of the North Atlantic nations in terms of the scientific rather than religious orientation of their ruling classes. After the Liberal triumph, positivist technocrats formed much of Juárez's inner circle. One of them, the French-trained lawyer Gabino Barreda, founded a National Preparatory School dedicated to education according to the positivist model. The ENP focused on science over the humanities, and its teachers instructed many of the men who would become Porfirian technocrats. During the Porfiriato, Barreda's positivist creed became government doctrine. Once reintroduced into the governing elite, doña Carmelita's father, Manuel Romero Rubio, became the centerpiece of a group committed to modernization in accordance with French and US models.[18]

Known as the *científicos*, this group of about two dozen became the most influential faction in the Díaz regime. Their approach to political issues was *menos política, más administración* (less politics, more administration). This theme highlighted the positivist belief that educated men could find an administrative solution to any political problem. They disdained democratic processes that involved people whom the científicos considered unfit to make political decisions. The científicos also amassed considerable wealth by using their influence to gain control over formerly public lands, and by brokering agreements between the government and foreign investors. The científicos came to represent the worst aspects of the Porfiriato: authoritarian rule, foreign economic influence, and cronyism. The revolutionaries of 1910 would rally in part to end their influence. Yet the political system in which the científicos thrived—a military clique wedded to a circle of technocrats—would survive the revolution, and Obregón would recognize the utility of loyal intellectuals as much as Díaz had done.[19]

Born in the early years of the Porfiriato, Obregón's generation revealed the imprint of their age. They grew up under the Díaz regime, and in many cases, witnessed state- and local-level politics as the rule of the same clans allied with the Porfirians. One cannot understand Obregón or his contemporaries without reference to the antidemocratic context in which they grew up. To be sure, Obregón and many others would grow to resent the *científico* clique for their corruption and extensive hold on power. Yet they became inured to their political methods, and they agreed that material progress constituted the most important goal for a developing nation. To achieve material progress, they believed, the ends often justified authoritarian means. What would set Obregón and other revolutionaries apart from the Porfirians was the awareness that modernization required a modicum of social justice. How Obregón blended Porfirian precedents with new revolutionary ideas is the central story of the chapters that follow. But that story cannot be understood without reference to the state in which Obregón grew up.

The Sonoran Background

Obregón has often been described as a typical Sonoran: a member of a frontier society different in many ways from the rest of Mexico. He founded a political dynasty of Sonorans that would account for four out of six presidents of the period 1920 to 1934. This fact is even more astounding when one considers Sonora's population of 140,000 at the time of Obregón's birth; only one out of a hundred Mexicans lived in the nation's second largest state. The Sonoran background therefore served as an important building block of the post-revolutionary state that Obregón and his allies helped create. It allows historians to understand one of the fundamental dramas of the revolution: the conquest of central and southern Mexico by northern frontiersmen who, as historian Héctor Aguilar Camín exaggerated, "had little idea of the inner history or human reality" of most of the nation they had just conquered.[20]

Like the rest of the north, Sonora experienced only sparse Spanish colonization during the colonial period. The northern frontier held few attractions for the conquistadors who first came to this distant region in 1530. Land was abundant but arid, with scorching hot summers in which temperatures exceeded 120 degrees Fahrenheit (49 degrees Celsius). Initially, neither silver nor gold lured the conquistadors, although the southern city of Alamos became an important center for silver mining in the late eighteenth century, and vast copper deposits in the north awaited their discovery in the late nineteenth century. Those wayward Spaniards who found themselves in what is now Sonora faced an indigenous population able to preserve its autonomy. One historian has characterized the colonial northwest as the land of "wandering peoples," as many of these indigenous civilizations, and particularly the Apaches, lived a nomadic lifestyle.[21] Ranging across an area that included today's Sonora and Chihuahua as well as much of what is now the US Southwest, the Apaches held tough against Spanish attempts to subdue them from *presidios*, or garrisons. Even today, thick-walled churches in eastern

Sonora remind residents of a time when settlers feared Apache depredations on the "nomadic frontier."[22]

However, two major indigenous communities—the Yaqui and the Mayo—made their mark as sedentary peoples, and both of these peoples would greatly affect Obregón's career. They lived near the two most significant rivers of the region, and the former inhabited a wide swath of territory north of the Yaqui River. Due to the availability of water for irrigation, these communities claimed the prime farmland of Sonora. During the seventeenth and eighteenth centuries, Jesuit missions made this area into one of their most profitable holdings in the Americas. As elsewhere, Spanish settlers in this arid region coveted arable land, sowing the inevitable conflict that marked the encounter of indigenous and European cultures. By the time Mexico became independent in 1821, the Mayo and Yaqui held on to most of their land three centuries after the Spaniards had subdued the Aztecs. They also asserted their right to remain independent, and they would not pay taxes or tolerate the presence of government soldiers. Throughout the nineteenth century, they allied with those who would help them maintain their autonomy from the Mexican republic and the Spanish-speaking people they called Yori. For example, they forged a strategic alliance with the Gándara clan. During the age of Santa Anna, Manuel María Gándara had established his supremacy over the state. He hailed from Ures in east-central Sonora, an arid district with little potential for economic development, but one that featured a number of former *presidios* set up to defend the area from Apache incursions. Gándara allied with indigenous chieftains, and specifically the leaders of the Yaqui, whom he regarded as natural allies against the Apaches. During the 1850s, he lost out to Ignacio Pesqueira, a Juárez ally from the northeastern district of Arizpe. Pesqueira saw indigenous Sonorans as an obstacle to economic development. Not surprisingly, the Mayo and Yaqui realized that the building of railroads and the construction of a stronger central state threatened their status quo. Therefore, in 1875, they joined forces to proclaim their independence from Mexico. It was not until 1886 that the government crushed this indigenous holdout.[23] Most Yori continued to fear the indigenous Sonorans; in this regard, Obregón would prove to be an important exception, as he recruited both Mayo and Yaqui to fight with him.

Another significant difference between Sonora and much of the rest of Mexico was the role of the Catholic Church. In central and southern Mexico, thousands of priests tended to the spiritual needs of their parishioners. In those areas, Catholicism became deeply ingrained into the cultural fabric, and as evidenced by the plethora of ornately adorned churches and cathedrals, the Church emerged as the wealthiest institution in the colony. In Sonora, however, the Jesuit missions among the Yaqui constituted the most important footprint of the Church. Not surprisingly, Catholicism played a more important role among the indigenous communities than among the Yoris. Upon the expulsion of the Jesuits from the Spanish empire in 1767, few priests remained in northwestern Mexico. By 1830, one year after Spain's failed attempt at reconquest led to the exile of most Spanish-born clergy, there were only eighteen priests in an area the size of the US state of Montana.[24]

Yet another difference between northern Mexico and the rest of the nation lay in the fluidity of social relations. Spanish-speaking Sonora remained a frontier society engaged in the conquest of the environment and the state's indigenous population. The scarcely present Catholic Church could not regulate social relations: births out of wedlock were common, and in many cases, wives could desert unfaithful or cruel husbands by running away and starting a new life. Social pedigree—so important in the center and south—held less importance than individual achievement. In part for that reason, many Mexicans called Sonorans the "Yankees" of their nation.[25] Patron-client and familial relationships of the sort that Obregón would use to his own benefit structured this fluid frontier society. The handful of notable families who dominated Sonora learned the importance of personal relationships in acquiring wealth and power. In the absence of central political authority, they acquired these two signifiers of social status by fiat rather than by law, and by means of personal alliances rather than legal titles.[26]

Sonora not only differed from states farther south, but also from other northern states such as neighboring Chihuahua, the largest state of the republic. In Sonora, most land belonged to medium-sized and large holdings, with very few exceeding one thousand hectares. Therefore, with the exception of the indigenous communities mentioned above, there were few *rancheros* (smallholders) and landless peons. Not coincidentally, the Sonoran military forces in the revolution comprised a large number of farmers, shopkeepers, teachers, and other middle-class rebels. In Chihuahua, on the other hand, large estates abounded along with thousands of smaller properties. For example, Luis Terrazas and his family owned the largest land holdings in the entire republic, which exceeded the US state of Maryland in territorial extension. But that state also featured a sizable population of landless campesinos, rancheros, and squatters, a population that mobilized in the very first days of the revolution. Under Pancho Villa's leadership, they remained at the forefront of the fighting until Obregón's forces emerged victorious.

A final peculiarity of nineteenth-century Sonora lay in its proximity to the United States. Following the US annexation of the Mexican Northwest in 1848 and the Gadsden Purchase of 1853, Sonorans interacted to a greater extent with the inhabitants of the United States than with those of neighboring Baja California and Chihuahua. Baja California remained virtually unpopulated until the early twentieth century; and the tall peaks of the Sierra Madre Occidental limited interaction with the state of Chihuahua. With the exception of Sinaloa, which abuts Sonora to the south at the Sea of Cortez, communications with the rest of Mexico were even more difficult. By the time of Obregón's birth, there were no railroads in Sonora; port facilities were in abysmal shape, and overland travel could only be accomplished by donkey or mule. By contrast, the border crossing to the United States was easy. Sonorans looked to Arizona as refuge, employment opportunity, and a source of money and arms.

The Sonora that the young Obregón knew firsthand, of course, was that of the Porfiriato (see Map 1.2). Porfirian modernization affected Sonora more profoundly than many other states. Its location on the border made the state a keystone of efforts to link the Mexican and US economies. As part of their strategy to centralize and modernize the nation, the Porfirians and their US supporters turned Sonora from a sleepy backwater at the periphery into a crucial state at the very center of the modernization effort. Three critical infusions of foreign capital helped accomplish this goal. First, in 1882, British and US investors funded the Sonora Railroad that connected the port of Guaymas to the Arizona border. By the dawn of the new century, this railroad extended beyond the Sinaloa border under the name of the Southern Pacific Railroad. Second, in 1890, a US investor obtained the rights to most of

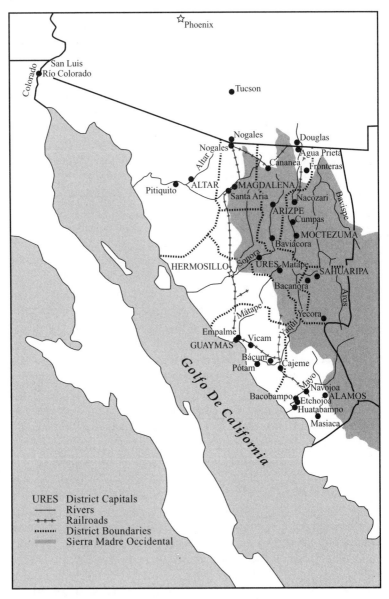

Map 1.2   Sonora in 1910.

the waters of the Yaqui and Mayo Rivers. Reduced to the Yaqui River valley, this concession later ended up in the hands of the US-owned Compañia Constructora Richardson. Finally, in 1897, the Phelps-Dodge Corporation invested in a copper mining site near the northeastern town of Nacozari, and two years later, Colonel William Greene founded the Cananea Consolidated Copper Company. Together, railroad construction, irrigation, and copper mining engendered an unprecedented boom. As a result, the state's population doubled between 1880 and 1910, as thousands of migrants came looking for work on the farms and in the copper mines. By contrast, the population of central and southern Mexico grew far more slowly.[27]

Modernization entailed a far greater presence of central government in this distant state. In particular, a triumvirate of leaders—Luis Torres, Rafael Izábal, and Ramón Corral—helped the Porfirians extend their political hold into Sonora. The triumvirate came to dominate state politics by doling out contracts and other favors backed by a federal government that at last commanded significant enough revenue to buy influence in state governments. Of the three politicians, Corral was the only native Sonoran, and probably the most important of the group. He was the only Sonoran member of the *científico* group that dominated the Porfirian inner circle. Beginning in 1904, he served in the new office of Vice President—an appointment that illustrated the rising importance of the state in national politics.[28]

During their thirty-year hold over the state, the triumvirate attempted to break the power of the notable families, and especially the Pesqueiras, who never reconciled themselves to the new order. They also used their political offices to become the crucial intermediaries between foreign investors and local governments. Yet resistance persisted: the Pesqueiras retained powerful friends, especially the Maytorena clan, a landowning family from the Guaymas area. In the copper mines, adherents of the Flores Magón brothers organized labor along anarcho-syndicalist lines. Anarcho-syndicalists believed that the central government repressed the workers in alliance with the copper companies, and that freedom for the workers could only come through the abolition of both private capital and the state.[29]

Porfirian modernization dealt a decisive setback to indigenous aspirations for continued autonomy. In 1886, the army's defeat of the Mayo opened their land to exploitation by Yori settlers, the government, and foreign investors. That same year, the government also crushed the Yaqui army. None other than Corral led the charge against the Yaqui, which lost not only the war, but also their leader, José Leyva de Cajeme, who was executed by the government. One year thereafter, however, Cajeme's second in command, Tetabiate, led the remaining Yaqui rebels into the Sierra de Bacatete mountains east of the Guaymas region. Even as the Porfirians seized most of their land and deported thousands of Yaqui into slavery in Yucatán, Tetabiate and his successors would continue defending their independence well into the 1920s. There was no prominent Yori in the central and southern parts of the state not affected by the endless conflict with the Yaqui. Even those who hated the Yaqui and sought a military victory at all costs needed their labor and enlisted their assistance as military allies.[30]

Modernization also exacted a toll on the population working in the copper mines. To be sure, the copper boom brought rapid population growth to the northeast of Sonora, and the miners received better wages than those paid in mines elsewhere in Mexico. But workers in the mines of Cananea and Nacozari observed that their North American co-workers received much higher pay for the same work; in Cananea, for example, Mexican workers received 3.50 pesos while North American workers earned 5 pesos per day. In addition, the Mexican miners worked in deplorable conditions. In this atmosphere, an anarchist and socialist opposition party led by the Flores Magón brothers, the Partido Liberal Mexicano (PLM, or Mexican Liberal Party) found ready converts. On June 1, 1906, more than five thousand Mexican miners went on strike, demanding the removal of a particularly abusive foreman and a pay rate of 5 pesos per day. When the company rejected the demands, the workers organized demonstrations, and in response, the company called in a posse led by Arizona Rangers. The brutal suppression of the strike left 23 miners dead, and a legacy that would later reverberate in the Mexican Revolution.[31]

This sketch of Obregón's historical context would remain incomplete without a brief look at southern Sonora, and particularly the district of Alamos in which he spent most of his life. The district was wedged between the Gulf of California to the west, the Sierra Madre mountains to the east, and the state of Sinaloa to the south. The border with Sinaloa made the region into the gateway to the center. Obregón and many other small entrepreneurs from the district were more likely to travel to northern Sinaloa than to the state capital of Hermosillo. Not surprisingly, the region was more oriented toward the rest of Mexico than the United States. For example, while Sonora enjoys national renown for the quality of its beef, the city of Navojoa remains famous for its roasted chicken and seafood. As another example, ethnic relations in the Alamos district resembled those in regions farther south in that the Mayo defeat during the 1880s ushered in a relatively stable ethnic hierarchy. Unlike the Yaqui, the Mayo found a tenuous arrangement with the Yori who had defeated them in battle.[32]

To sum up, both Obregón's historical (Liberal-Porfirian) and regional (Sonoran) background influenced his generation's role in the revolution in important ways. Modernization in the late nineteenth century led to rapid economic growth in Sonora fueled by foreign investment and the growth of a transportation and communication infrastructure. Obregón grew up in a dictatorship in which the practical ends of politics reigned supreme over deliberative processes that would have involved democratic decision-making and consensus-building, on whatever scale such processes could have occurred in a regionally diverse and largely illiterate society. Likewise, the Sonoran tradition instilled in him several important attitudes, including an abiding faith in individual initiative; a critical attitude toward the Catholic Church; a belief in modern, privately-owned agriculture on a small to medium scale; a reliance on extensive familial and clientelist networks; and an abiding belief in a hard-headed political pragmatism as opposed to a commitment to representative democracy.

2

An Improvised Leader, 1880–1913

I am used to fighting with the elements of nature
How could it be hard for me to defeat men, whose passions, intelligence,
and weaknesses I understand? It is easy to switch from being a farmer to
being a soldier.

Alvaro Obregón (1912)

A lvaro Obregón Salido was already noted for his humor when he
bought a farm near the town of Navojoa in the district of Alamos,
Sonora, in 1906. Obregón called his new acquisition "La Quinta Chilla"
(the penniless farm). The ranch was 180 hectares, or 450 acres: small by
Sonoran standards. But the land was not too shabby. Navojoa lies in the
fertile valley of the Mayo River, and the availability of water made the
land in the area some of the most productive in the state. A former
mining center, Navojoa was about to experience substantial growth with
the arrival of the Southern Pacific Railroad in 1907. Just about anything
grew on "La Quinta Chilla," but Obregón specialized in chickpeas, a
staple in high demand as far away as Spain. He definitely did not remain
penniless and, by 1910, he numbered among the most promising young
agricultural entrepreneurs of the Navojoa region.

Obregón spent much of his young life in search of a suitable profession that would enhance his family's wealth and status—a search that
profoundly affected his political outlook. His rise to prosperity as a
farmer informed his approach to the problems of the countryside, and,

The Last Caudillo: Alvaro Obregón and the Mexican Revolution. Jürgen Buchenau
© 2011 Jürgen Buchenau

in particular, the thorny issue of land tenure in a nation in which a small number of proprietors held most of the arable land. In addition, as Obregón's fortunes grew, he came to understand the relationship between wealth and power and, most specifically, the arbitrary and corrupt aspects of political careers in Porfirian Mexico. Finally, the way in which Obregón came to participate in the revolutionary wars of the 1910s presaged important patterns in his later career. Far from an ardent revolutionary, Obregón sought consensus and stability where others desired either the status quo or radical change.

Obregón's Early Years

In his carefully cultivated public persona, Obregón always described himself as a self-made man who was pulled up from poverty by his own bootstraps. While this characterization constituted an exaggeration, his childhood was not easy. Alvaro was born on February 17, 1880 on the hacienda of Siquisiva located on the banks of the Mayo near the village of Huatabampo.[1] Huatabampo was a small settlement of no more than three or four streets, and a population of a few hundred people. Many of the inhabitants of the area were Mayo, producing a bilingual environment of Mayo and Spanish. Obregón was the youngest of eighteen children. The family was so large that, as Alvaro later joked, "when we ate Gruyere cheese, only the holes were left for me."[2] Most of his siblings were significantly older, giving him a multitude of parental authority figures. This large family was important in helping his mother, Cenobia Salido, weather the death of her husband, Francisco Obregón, just a few months after Alvaro's birth.

Unlike the other phases of Obregón's life, which are well documented in historical memory, there are not many sources on his early years. Because Obregón did not include a discussion of his origins in his famous account of his military career, and in the absence of extensive documentary evidence, historians primarily rely on the writings of a number of individuals who interviewed the famous leader regarding his childhood, including E.J. Dillon's 1923 book, *President Obregón: A World Reformer*. Scholars must take the fact into consideration that Obregón embellished many aspects of his upbringing during his conversations, and that the book's title indicates that Dillon was an admirer of his. Indeed, Dillon's work was a propaganda piece, written to impress its English-speaking public in order to achieve diplomatic recognition from the government of the United States. Nonetheless, the book includes fascinating insights into Obregón's personality, and especially into the way he told his own history to a US journalist. The discussion that follows relies on Dillon's as well as other accounts based on interviews, and recent research that has shed further light on Obregón's family connections.[3]

Unlike most Mexicans, who combined indigenous, European, and sometimes African ancestry, Alvaro Obregón was the product of a wholly Spanish family tree. His whiteness stood out from the mestizo origins of the majority of Mexicans, and even President Díaz himself. With quite a bit of hyperbole, Spanish novelist Blasco Ibáñez would describe Obregón thus, following a 1920 interview:

> It would be ... erroneous to imagine him as a Mexican chieftain of the type which we so frequently see in the movies ... a copper-colored personage with slanting eyes and thick, stiff hair, sharp as an awl; in short, an Indian dressed up like a comic-opera General. Obregón is nothing of the sort; he is white, so positively white that it is difficult to conceive his having a single drop of Indian blood in his veins. He is so distinctively Spanish that he could walk in the streets of Madrid without any one guessing that he hailed from the American hemisphere.[4]

Although rumor had it that the name of the Obregón family reflected a Hispanicization of the Irish name O'Brien, recent research has conclusively established that his grandparents were immigrants from Spain. Obregón claimed Spanish ancestry in his interview with Ibáñez, but emphasized that he descended from poor immigrants rather than conquistadors. Speaking of his grandparents, he said: "they must have been poor folk driven to emigrate by sheer hunger."[5]

While we will probably never know the material circumstances of Obregón's ancestors who crossed the Atlantic, they found opportunities once they established residence in Sonora. The paternal grandfather, Francisco Obregón, came to the New World during the waning days of colonial rule. Two decades later, he numbered among the thousands of Spaniards threatened by expulsion after the former mother country's failed attempt at reconquest. That was a sign that he had achieved some prosperity, as the republican authorities did not worry about penniless *peninsulares*. Like the Gándaras and Pesqueiras—other native Spaniards whose nationality made them undesirable at that time—he managed to find a way to stay in Sonora. However, unlike those founders of powerful dynasties, the Obregóns remained of minor importance. One of the reasons for their lack of success lay in the fact that some family members continued to pick the wrong side in political disputes. This step entailed egregious consequences in a nation in which political mistakes cut off sources of revenue. For example, in the 1860s, Alvaro's father, also named Francisco, became a business partner of a prominent supporter of Emperor Maximilian. At that time, he occupied a number of significant municipal posts and owned real estate in Cuernavaca and Mexico City, both far away from Sonora. After Maximilian's execution, the Juárez government expropriated these properties. Thereafter, Siquisiva remained the last holding of his father, and the farm suffered a number of successive disasters, including a devastating flood and an attack by members of the Yaqui tribe, who burned down the family residence and stole all of the remaining cattle.[6]

Alvaro's mother, Cenobia Salido, came from a far more fortunate background. She hailed from one of southern Sonora's most distinguished families, a clan that had shown better political acumen than the Obregóns. The Salidos allied with the Pesqueiras at the time when Juárez's Liberals swept to power, and they continued this alliance through Maximilian's empire. After enduring the vexations of the Conservative/Maximilian era, they enjoyed the favor of the federal and state governments and came to own thousands of fertile acres in the Navojoa area. The Salidos also developed a reputation for fearlessness and valor. For example, one story told in the Obregón household featured Alvaro's aunt defending a neighbor's house under attack by five bandits. According to family legend, the aunt pursued the perpetrators on horseback and, upon catching up with them, shot one of them dead. The Salidos considered the Obregóns poor relations.[7]

Young Alvaro thus grew up focused upon helping his large family. Doing so required flexibility and pragmatism. As a young child, he could not pursue a formal education, as Siquisiva lacked a school. Three of his older sisters, who had attended school in more prosperous times, served as his principal teachers. Alvaro went to work at ten years of age, when he labored as a carpenter's assistant, followed by work in the shop of a blacksmith. He distinguished himself by his capabilities for menial labor. For a while, he attended an elementary school directed by his brother, José J. Obregón, a "rank agnostic" known as the leading intellectual of Huatabampo principally for his anticlerical disposition.[8] While few Sonorans, as we have seen, were devout Christians, intellectually based anticlericalism remained as rare as book reading. Influenced by José, his younger brother never embraced Christian doctrine, but unlike many other revolutionaries, he never rejected Catholicism either. His practical mind remained uninterested in ideological, theological, or philosophical subtleties. Even though Alvaro dropped out of school when he was thirteen, he loved literature and became an avid reader, no doubt influenced by José and his siblings, who published poetry in a regional newspaper. Meanwhile, he continued to work for his family as a mechanic on a nearby hacienda, and he also participated in many other activities that helped his family make ends meet. He also worked as a hairdresser, carpenter, photographer, and blacksmith, among other occupations. He even conducted a small orchestra composed of members of his extended family with self-made instruments, as none were available in the region.[9]

One particular episode testified to Obregón's ingenuity. When he was thirteen years old, he acquired a small patch of land. On this land, Alvaro cultivated tobacco, which he harvested, dried, and rolled into cigarettes. Branded "Américas," these cigarettes did not find any buyers until the youngster enjoined his friends to ask for Américas in nearby stores. Reportedly, the ruse worked for a while as the storekeepers bought some cigarettes from him, which they hoped to sell to their customers. Eventually, however, the scheme failed as the cigarettes were of poor quality.[10]

Whether these stories are true or not, they illustrate the fact that Obregón became known as a pragmatic jack of all trades. One biographer has characterized him as a "lighthearted, genial, romantic, and very likeable person, with a creative and alert mind."[11] Among his many skills, he excelled as a repair man for agricultural machinery. He was also famous for his photographic memory. Many eyewitnesses reported that Obregón could look at the cards in a deck arranged at random and recite their sequence from memory. Later on, he was so feared as a poker player that one proprietor gave Alvaro money not to play. Finally, Obregón's mix of realism and empathy allowed him to work well with other people, often serving as an arbiter of conflict.[12]

One example of Alvaro's conciliatory nature as a youth was his attitude toward indigenous peoples, and particularly the Mayo culture in his own vicinity. Unlike many other Yoris who despised the native population of their state—some of them, future revolutionary leaders such as Plutarco Elías Calles—he respected indigenous cultures, and particularly the Mayo. Many of his childhood friends were Mayo, and Alvaro himself was as fluent in their language as in Spanish. As one story had it, he once made a wooden sword when playing with his Mayo friends and brandished it because he wanted to defend the indigenous children. Later, he named one of his sons Mayo, and indigenous troops would constitute a large part of his military contingent in the revolution. Reportedly, he also spoke the Yaqui language.[13]

After the death of his mother in 1895, Alvaro aspired to restore himself to the social status to which he felt entitled as a member of two prominent Sonoran families. In 1898, he left Huatabampo in search of new opportunities and worked as a teacher, mechanic, and itinerant shoe seller, among many other occupations. He crossed the state line to work as a mechanic at the sugar mill of Navolato, Sinaloa, an enterprise owned by his mother's relatives. The job at Navolato was Alvaro's first significant employment, and it emphasized the importance of familial relationships. However, working for his wealthier uncles also impressed upon him the fact that he was still a poor relative. Thus we can detect in this employment the origins of the ambivalent position toward capital and labor evident in the epigraph to this chapter. As someone who knew hard menial labor, Obregón empathized with the plight of poor laborers. At the same time, this scion of a distinguished Sonoran family worked hard for a future in which he, like his relatives, was a *patrón*, or boss, rather than an employee.[14] That experience later allowed Obregón to construct himself as either a worker or an entrepreneur as the situation dictated. As he later wrote in his *Ocho mil kilómetros de campaña* (eight thousand kilometers of campaigns), his sometimes rambling account of his involvement in the revolution: "in the ten long years when I belonged to the brotherhood of workers and later, when I managed several haciendas, I could note precisely the treatment they received from

overseers and bosses ... and I could also appreciate the immense dise-
quilibrium that existed between the privileged castes and the working
classes. ..."[15]

The first turning point in Obregón's life came in 1903, a few years
after leaving the job at Navolato. Even as he continued to dabble in different professions as a shoe salesman and school teacher, it was time to
start a family. In Mexico, a man remained in the care of female family
members—whether a mother or a sister—until he got married. Therefore,
matrimony occurred relatively early in life, and Obregón was no exception. In 1903, at the age of twenty-three, he married the Alamos native
Refugio Urrea, with whom he had four children. Then tragedy struck in
1907, when his wife and two of the children died. Refugio's death left
Obregón's older sisters to care for him and his two remaining children,
Humberto and Refugio, whose birth had cost her mother her life.[16] Less
than two years later, he wrote a poem entitled *Fuegos fatuos,* or "Foxfire"
that reflected on this traumatic experience:

Our lives are the rivers
That lead to the sea
That is the process of dying
There go the lordships
Rights that are ending and expiring ...

Together, they are equal:
Those who work with their hands
And the rich.

... Humanity in its loss
Hauls along so much fruitless vanity
Forgetting the tribute
That it will have to render to the cemetery

There, everything is the same; Calvary
Is equal to the bone yard
And although they may come from different lineages,
The men and the women, the old, and the infants,
In the dark nights
Foxfires, unreal, they all promenade together. [17]

Historian Enrique Krauze has argued that this poem revealed an early obsession with death.[18] More likely, however, it shows Obregón's view of human beings as equal in the face of death, and, hence, in life as well. The poem suggests the inevitability of death which Obregón had witnessed at a young age, and potentially an affliction with depression. At twenty-nine years old, he had already lost his father and mother, as well as his wife and two children.

Thus chastised by fate, Obregón plunged headlong into his business. As someone who produced chickpeas, an export commodity, he became one of the beneficiaries of Porfirian modernization. While his ancestors would have had to transport the chickpeas by mule to Guaymas and from there to the United States around the tip of Baja California, the Southern Pacific Railroad quickly conveyed his legumes to Arizona. From there, they could easily reach the rest of the world, including Spain—Obregón's ancestral country, and the primary market for chickpeas. We have few sources that attest to the early days of "La Quinta Chilla." (see Figures 2. 1 and 2.2). However, we do know that Obregón held a series of minor political offices, a sign of some fortune. In the period 1905–1907, he served as first *regidor*, or senior town council member, of Huatabampo,

Figure 2.1 The Ranch House at "La Quinta Chilla." Source: Fideicomiso Archivos Plutarco Elías Calles y Fernando Torreblanca (FAPEC).

Figure 2.2   Corn Harvest Time at "La Quinta Chilla." Source: FAPEC.

and he won re-election for the following term. In 1908, he managed the town's public works projects, and he paid special attention to irrigation and the provision of water to urban residents.[19]

In 1909, Obregón's creativity and hard work paid off with the invention of the chickpea harvester, probably the only technological innovation ever credited to a future Mexican political leader. Within months, Obregón manufactured this harvester for sale to other farmers in the Mayo Valley, and chickpea cultivation skyrocketed throughout the region. His new invention brought him a fair degree of prosperity, and, more importantly, a newfound status as a social and economic networker. The Navojoa region avoided much of the downturn that affected most of the rest of the nation, as a global economic crisis sharply reduced the price of silver and other export commodities, while chickpeas and other foodstuffs remained in high demand. The chickpea venture turned Obregón into one of the aspiring capitalists of the region, allowing him to set his sights on the *cacicazgo* of Huatabampo, a status much higher than his own. At the moment, political and economic power remained concentrated in the hands of the town's long-standing cacique, or local strongman: José Tiburcio Otero, the commander of government troops during the Yaqui War of the 1880s. Otero owned a 7,000-hectare hacienda, the largest of the region.[20] Nonetheless, Obregón had staked his claim among the landowning bourgeoisie and the ascendant political class.

Therefore, it was not surprising that in 1910, the residents of Huatabampo chose him, along with his brother José and one other citizen, to represent their town in Mexico City during the celebrations commemorating the centennial of Miguel Hidalgo's rebellion against the Spanish Crown. Otero had passed on this honor, which involved a long and arduous trip, as there was no direct rail service. Like other Sonorans wishing to travel to the national capital, Obregón took the Southern Pacific Railroad to Mazatlán, and then a boat to the port of Manzanillo, Colima, from where he once again continued by train via Guadalajara. Although no historical records have survived that display Obregón's reactions to his visit, the trip must have been an overwhelming experience. Unlike the sleepy Sonoran towns, the national capital was a city with world-class aspirations. Centuries as the administrative nexus of New Spain and the Mexican republic, successively, had produced a city of 350,000 inhabitants that aspired to a place among the world's foremost capitals. To a small-town Sonoran, Mexico City was a great metropolis. This trip began a long love-hate relationship with the national capital, as Obregón simultaneously admired the city's power and detested its culture.[21]

Obregón found in Mexico City a microcosm of the internal contradictions of the Porfiriato. European-style boulevards showed off the city's wealth, and French and German immigrants had opened department stores that sold the finest clothes from Paris and the sturdiest hardware from western Germany, Great Britain, and the United States. On the other hand, the eastern half of the city was poor, and just a few blocks off the Zócalo, or central square, tens of thousands of people serving the wealthy as workers or servants lived in squalor. These same contradictions found themselves highlighted during the centennial, which the Díaz regime had turned into a month-long celebration. The government unveiled two grandiose monuments in the capital, including the Angel of Independence on the city's main boulevard, the Paseo de la Reforma—a street designed by Empress Carlota in the 1860s to look just like its counterparts in Brussels or Paris. It sponsored a series of balls and cocktail parties that cost more than the annual federal education expenditure in a nation where only 15 percent of the adult population could read. Having invited hundreds of foreign dignitaries, entrepreneurs, and thousands of statewide and local Mexican leaders such as Obregón, the Porfirian regime also took great pains to hide the social reality of the capital. For example, the police whisked beggars off the streets so that visitors would not witness the stark poverty and draw the inevitable conclusion that the prosperity brought by modernization had only benefited a minority.[22]

Indeed, the centennial celebrations marked the last hurrah of a dictatorship that had become a decrepit gerontocracy. The day before Independence Day, Díaz had celebrated his eightieth birthday, and many of his cabinet ministers were over seventy. In a 1908 interview with the US journalist James Pearson, the old dictator had expressed a desire to step down at the end of his current term in 1910, and he had encouraged the formation of an opposition party. However, as soon as the long-dormant opposition stirred in anticipation of finally winning political office, Díaz reversed course and announced his intention to run for yet another six-year term.[23]

Díaz's about-face disappointed opponents such as the northern landowner Francisco I. Madero. A native of the northern state of Coahuila, Madero belonged to a family that had greatly benefited from Porfirian modernization, and particularly the irrigation of the Laguna region, where the Maderos and other clans cultivated cotton. When the state's Porfirian governor failed dismally, which allowed one opposition clan—the Carranzas—to seize Coahuila's Senate seat, the Maderos could not capitalize on this failure. A diminutive, idealistic man and a follower of spiritism, Madero set his sights on the vice presidential position occupied by Ramón Corral, the former Sonoran governor, only to find that the dictator did not intend to share any power with members of the opposition despite the promises he had made in the Pearson interview. In 1909, Madero published a book-length treatise assailing the Díaz regime as a repressive dictatorship in cahoots with foreign investors. Other influential political figures soon joined Madero, for example, fellow Coahuilan Venustiano Carranza and the Sonoran hacendado José María Maytorena. Thus encouraged that he had a significant following, Madero undertook a grand tour of the nation that also took him to Sonora. In so doing, he rallied thousands against the continuation of one-man rule and antagonized the old dictator. A few months before Obregón arrived in Mexico City to celebrate the centennial of independence, Díaz had jailed Madero and proceeded to win another term in office along with Vice President Corral. This triumph, however, was to be don Porfirio's last. Feeling magnanimous in victory, the dictator ordered Madero's release from prison. It proved to be a mistake. Madero escaped to the United States, from where he issued his Plan of San Luis, postdated to November 20, 1910 so that he was not violating US Neutrality Laws. Calling for the overthrow of Díaz and free elections, this plan aimed to bring democratic rule after three decades of dictatorship. Little did Madero know that his plan would unleash an avalanche that produced a decade of violence, at least one million deaths, and the first social revolution of the twentieth-century world.

Obregón and the Beginning of the Mexican Revolution

This revolution began as a grass roots movement, and in the north. Without diminishing the contributions of the campesino followers of the legendary Emiliano Zapata, who attacked the Porfirians in the southern state of Morelos in a quest to recover land lost to the great sugar estates of the region, it is fair to say that the first phase of the revolution centered on Chihuahua. Like Morelos, that state featured a home-grown rebellion that acted on its own accord. Two former muleteers from humble origins headed the Chihuahuan revolution: Pascual Orozco and the Durango native Doroteo Arango, better known as Pancho Villa. Both Orozco and Villa organized small forces in the state's mountainous regions, areas with a long history of resistance against central authorities. Orozco initially played the leading role, assembling several thousand men who pledged their allegiance to Madero and waged an effective guerrilla campaign against the federal army. In May 1911, Orozco's troops took the border town of Ciudad Juárez, precipitating don Porfirio's resignation later that month. Villa supported Orozco at the head of a smaller military force; his own chance for greater glory would come later on. Significantly, the Chihuahuan revolutionary armies remained amorphous, composed primarily of poor *rancheros* who sought to defend their way of life—and often, their *municipio*—from the encroachment of federal and state authorities.

Sonora remained only a sideshow to the insurrection that would thereafter be known as the Revolution of 1910. Obregón's home state, too, harbored revolutionaries with aims that blended only imperfectly with Madero's national movement. However, theirs remained a far less significant movement that belied the enormous role that Sonorans would play in later phases of the revolution. Even more importantly, and fitting for a state with a relatively large population of landowning farmers, many of its leading figures hailed from the middle and upper classes. In fact, class differences divided the Sonoran revolutionary movement of 1910 into two different groups.[24]

The figurehead of the Maderista movement in Sonora, José María Maytorena, represented the first group. Maytorena was a middle-aged landowner from one of the state's foremost opposition clans. He was primarily interested in political change and reiterated Madero's demands for democracy at both the national and the local level. Two leaders of great subsequent importance—both of upper middle-class origins—supported Maytorena: Adolfo de la Huerta and Obregón's nephew, Benjamín G. Hill. De la Huerta, an artistic and intelligent man from Guaymas, was one of the few Sonorans with a high school education—a level that he could only achieve by studying in Mexico City. A native of Sinaloa, Hill was the grandson of a doctor in the Confederate army. He settled on a ranch near Navojoa with a European countess and served as a local councilman, only to become involved with the Maderista opposition in Díaz's waning years.[25]

The second group of the revolution in Sonora included a set of characters from the lower middle class influenced by the anarchist and socialist ideas swirling around the strike in Cananea four years before; radicals who pushed for social rather than political change. Jalisco native Manuel M. Diéguez had received his political education in the Cananea mine and had been a first hand witness of the brutal suppression of the strike. Salvador Alvarado had also experienced this historic event as a shopkeeper in Cananea. In late 1910, he spearheaded an assault on the headquarters of the federal army in the state capital of Hermosillo—one of the first revolutionary acts in the state. Finally, strike participant Juan Cabral later distinguished himself as one of the few Sonoran revolutionaries to push for land reform as a solution to his state's and his nation's social problems. Maytorena, de la Huerta, Hill, Diéguez, Alvarado, and Cabral all figured to benefit from Madero's triumph, yet they pursued drastically divergent political objectives.[26]

Obregón belonged to yet another group of Sonorans: a group that sat out the 1910 revolution altogether. Even though Hill attempted to involve him in the Maderista campaign in Navojoa, Obregón refused.[27] In his account of his involvement in the revolution, Obregón admitted he did not do anything beyond "cowardly" verbal support: he refused to sign a petition in support of Díaz by the Porfirista *presidente municipal*. He attributed his decision to stay home during the initial phase of the revolution to fear, as well as the fact that he had to take care of his family. He called himself and others who did not participate in the revolution "inactive Maderistas."[28] This seemingly contrite formulation was based on hindsight and constituted an excuse. In fact, his agribusiness flourished during the late Porfiriato, and Obregón did not see a need to take up arms against the government. This action would have invariably entailed adverse consequences for his business interests. He also needed to care for two small motherless children. Those Sonorans who did participate in the revolution of 1910 would never let him forget his inaction, and Obregón could not close the chasm that separated him from the real Madero supporters. Strikingly, however, his group of non-participants would end up being the most important faction of Sonoran revolutionaries in the end, as his successor as president, the Guaymas native Plutarco Elías Calles, also did not participate actively in Madero's revolution. Despite their lack of involvement in the beginning of the revolution, Obregón and Calles would dominate Mexican politics for a decade and a half.[29]

Obregón soon realized that his inaction did not cost him politically. The October 1911 elections gave all candidates a fair chance of success: whether Maderistas, their Porfirian opponents, or opportunists who called themselves Madero supporters only after the triumph of the movement. In fact, it would be fair to say that Madero's triumph brought about the freest elections the nation had known up to that point—a fact that mobilized an unprecedented number of people to political involvement. Even more importantly, the freedom of the vote extended to the state and municipal level and gave the former political "outs" a chance to win office after decades of Porfirian cronyism. Thus, despite the fact that much of the structure of the Old Regime survived under Madero, the revolution shook up the old boss system.[30] This new trend became apparent in the Mayo Valley, where most of the candidates for local office had followed a fairly predictable trajectory under the Porfiriato. Having occupied various offices during that period, many of the entrepreneurs of the region had not actively participated in the revolution, but had instead focused on their businesses. They had sympathized with Madero and quickly proclaimed their allegiance to him after his victory, yet their support remained tepid at best. Obregón's record as a minor Porfirian office holder and lukewarm Madero supporter therefore did not constitute political baggage, and he got an opportunity to claim his first executive position under the new regime.

In October 1911, in the same elections that elevated Madero to the presidency of Mexico, the citizens of Huatabampo elected Obregón as their *presidente municipal*, or mayor, over an opponent, Pedro H. Zubarán, allied with the town's old cacique, José Tiburcio Otero. Obregón carried the vote in the rural areas, while Zubarán dominated the vote in the town of Huatabampo. Although Zubarán claimed an older and more consistent allegiance to Madero's cause, his association with the openly Porfirista Otero hurt him. In addition, Obregón found the support of most of the Mayo residents of Huatabampo as well as that of a considerable number of hacienda peons. Not surprisingly, Zubarán attempted to have the election annulled with the argument that most of the Mayos could not read and write; according to the electoral code, literacy was a requirement for voter eligibility. As mandated in the state constitution, the Sonoran legislature charged an election commission with resolving the dispute. The committee chair was Guaymas representative Adolfo de la Huerta, a friend of a mill owner associated with Obregón and—as we have seen—an ardent Maderista.[31]

De la Huerta's involvement in the Huatabampo election dispute was a lucky break for Obregón in more ways than one. It not only promised a favorable adjudication, but it also marked the beginning of a long and beneficial political alliance. The two men had met shortly after Madero's triumph in May 1911, and we only know de la Huerta's version of their initial conversation, related in his memoirs more than ten years after his conflict with Obregón had initiated a cycle of fratricidal conflicts among

Sonoran leaders in the 1920s. Thus historians need to take de la Huerta's opinion with a grain of salt. According to de la Huerta, Obregón remained skeptical about the Madero movement even after its triumph:

Obregón:	Well, you have already won! What exactly have you won?
De la Huerta:	Well, of course, the right of all citizens to freely choose their representatives and leaders.
Obregón:	And will this be a fact?
De la Huerta:	Without a doubt; were it not so, the blood spilled would be useless …
Obregón:	May it be so.
De la Huerta:	And let it be said that we fought not only for ourselves, but also to give you guys the right to vote. All, not just friends, but also enemies, can choose … our government.

In a reference to the unequal resources at the disposal of Mexican citizens, Obregón then said: "So whoever has the most saliva will have to swallow the most pinole," a sticky food made from parched ground grains.[32]

De la Huerta's rendition of the first conversation between the two men yields a glimpse into the political differences between a self-made man who believed in results, and an educated leader who put his faith in the democratic process. It also shows Obregón's uncanny sense of the difference between political theory and the political practice that he himself would work hard to perpetuate. Unlike de la Huerta, Obregón recognized the limits of Madero's appeal. As he knew, political equality alone could not solve economic backwardness or social inequities. Of course, historians need to employ skepticism with regard to a historical document written more than two decades after the fact. In particular, de la Huerta, bitter about his defeat at the hands of Obregón in 1923, might well have exaggerated Obregón's reluctance to embrace Madero's revolution. In any case, however—and just like the Porfirian officials under whom he had grown up—Obregón never demonstrated much affinity for democratic processes, instead focusing on administrative and political solutions to specific problems.

When Obregón's victory stood up on appeal, he had gained his first significant political post as well as something more valuable— acquaintance with one of the rising stars in Sonoran politics. It is likely that Obregón prevailed due to the influence of his vast family network in Huatabampo and its environs. Zubarán was correct in contesting the outcome. In support of Obregón, hacendados had carted in Mayo peons from outside the municipal boundaries, and many of these peons were under the legal voting age. In addition, the Mayo chieftain Chito Cruz had strong-armed his followers into voting for Obregón, and many voters cast two ballots. This gesture shows the strength of Obregón's support among Huatabampo's indigenous population, but it also demonstrates the persistence of boss rule tactics even in an election that was supposed to herald the coming of true democracy. In fact, his association with Cruz taught Obregón two important lessons: how to use coercion to achieve political ends; and the potential of alliances with indigenous Mexicans. As *jefe municipal*, Obregón would rely on Cruz to help keep order in Huatabampo.[33]

Obregón's upbringing in Porfirian Sonora provided the toolbox that he would use in his subsequent career in the revolution. Among his innate talents, his outgoing nature, his ability to take calculated risks, and his prodigious memory all helped steer him toward success in these areas. His notable provenance produced much of the ambition that would one day carry him to the presidency of the republic. Obregón's experience with the Mayo people of his native village created the germs of an alliance that would prove crucial in the revolution. His experimentation with various careers—and particularly his successful stint as a farmer— brought him into contact with Sonorans from different walks of life. It also instilled in him an abiding faith in individual initiative, a belief in a free capitalist system that resembled that of North Americans. Yet in dealing with campesinos and workers, Obregón would always remember his days as a poorly paid day laborer, and depending on his audience, he could either portray himself as a working man of humble origins or as an enterprising farmer. As he became more wealthy and influential in Huatabampo, the late Porfiriato and the Madero presidency afforded him a useful political laboratory. In those turbulent years, he rose from the position of *regidor* in the late Porfirian period to *presidente municipal*.

At the time, Obregón's election as Huatabampo's new mayor signaled a political and business opportunity. He stood in line to challenge Otero, a man who had become synonymous with local politics. Indeed, local political authorities had always used their offices as a springboard to secure access to land, water, credit, and even income, and Madero's election—while raising hopes for democracy—looked unlikely to change that dynamic.

Obregón's First Campaign

However, this was not a time of peace, as a multitude of enemies beleaguered Madero's new, democratically elected government, and many with the force of arms. As a result, Obregón's new post became an opportunity for redemption for someone who had missed Madero's revolution in order to chase material objectives. Within months, Obregón found himself in eastern Sonora, hundreds of miles away from his home town on an expedition that would presage much greater military adventures the following year.

The trouble that led to Obregón's involvement in the revolution stemmed from the weakness of Madero's government. Carried to office by a broad but fractious coalition, Madero ran into trouble within weeks of his inauguration. At once, he found himself facing competing political agendas, as former Porfirians worked to keep the social status quo, while agrarian revolutionaries like Emiliano Zapata pushed for the distribution of hacienda land to campesinos. For Madero, all of this happened too fast, and he attempted to strengthen the newly elected institutions before moving ahead with significant social reforms. Moreover, he had inherited the repressive Porfirian apparatus, and especially the federal army, and Madero knew that the stability of his government depended on these *federales*. Following his agreement with the Porfirians, he therefore insisted on the disarming of all former revolutionary fighters, and he also refused to take rapid action on the land reform desired by the Zapatistas. As a result, on November 25, 1911—less than three weeks after Madero took office—Zapata declared himself in rebellion. His Plan of Ayala called for the president's overthrow and the restitution of all village lands. By the end of the year, Madero had faced two other rebellions, including one spearheaded by a powerful Porfirian general, the erstwhile vice presidential candidate Bernardo Reyes, and another led by the brother of a prominent Maderista. Only two months into its term, the Madero presidency appeared headed for disaster. However, none of these early rebellions affected life in distant Sonora, and they passed without scarcely any notice to the inhabitants except the state government.[34]

That changed dramatically when the unrest came to neighboring Chihuahua. In March 1912, Pascual Orozco rebelled against the national government. The most important military commander in the revolution against Díaz, Orozco was upset because Madero refused to endorse him for the governorship of his native state, instead backing his rival, Abrahám González. Madero considered Orozco a ruffian fit to fight, but not to govern. Orozco's rebellion threatened the Madero administration because the Chihuahuan leader enjoyed a broad regional base of support. After all, his supporters had constituted the largest contingent of the revolutionary forces, and they had played an indispensable role in Díaz's defeat. Orozco charged the president with nepotism and declared his administration null and void. In response, Madero sent a contingent under General José González Salas into the field. However, in late March, the Orozquistas dealt González a humiliating defeat, and the general committed suicide rather than face a shameful return to Mexico City. While the president readied another contingent under the old Porfirista General Victoriano Huerta, Orozco took the offensive. In July, as part of this offensive, the Orozco rebellion spilled over into Sonora. Orozco diverted troops to this maneuver in order to cause trouble for Governor Maytorena, a staunch backer of Madero.[35]

Maytorena did not have the luxury of waiting for the arrival of the federal army. Aware of the failure of the first Federal expedition, the governor questioned whether Madero could organize a more effective response. He also knew that the federal army would strike at the heart of the rebellion in Chihuahua rather than defending Sonora, a state even more distant from Mexico City than its neighbor. As he realized, Orozco counted on significant support in eastern Sonora, mainly local leaders who opposed Maytorena and his Guaymas- and Hermosillo-based political establishment. Instead of relying on the small federal garrisons, most of which lay far away from the area of conflict, Maytorena organized a militia to address the problem. Formed by local leaders who received the rank of lieutenant colonel from the governor, irregular battalions, the *batallones irregulares,* aimed to defend their state from the incursion. Obregón saw this militia as a chance to wash himself of his shame: as he put it, "duty told me that I had an opportunity to redeem myself." In April 1912, Obregón organized a battalion of three hundred local volunteers, most of them ranchers like himself.[36] He did not take the field out of enthusiasm for Madero; rather, he did so in order to protect the sovereignty of his state and as well as to vindicate himself for his earlier failure to participate in the revolution.

The nucleus of Obregón's eventual army, his *batallón irregular* therefore differed from ordinary revolutionary forces in important ways. Orozco's army consisted of a makeshift array of poor artisans, workers, and ranchers, with important Porfirian supporters behind the scenes. It had defied the Chihuahuan state government in its insurrection. On the other hand, Obregón's force enjoyed the protection and support of the state governor, who had never enforced Madero's order to disband and disarm all revolutionary troops. Though nicknamed "the rich battalion," it included at least some Mayo and Yaqui farmers in addition to a large number of well-to-do ranchers (see Figure 2.3).[37] The battalion resembled a regular army contingent in its composition and discipline.

Initially, the battalion possessed only minimal weaponry: eight rifles and sixty rounds of ammunition. Therefore, Obregón's small and inexperienced force almost did not get very far on their arduous way to the

Figure 2.3 The Rich Battalion (Alvaro Obregón is in the center of the bottom row; Francisco Serrano is on the far right). Source: FAPEC.

eastern part of the state. Yaqui rebels held up the train that carried his troops to the state capital of Hermosillo. In what constituted their very first military engagement, Obregón and his men attacked and chased off the Yaqui, killing several of them in the process. Afterward, the battalion camped just south of the state capital, where they received additional weapons and ammunition. Maytorena constituted the force as the Fourth Irregular Battalion. He also awarded Obregón the rank of lieutenant colonel, his first military rank.[38]

On June 2, the Fourth Irregular Battalion traveled northeast to the US border, first to Naco, and from there on to Agua Prieta. From Agua Prieta, the force needed to continue on foot, so Obregón and his men spent two weeks in that city getting provisions and reinforcements. It was the beginning of summer, a time of unbearable heat. Now five hundred strong, the battalion faced a march through dozens of miles of scorching desert without access to water and food. Even before meeting the enemy, death from hyperthermia, dehydration, or starvation loomed for many of the members of the battalion, as it does for many prospective Mexican immigrants to the United States today who attempt to brave that brutal desert during the summer. It therefore appeared unlikely that the stay in Agua Prieta would amount to anything but a respite for Obregón in advance of his difficult march to the Sierra Madre.[39]

However, his sojourn in Agua Prieta began his most enduring and significant political alliance: that with Plutarco Elías Calles, the town's *comisario* (police chief). Calles was a childhood friend of state congressional representative Adolfo de la Huerta, whom Obregón had met the previous year after Madero's triumph. In many ways, Calles's background resembled Obregón's. A native of Guaymas, Calles hailed from a distinguished Sonoran family that had fallen upon hard times during the 1860s and 1870s, as his father slipped into alcoholism. Three years older than Obregón, he was also a half orphan, having lost his mother at a very young age. Like Obregón, Calles had tried his hand at a variety of professions, including teacher, hotel manager, farmer, and mill operator; he had served in various minor political offices during the Porfiriato; and he had joined the revolution as a lukewarm latecomer. The differences between the two leaders, however, were just as important. Calles had received a middle-grades education, and his mind was theoretical rather than practical. Unlike Obregón, he had failed in his business ventures. Even more importantly, the sullen and brusque Calles did not share Obregón's winning personality. However, Calles possessed a gift that Obregón lacked: a splendid administrative mind with the ability to analyze complex political situations and to tackle multiple problems at once. Obregón excelled due to his photographic memory and interpersonal relationships, while Calles boasted a brilliant political vision that contributed in important ways to the success of his emerging faction. In a world in which erstwhile friends often became enemies, Calles and Obregón remained allies of convenience even as they pursued different political aims.[40]

Calles and Obregón also differed in their enthusiasm for military service, as the former did not relish the opportunity to fight the Orozquistas. Located east of Cananea, Agua Prieta lay in a strategic position. It was the northern terminus of a rail line bringing copper ore from the US-owned mine "El Tigre," and it guarded the approach to the Paso del Púlpito, the only access route to and from Chihuahua in the northern part of the state. Not surprisingly, the Orozquistas took the "El Tigre" mine and then targeted the copper mine in nearby Nacozari and the Agua Prieta area as their next steps in an effort to control the entire railroad line and thus, northeastern Sonora. Calles's troops, however, were not up to the task of stopping the rebels. At one hundred troops, the Agua Prieta battalion was relatively small, and even when Obregón's forces appeared, Calles showed no inclination to join their march toward the Sierra Madre. Obregón soon found out that Calles was most effective in his role as an official on the border, procuring weapons and ammunition and gathering intelligence across the border. These first interactions with Calles convinced him that the comisario's administrative skills far exceeded his military abilities, a belief confirmed the following year when Calles's first significant military engagement ended in defeat. Years later, when both men had attained their general's stripes, Obregón stated that his friend was the "least general-like of the generals."[41] Thus it was not surprising that he ordered Calles to remain in Agua Prieta rather than accompany him in his offensive against Orozco.

Along the way toward the Orozquistas and the Sierra Madre, Obregón received further reinforcements. On June 23, Salvador Alvarado and 150 troops joined Obregón, and a few days later, 150 members of the federal cavalry followed suit. Two weeks later, Obregón's nominal superior, Brigadier General Agustín Sanginés, incorporated the Fourth Irregular

Batallion into the so-called "Sonoran Column" and named Obregón the chief of the cavalry division.[42] It was a premature, but ultimately provident honor. The Sonoran Column was ready to engage the enemy. As the march wore on, Obregón—an "inveterate smoker of cigarettes"—kicked the habit out of necessity during his first weeks in the Sonoran desert, and only smoked an occasional cigar thereafter. He also learned to sleep at any time of the day and in any posture.[43] After almost a month in the desert, the column reached the Sierra Madre, and on July 18, Sanginés and Obregón passed through the Paso del Púlpito and entered the state of Chihuahua. Forty kilometers east of the state line, the column paused at the hacienda of Ojitos. When Sanginés learned that a contingent of Orozquistas was advancing on the hacienda, Obregón figured out a military strategy in a terrain that he did not know. Most importantly, following the dictum of Prussian strategic theorist Carl von Clausewitz that defense is inherently the stronger form of war, he knew that a well-organized defensive position could withstand an enemy attack and mount an effective counterattack. Disdaining the time-honored practice of digging collective trenches, he suggested that the soldiers of the column carve out foxholes. These were deep, bottle-shaped holes large enough for one fighter, who could either crouch down or stand with his head and shoulders exposed. One of the newest strategies used in warfare, this effective defensive fighting position would soon find widespread adoption in World War One. Protected by fire from the soldiers in the foxholes, the column weathered the Orozquista charge before Obregón's cavalry chased away the attackers. A few hours later, he defeated another nearby rebel contingent.[44] The victorious column then proceeded northeast toward Ciudad Juárez, while a federal army unit under General Victoriano Huerta (under whom Sanginés and Obregón nominally served) advanced on the Orozquistas from the south.

On September 1, Sanginés's and Huerta's troops met at the Estación Sabinal train station not far from Casas Grandes. At an elevation of almost 5,000 feet, the mountain air was crisp and clear as the commanders presented their arms. The contingents could not have been any more dissimilar. One—the federal army, or Federales—featured clean-shaven men in uniform, well fed and well equipped. The rank and file among the Federales could not wait to get back home, as many of them had been pressed into service in some distant region. Their commander, Huerta, was a graduate of Mexico's finest military academy. For now, he remained loyal to President Madero. The second, the Sonoran column, consisted of a makeshift force in shabby clothes and carrying outdated weapons. Obregón's battalion marked the first military service for many of its members. This included their chief, whose rank of lieutenant colonel derived from the Sonoran state government rather than the formal nomination of the Secretary of War in distant Mexico City. Sanginés introduced Obregón to Huerta as one of his young colonels who had distinguished himself in the campaign. As Obregón related, Huerta replied: "Let's hope that this commander will be a promise for the fatherland!"[45] They then went their separate ways, as Obregón's forces returned to Agua Prieta, and Huerta's, to Mexico City.

This meeting not only signaled Obregón's ascendancy as a promising young military commander, but it also epitomized the clash between Mexico's past and future. Huerta's service in the Federales represented one example of Madero's failure to root out the Old Regime: the first revolutionary government continued to rely on Porfirian generals and bureaucrats. Obregón's *batallón irregular*, on the other hand, represented a volunteer force more connected to the needs and desires of ordinary Mexicans than the Federales. To be sure, the Fourth Irregular Battalion included many middle-class Sonorans, not lower-class rancheros like the Orozquistas or the forces of Pancho Villa, let alone the indigenous campesinos who served under Emiliano Zapata in distant Morelos. However, Obregón, like Orozco and his commanders, had received his military training on the battlefield rather than in the academies that had produced the Porfirian army officers. Obregón's batallion thus constituted a middle ground between the professional army commanded by the federal government and the ragtag forces that had put Madero in power. No matter what policies Obregón would pursue at the national level, he would always remember the men whom he had led into the Sierra Madre in the late summer of 1912. One of them—his protégé, Francisco Serrano, whose sister, Amalia, had married Obregón's brother, Lamberto—would accompany him all the way to the national government. Without question, Obregón had experienced the revolution so far as an essentially agrarian phenomenon and he would cultivate his connections to the majority of Mexicans who lived off the land.[46]

However, Obregón could not yet look ahead, as the Orozquistas crossed into Sonora and threatened Agua Prieta and Nacozari. As Huerta had returned to Mexico City, Obregón and his friends alone confronted an invasion force that numbered approximately 1,500 troops. After Maytorena had failed in his attempts to convince Huerta to return to the north to finish the job, he made contact with Madero, who asked Huerta to order the Sonoran Column to return to their native state to confront the Orozquistas. In addition, the president procured US permission for the column to travel through US territory, which allowed Obregón, his troops, and his horses to reach Agua Prieta on September 12, with the Orozco contingent already in view of the town. As a result, the Orozquistas decided to withdraw from Agua Prieta; instead, they seized the US-owned El Tigre copper mine south of the town, from where they threatened Nacozari. Nacozari was not only the location of another copper mine, but it was also the terminus of the railroad line that shipped the copper from both Nacozari and El Tigre to Agua Prieta and Arizona. Sanginés ordered Obregón to reinforce Nacozari with a mere 150 troops, a force that possessed the grand total of one machine gun controlled by the German-Mexican Maximiliano Kloss.[47]

On September 17, 1912, after Calles had organized the provision of his troops, Obregón and his battalion traveled to Nacozari by a train with a number of ore cars. Once there, he learned that the Orozquistas had evacuated El Tigre, but that 900 enemy troops had camped at the hacienda of San Joaquín, 120 kilometers north of Nacozari and not far from the village of Fronteras where Calles had served as a mill operator just a few years before. As Obregón's troops reversed course and traveled northward toward Fronteras, the enemy cut the telegraph lines, leaving Obregón incommunicado with his headquarters. The contingent could have returned to safety in Nacozari, but Obregón announced to his troops that they had not come "to turn our backs to the enemy."[48] Based on detailed information furnished by Calles, he knew that the area was full of bogs and wire fences. These elements limited the usefulness of the Orozquista cavalry. When spies reported to him that five hundred Orozquistas were advancing on the railroad, he switched the engine to the back of the train and the caboose to the front and mounted Kloss's machine gun onto the caboose. The train then advanced toward the rebels, with the troops lying down in the ore cars so that they remained hidden from view. Once the Orozquista cavalry charged the train, the soldiers jumped out of the ore cars and began shooting at the rebels, while Kloss's machine gun fire gave them cover. When the Orozquistas retreated, Obregón's men pursued them into their camp, where they surprised five hundred enemy soldiers having lunch. After several hours, the men of the Fourth Irregular Battalion returned to the train, having captured 228 horses, 150 rifles, and a machine gun. With the help of strategic genius, Kloss's gunfire from the train, and the element of surprise, Obregón's troops had defeated the numerically superior Orozquistas.[49] This defeat sent the rebels scrambling toward the Chihuahua border and constituted their final and decisive defeat in Sonora.

Even as Obregón returned to his farm after Orozco's defeat, Maytorena recognized his abilities on the battlefield. Eager to divert attention from reports that he and his men had squandered and misappropriated money in the state treasury, he ordered him and his troops to Agua Prieta when new unrest threatened that town. Thereafter, Obregón alternated between his old life as a farmer and local political official, and his new life as a military officer, even though he resigned from the state militia in December 1912. While many other Sonorans demobilized their battalions, he kept his troops at the ready on the governor's orders. He already cultivated an image that would become ever more powerful in the later years of the revolution: that of a farmer who only reluctantly left his land in order to defend his native state and nation against its enemies.[50]

Thanks in part to new military leaders like Obregón, both the Madero government and Governor Maytorena had appeared to have weathered a serious storm. For now, Sonora appeared at peace, governed by a loyal Madero supporter and landowner who opposed drastic change. But the government owed the Porfirian military officers such as Huerta a debt of gratitude as well. When the year 1912 drew to a close, the state and national governments found themselves wedged between popular demands for social change and the elite's unwavering support for the status quo.

For his part, Obregón had experienced the unrest as an essentially agrarian phenomenon, and he knew that lasting peace would be ephemeral if the government did not address at least some of these social demands. With his victories at Ojitos and San Joaquín, Lieutenant Colonel Obregón had made a name for himself as a military commander and at last erased the shame of not having joined Madero's revolution. His command of an irregular battalion had demonstrated his own considerable abilities as a military leader, and Obregón stood poised to take advantage in case of further unrest.

3
Chaos and Triumph, 1913–1916

If Cain does not kill Abel, Abel will have to kill Cain.

Alvaro Obregón

Following the Orozco revolt, the generals of the federal army who had saved the Madero administration wondered whether the country would ever see the restoration of political stability. In Morelos, far away from Sonora, the campesino army of Emiliano Zapata continued to wreak havoc with its attacks on federal troops and its demand for land reform. Everywhere, schemes and plots abounded, and US Ambassador Henry Lane Wilson and his colleagues in the diplomatic corps grew impatient with Madero's inability to maintain effective control of the nation. Moreover, Madero's penchant for appointing his own relatives to political office elicited widespread opposition.

As a result, Madero confronted new rebellions, each one more serious than the last. In October 1912, don Porfirio's nephew, Félix Díaz, led an uprising that seized the port of Veracruz. For lack of support from the Porfirian officers of the federal army, the revolt collapsed. Sentenced to death, Díaz awaited the firing squad, only to have President Madero commute his sentence to life in prison. Nonetheless, Madero's fledgling

The Last Caudillo: Alvaro Obregón and the Mexican Revolution. Jürgen Buchenau
© 2011 Jürgen Buchenau

democracy appeared to be living on borrowed time, and it was only a matter of time until either the Porfirians or agrarian revolutionaries such as Zapata overthrew the government.

This highly unstable situation gave Obregón and other military chiefs in Sonora new opportunities for involvement in a conflict that was widening geographically and deepening socially. Beginning in 1913, the revolution entered its most destructive phase, once again calling upon the scene the Sonoran batallions created during the war against Orozco. The spreading civil war made Obregón into a national figure, and ultimately an aspirant for the highest office of the nation.

Obregón and the War Against Huerta

In February, Madero's government finally buckled under the weight of its adversaries. From prison, Félix Díaz and General Bernardo Reyes, a Porfirian ally who also served time, planned a coup d'état that could not succeed without outside help. At that point, US Ambassador Henry L. Wilson brokered a pact between Díaz and Huerta. Huerta's men went to the National Palace and forced the resignation of Madero and Vice President José María Pino Suárez. In the wee hours of February 18, an intimidated Congress confirmed Huerta as president. Hours later, the usurper ordered all state governors to recognize his regime.

But Huerta's coup only brought new unrest to the nation. As Madero had never managed to disarm the Zapatistas and other revolutionary armies, those forces fought Huerta just as they had Porfirio Díaz, and, in Zapata's case, Madero. Nor did the new dictator bring all of the governors into line, as the governors of the northern states of Chihuahua, Coahuila, Sinaloa, and Sonora refused to recognize the new order in Mexico City. Upon receiving Huerta's telegram informing him of his ascension to the presidency, Maytorena immediately congregated the state's military chiefs, including Obregón. These chiefs urged the governor to take immediate action against Huerta, who already knew that trouble was brewing in the north. When a subordinate warned the new dictator to keep an eye out for Obregón, Huerta reportedly exclaimed: "Well, we will buy him off. And if we cannot buy [him off], we will just have to kill him!"[1]

The dictator immediately demonstrated that he was serious about killing his opponents. Assassins most likely in his employ murdered Madero and Pino Suárez on February 22, and word spread quickly, leading to spontaneous demonstrations and protests throughout Sonora. The heinous crime had a chilling effect on the recalcitrant governors and state legislatures. The state government of Sinaloa began to veer toward its eventual recognition of Huerta. Chihuahua offered another reminder of Huerta's power, further demoralizing his opponents. On February 25, the Federales entered Chihuahua City and forced the resignation and arrest of Governor Abraham González, a mainstay of Madero since the early days of the revolution. Less than two weeks later, they murdered González on Huerta's orders. Given these events, it was not surprising that Maytorena wavered in his resolve to defy Huerta. The day after González's arrest, the governor asked the state congress for a leave of absence and left for exile in nearby Tucson, Arizona. There, Maytorena met several fellow émigrés, including Pancho Villa.[2]

Maytorena's departure left Ignacio L. Pesqueira as interim governor, a scion of the famous Liberal clan that had governed Sonora throughout the 1860s and 1870s. Pesqueira initially considered recognition of Huerta but was dissuaded by the energetic protests of the military commanders. On March 5, 1913, Pesqueira and the state congress issued separate declarations that disavowed recognition of the Huerta regime because of its violent seizure of power. As his first action, Pesqueira appointed Obregón chief of the military section.[3]

This appointment marked Obregón's first major statewide position. As section chief, he oversaw the defense of three military zones: the north, under Cabral; the center (including Hermosillo), under Alvarado; and the south, under Hill. Pesqueira created a fourth, northeastern zone under the command of Calles, who reported directly to him rather than to Obregón. To the chagrin of Alvarado, Cabral, and Hill, all of whom had served in Madero's revolution, the newcomer Obregón had scored the most significant military post in the state, and another newcomer—Calles—was equal to them. The five military leaders would work together over the next seven years, but Obregón's appointment sowed the seeds of mistrust between the Maderista generation of 1910 and the generation of 1912, which had entered into action only when the Orozco rebellion threatened their state.[4] Not surprisingly, the Sonoran Maderista military officers resented the choice of Obregón as their nominal superior, while Calles sensed an opportunity.

With Pesqueira's support, Obregón and the other commanders got ready to fight the Federales. First of all, they found new recruits. Although his old irregular battalion remained at the core of his forces, Obregón assembled a more diverse contingent, including a large number of Yaqui, who remembered the Porfirian deportations and thus wanted no part in a renaissance of the Old Regime. Drawing a stark contrast with the other soldiers, the Yaqui wore cotton pants, sandals, and embroidered shirts. Although the federal army maintained a significant presence in the state, including well-fortified garrisons in Guaymas and other towns, the rebels took heart in the fact that newly inaugurated US President Woodrow Wilson refused to recognize the Huerta regime. In the absence of diplomatic recognition, the Mexican government could not legally import arms or ammunition from the United States or obtain loans from US banks. Of course, neither could the rebels; led by the capable efforts of border agents such as Calles, they found ways around this embargo, importing arms from the United States through middlemen or outright smuggling.[5]

Further help came from other states. The assassination of González, and Maytorena's voluntary exile, left the governor of Coahuila, Venustiano Carranza, as the only elected state governor to defy the Huerta regime. A wealthy landowner and former Porfirian senator, Carranza had numbered among the major supporters of Madero, a fellow Coahuilan hacienda owner. On March 26, he issued a plan on his hacienda of Guadalupe that denied recognition to Huerta and called upon all Mexicans to resist the usurper. The "Plan of Guadalupe" asked all those who opposed Huerta to recognize Carranza as First Chief of the "Constitutionalist" movement, a clear sign that he intended to serve as president upon the removal of the dictator. Pesqueira signed up to this plan, as did the primary military leader who supported Carranza, Pablo González Garza, and rebel leader Pancho Villa in Chihuahua. A poor muleteer who had been forced to flee his native state of Durango after avenging the rape of his sister, Villa had become a social bandit in the late Porfiriato and joined Orozco in rebelling against the Díaz regime. However, he remained loyal to Madero during the Orozco rebellion and fought the rebels alongside General Huerta. Huerta viewed him as a likely competitor and had him arrested and sentenced to death on trumped-up charges, before Madero commuted his sentence to a prison term. Villa escaped from prison and crossed into the United States, from where, encouraged by both Maytorena and de la Huerta, he returned to Chihuahua to take the fight to the Huerta regime. This constellation would prove to be of great importance, as Villa trusted both of these Sonoran leaders—but not so much the group surrounding Obregón.[6]

Soon after the proclamation of the Plan of Guadalupe, Obregón went on the offensive against the federal army. He was fully aware that the war against Huerta might end up as a death mission. Even before Pesqueira had sent him into battle, he had contemplated a hero's patriotic death. As he wrote to his son, Humberto "if I should find the glory of dying for this cause, bless your status as an orphan, as you will be able to proudly proclaim yourself the son of a patriot."[7] Supported by zone commanders Cabral and Calles, who organized the provision of troops from across the US border, Obregón first targeted the north of the state. The border town of Nogales was the first to fall to the Constitutionalists, and the Federal garrison in another border town, Naco, surrendered after a siege of two weeks. Soon thereafter, Obregón's and Cabral's forces marched south and conquered Magdalena and the capital of the state, Hermosillo. In Obregón's homeland the far south of Sonora, Hill secured the District of Alamos. By May 1913, only the Federal garrison of Guaymas held out against the rebels in Sonora.[8]

Obregón's successes contrasted with the Constitutionalist fate in Chihuahua and Coahuila. In the former state, the Federales seized the administration following the assassination of Governor González. Next, the federal army forced Carranza's state government out of Coahuila. By August 1913, Pesqueira was the only governor who continued to defy Huerta from his state capital. Sonora had become the center of the revolution, and Obregón and the other Sonorans intended to capitalize on this status. So did Maytorena, who finally returned to his post to reap what Pesqueira's commanders had sowed.

Therefore, Obregón invited Carranza to take refuge in Sonora. Accompanied by a warm welcome back to Maytorena, this invitation proved a brilliant political move. The First Chief's presence in Sonora afforded Obregón unprecedented visibility in the Constitutionalist alliance. It also allowed him to coordinate negotiations between Carranza and Maytorena about the direction of the Constitutionalist campaign. Carranza and the Sonorans watched while Villa's forces bore the brunt of the military campaign in Chihuahua, once again the locus of the most intense fighting. While Carranza remained in Sonora for a full six months, Villa's troops softened up the Federales through a series of guerrilla strikes. In March, Carranza transferred his headquarters to Veracruz. In Sonora, the First Chief got first hand experience with a rebel group that had entered the war primarily in order to defend their native state rather than for any overarching political and social goals. Indeed, the Sonoran Constitutionalists showed their distance from the agrarian revolutionaries who followed Villa and, farther south, Zapata. Reportedly, Obregón told Carranza: "we have no *agraristas* here, thank God! All those of us who are involved in this effort are doing it for patriotism and to avenge the death of Mr. Madero..."[9]

This comment perceptively defined the differences between the Sonoran revolution and that in Chihuahua. It also reminded its audience that Obregón and many of his Sonoran allies had not played major roles in Madero's revolution. Instead of fighting for political principles, they got involved in defense of their native state against Orozquistas and Huertistas. Their political program would only evolve in the next two years as part of what historian Alan Knight has labeled the "logic of the revolution."[10] In this process, leaders absorbed the social and political aims of their followers in order to ensure their own political survival. Based upon an army recruited, in the words of one Huertista, "from the ranks of foremen, muleteers, policemen, clerks, milkmen, and [including] quite a number of drudges, farm hands, peons, and jailbirds," Obregón and the other Constitutionalist commanders would learn the need to embrace land reform, economic nationalism, and the goals of organized labor.[11]

No revolutionary leader represented Knight's "logic of the revolution"—expedient and pragmatic—more than Obregón himself. One of his eventual political enemies, the novelist Martín Luis Guzmán, who first met Obregón during Carranza's stay in Sonora, later described these qualities in dark hues. He was, Guzmán wrote:

> ... a man who felt assured of his immense value even though he appeared not to give this any significance. ... Obregón did not live on the terrain

of everyday sincerities, but on a platform; he was not a real person, but an actor. His ideas, his beliefs, his sentiments were like the world of the theater, to sparkle before the public; they lacked any personal conviction or inner reality. .... He was a phony, in the direct sense of the word.[12]

Although bitterness colored Guzmán's views, his words capture one essential aspect of Obregón's persona: his ambitions became a vehicle for the objectives of his followers. Unlike many other Latin American leaders of the twentieth century, Obregón did not subscribe to a recognizable ideology. Instead, he would seek to balance competing agendas for the purpose of achieving his greater military and political ends.

Obregón's association with Carranza made him a national revolutionary leader. In particular, he gained national stature by Carranza's nomination as leader of the Division of the Northwest, a position defined to include command over the Constitutionalist forces in Baja California, Chihuahua, Durango, Sinaloa, and Sonora. The title thus gave him nominal authority over Pancho Villa. With that title came a general's rank, one of the first conferred by the "First Chief" upon a Constitutionalist military leader. Obregón immediately took the fight south to Sinaloa. Henceforth, he would conduct most of his battles outside of his native state; a national military leader who left the fighting in Sonora to his subordinates. He was fortunate to subtract himself from the turbulent political scene in his native state, as the Constitutionalist coalition in Sonora soon thereafter fell victim to factional politics and rivaling personal ambitions.[13]

For Obregón, the overarching importance of Carranza's sojourn therefore lay in the fact that it marked the beginning of the establishment of a national network of political allies. No general himself, Carranza needed Obregón's military leadership, as well as that of González, the commander of Constitutionalist forces in the northeast. While most other military leaders gained renown by building a strong local and regional network of supporters, Obregón's strength emerged at the national level. Historian Linda Hall cites this phenomenon to dispute the notion that Obregón was a caudillo, since he never emerged as the primary political force in his own state. Indeed, it would not be until the 1920s that Obregón commanded both state-wide and national prominence, and it was not until then that he attained the stature of a caudillo.[14]

After Carranza's departure, the Constitutionalists coordinated a three-pronged attack from north to south, while Zapata besieged Cuernavaca to the south of Mexico City. At the head of the Division of the Northwest, Obregón began marching toward the capital along the western railroad. The División del Norte led by Villa, now provisional governor of Chihuahua, used the central railroad in their offensive. During the offensive, what had once begun with a group of eight men grew into the largest army the nation had ever known, a legendary force often referred to by its Spanish name even in English-language scholarship. Meanwhile, the Division of the Northeast advanced along the eastern railroad under the leadership of González. On April 21, 1914, all four armies got a major assist from US President Wilson, who ordered the occupation of Veracruz by Marines. This action cut off Huerta from his supplies in Europe. Three days later, González captured Monterrey, an industrial city that constituted one of the major Huertista redoubts in the north. Obregón faced the longest odds of reaching the capital first, as the distance to Mexico City was greatest from Sonora. In addition, his army—unlike those of Villa and González—needed to traverse a part of the Sierra Madre on foot and horseback because the western railroad remained unfinished.

However, Obregón's forces beat those odds, in part due to some help from Carranza. When Villa stood only fifty miles north of the city of Torreón, Coahuila, the First Chief ordered him to advance upon Saltillo, a city almost two hundred miles to the east, and close to González's army. Caused in all likelihood by Carranza's unwillingness to let Villa reach the capital before Obregón, this diversion delayed the progress of the División del Norte, and Villa angrily resigned from his post under the First Chief's command. After occupying Saltillo, the division returned to take Torreón in what amounted to a 400-mile detour, and then marched south to the city of Zacatecas, where they squashed the Federales in the single bloodiest battle of the revolution, with over 5,000 casualties.

The delay ordered by Carranza gave Obregón's forces the chance to catch up. They advanced steadily along the Pacific Coast, then turned east toward Guadalajara. On July 15, 1914, Huerta resigned, and precisely one month later, Obregón occupied Mexico City. Carranza further showed his favoring of Obregón by rewarding him with the rank of *general de división*, or divisional general (the rough equivalent of a major general in the United States). The elevation in rank was a big deal indeed, as no divisional generals had been appointed since the Juárez era. It made Obregón the equal, at least in rank, of Porfirio Díaz, who was approaching his death in exile in Paris. Notably, Carranza did not bestow this rank upon Villa. Of course, Villa was furious. As he saw it, the División del Norte, which counted on more troops that González's and Obregón's forces combined, had borne the brunt of the war effort, and Obregón had stolen his thunder due in large part to the First Chief's manipulations.[15]

Obregón's entry into Mexico City allowed him to stake his own claim to national leadership. He entered the capital bent on seeking revenge for the city's sins during the Huerta period. Within three days of his arrival in the capital, Obregón visited the Panteón Francés, the French cemetery, to pay his respects to Madero, in the company of several congressional deputies. At Madero's grave, stark rhetoric illustrated his belief that Congress—and the rest of polite society in the capital—had behaved cowardly during the Huerta coup. On the occasion, he beckoned a woman to approach him. This woman, María Arias Bernal, had led a public protest of the coup and the murders of Madero and Pino Suárez. Obregón took his pistol out of its holster and handed it to Arias with the words: "since I admire valor, I give my pistol to María Arias, the only one worthy of wielding it."[16] In his mistaken belief that the high Catholic clergy, and particularly the archbishop, had played an important role in the Huerta dictatorship, he also levied a $500,000 peso fine on the church.

This stay in Mexico City produced an alliance with urban labor that would prove crucial not only for the Constitutionalist coalition but also for Obregón's own government in the 1920s. Obregón cultivated the Casa del Obrero Mundial (COM, or House of the World's Worker). Founded in the Madero years, the COM was an anarcho-syndicalist organization that represented the workers of the capital and surrounding areas. Huerta had suppressed the organization and driven its leaders underground. Obregón, by contrast, allowed the COM to reopen, assuring its loyalty to him over the other revolutionary factions. It was his first act of social coalition-building. While Carranza's Plan of Guadalupe had exclusively consisted of political objectives, Obregón realized that ordinary Mexicans had waged and won the war against Huerta. The struggle and the long treks away from their home had empowered them, and, as he knew, the new revolutionary government would need to satisfy their most important objectives.[17]

Obregón's embracing of social objectives came just in time, as Huerta's removal ushered in the most destructive period of the revolution. As in the case of Madero's call to arms, the factional leaders against the dictator had agreed on little more than his removal. As someone who was neither First Chief nor commander of the largest army, Obregón would face the delicate task of taking advantage of the conflict between these two rivals, a task that required an understanding of the grievances that motivated both the leadership and the rank-and-file of the revolutionary armies to continue an escalating cycle of war.

Obregón and the Clash Between Carranza and Villa

Following the First Chief's attempt to divert the División del Norte from reaching Mexico City first, relations between Carranza and Villa became increasingly hostile in the summer of 1914. A well-to-do, educated hacendado, Carranza considered Villa a pillaging bandit who could not play a constructive role in the future of Mexico. He charged that Villa desired a weak president who would merely bring about more war and chaos in a country that had already seen its fair share of violence over the past four years. Villa, on the other hand, viewed himself as the rightful arbiter of Mexico's destiny due to the fact that the División del Norte was by far the largest contingent among the Constitutionalist forces. He resented Carranza's claim to power as First Chief as well as his centralizing tendencies, and he portrayed himself as a defender of municipal and states' rights. Finally, Villa considered Carranza and his associates elitist leaders who were out of touch with the nation's poor majority.[18] He branded the Carrancistas "men who slept on soft pillows," notwithstanding the fact that his own coalition included many such leaders as well.[19] Zapata held similar views of Carranza, who stalled on the issue of land reform just as Madero had done; but for the time being, his power base remained separated from that of the Villistas. Clearly, Mexico was too small for the ambitions of Villa and Carranza even without taking into account those of Obregón or anyone else.

For his part, Obregón did not choose sides right away. Ideally, he would have desired the elimination of both of his rivals. Villa's leadership resembled his own in its northern origins and emphasis on pragmatic politics. However, Obregón considered Villa a bandit who would not keep his promises. He agreed with Carranza's economic nationalism, but he resented the latter's ambition and often arbitrary demeanor, as displayed by the First Chief's appointment of the civilian Pesqueira as the new chief of the Division of the Northwest. No doubt a product of Carranza's desire to prevent an excessive accumulation of power, this move offended Obregón, who had held the post since the spring of 1913.[20] He also did not like Carranza personally; as he once said, "Carranza is a great man for little things and a small man for great things … persistent and dogmatic as well."[21] Ultimately, Obregón saw both Villa and Carranza as his rivals for control over the revolution, and he knew that each of the other two leaders had plotted to gain the upper hand over the others.

Making matters even more complicated, Obregón experienced the downside of his national stature and extended absence from Sonora. Several of his associates in his home base pursued their own goals that often conflicted with Obregón's needs. In particular, Hill and Calles resisted the return of Maytorena as governor, whom they considered a coward. Hill was Obregón's stand-in as head of the Constitutionalist forces in Sonora. In August 1914, Carranza anointed Hill provisional governor, posing a direct challenge to Maytorena, who had been democratically elected in 1911 and still had a year of his term remaining. Boosted thus by the First Chief, Hill showed no inclination that he would agree to be his uncle's puppet, and the same held true of Calles. An admirer of Carranza, Calles was one of the administrative brains of the Division of the Northwest. Based in the border town of Agua Prieta, his group had played a major role in bringing arms and money across the border, and Calles harbored gubernatorial aspirations of his own. Hill's and Calles's ambitions raised problems for Obregón as he attempted to assert his power in his native state as well as profile himself as an alternative to both Villa and Carranza. Also they inevitably led to conflict with elected governor Maytorena.[22]

Sonora therefore offered an early view of what would become the war between the factions. Rather than what historian Friedrich Katz has called a "proxy war,"[23] a term that evokes a view of Cold War-era conflicts in Africa and Asia in which opposing superpowers let off steam by means of military conflict between their supposed clients, the struggle in Sonora followed its own logic and contributed to the brewing storm at the national level. The Sonoran Constitutionalists had not entered the war against Huerta as a united force. As soon as Obregón left to begin his long march toward the national capital, Maytorena's enemies moved against the governor. As we have seen, Hill claimed the title of provisional governor bestowed by Carranza, in direct competition with elected governor Maytorena. Calles, then the captain of the Hermosillo military district, attempted to strip Maytorena of his personal escort in order to help Hill's ambition, most likely with a view to improving his own political position for the future. Carranza supported Calles in his endeavors, and the governor appealed to both Obregón and Villa to help him protect his position. Inevitably, Maytorena and the Calles/Hill combination were headed for a military confrontation. When Obregón gave Maytorena equivocal responses, especially as regarded his nephew, Hill, the governor gravitated toward Villa, whom he had met in exile the year before.[24]

The Sonoran theater played a prominent role in Obregón's decision to enter into negotiations with Villa shortly after his occupation of the national capital. Obregón desired to assert his authority in Sonora at all costs, and to limit both Carranza's political authority and Villa's military power. Villa, on the other hand, hoped that the Sonoran might join him in an alliance that would remove Carranza from the national political scene, confirm Maytorena as governor, and destroy the governor's enemies, Calles and Hill. Initially, Obregón expressed interest in Villa's proposed solution, as he feared that Calles's and Hill's activities undermined his own power in his native state. During a meeting in Chihuahua, Obregón and Villa agreed to subordinate Hill and Calles to Maytorena, whom they named chief of the military forces in Sonora; to name Juan Cabral the new governor of the state; and to confirm Carranza as interim president of the republic. As Obregón and Villa agreed, the interim designation would have barred Carranza from seeking a full term during national elections that they envisioned for the following year. Not surprisingly, neither Carranza nor Obregón's subordinates played along, and Villa broke the agreement on his own by ordering Hill and Calles to report to Casas Grandes, Chihuahua. In mid-September 1914, Obregón and Villa met again to sort out the mess, just as open conflict erupted between Calles and Hill on one side, and Maytorena on the other. These developments demonstrated the limits of Obregón's abilities in his home state.[25]

Obregón's second trip to Chihuahua resulted in a famous face-off between two of the revolution's top alpha males that illustrated the nature of personalist leadership in dramatic fashion. At the dinner hour, Villa suddenly summoned Obregón to his camp. When Obregón arrived, he was treated to a violent diatribe. Villa called him a traitor and demanded that he send a telegram ordering General Hill to report to Casas Grandes. When Obregón assented, Villa threatened to have him executed by firing squad immediately following the sending of the telegram. His secretary, a young woman who overheard the rant in an adjacent room, later reported that she saw her boss with "eyes blazing in fury and using very harsh words."[26] Villa told Obregón: "I will now have you shot." According to Obregón's memoirs, the Sonoran calmly replied: "You will do me a favor, because your death will confer upon me a personality that I do not have, and in this case, the only one to suffer will be you."[27] Nonetheless, Villa remained unmoved and locked up Obregón in a guarded room inside his camp. While Obregón awaited his execution, General Felipe Angeles attempted to dissuade his leader from the bloody deed, and he managed to get to Villa's wife, Luz Corral. As Corral later wrote in her memoirs, she told her husband that he could not order the execution of a guest in his own home; and that doing so would "brand him in the eyes of future generations as a man incapable of respecting the rules of hospitality." To Obregón's surprise, Villa called off the execution and acted as if nothing had happened. As Obregón told it, Villa said "Francisco Villa is not a traitor; Francisco Villa does not kill defenseless people, and least of all you, *compañerito*, a guest of mine. I will prove to you that Pancho Villa is a man, and even though Carranza does not respect him, he will fulfill his duty to his country … Let's go eat, *compañerito*, everything is over."[28] Shortly thereafter, Obregón left unharmed, although his return voyage featured several more scares from Villa and his men designed to cow him into an open break with Carranza.

As told in Obregón's almost poetic recounting, the symbolic implications of this meeting loom large for a study concerned with the culture of leadership. His (likely feigned) acceptance of his impending death, as an act of martyrdom for the cause of the nation, appears

especially noteworthy. In addition, Obregón's memoirs shrewdly emphasized the role played by Villa's wife in order to undermine his counter-
part's macho image by suggesting that Villa took advice from women. In
fact, various associates weighed in on the decision on whether or not to
execute Obregón, and their recommendations generally ran along class
lines. Middle-class advisers such as the former Porfirian military instruc-
tor Felipe Angeles advocated clemency. On the other hand, lower-class
members of what Katz has called the "murderous" element of the Villista
coalition believed that their chief should seize this unique opportunity
to execute Obregón, whom they considered an even more dangerous
rival than Carranza.[29] In light of subsequent developments, one could
argue that the lower-class generals made the correct call if their top prior-
ity was the triumph of their cause as opposed to the strict adherence to
a code of honor.

   In fact, looking at this incident in the context of notions of honor
sheds important light on how Obregón constructed Villa's manhood, as
well as his own. Obregón's account attempts to emasculate Villa by
showing his deference to a woman's opinion—something a "real man"
would never do. It also emphasizes his willingness to die a martyr if such
death glorified him and his cause. Martyrdom in war is the ultimate
macho act, and by telling his readers that he was ready to die, Obregón
laid claim to a high moral ground. Although Obregón's fear for his own
life becomes evident in his account, his concern with his personal honor
figures even larger. And indeed, Obregón's trip to the lion's den aug-
mented his growing reputation as a courageous leader.[30]

   However, the incident did not determine Obregón's position in the
looming conflict between Carranza and Villa. Instead, he continued to
play his political cards with the utmost caution and kept his options open
as long as possible. He did not react when Maytorena raised the stakes
by formally disavowing Carranza as First Chief and announcing his alliance with Villa on September 23, 1914.[31] Even though Maytorena's dec-
laration made two of his clients, Calles and Hill, into enemies of Villa,
Obregón remained neutral. He knew that the factional conflict made the
establishment of a functioning central government impossible, but he
was not yet ready to go to war on the side of one faction or the other.

   Instead, he sought to press his advantage when Carranza invited
leaders from all revolutionary factions to a convention to be held in

Mexico City. When Villa objected to meeting in the capital city, the location of Carranza's quasi-government, mediators settled on the central-western city of Aguascalientes, located in neutral territory close to Villa's troops. Held from October 10 to November 9, 1914, the Convention of Aguascalientes included officers in the armies of Carranza, Obregón, Villa, and Zapata, apportioned according to their numbers. As Villa's División del Norte outnumbered the other three armies combined, its delegation constituted a majority. The convention only included military leaders; thus Obregón, Villa, and Zapata enjoyed voting rights as delegates to the convention, while Carranza, a civilian, did not.

Ostensibly, the convention represented a platform to resolve political differences through negotiation rather than warfare, and some delegates believed that they could, in fact, create a blueprint for a stable central government. In fact, hostilities had progressed too far to re-establish peace between the Carrancistas and the Villistas, who both regarded the convention as a forum to vent their grievances. Obregón hoped that both Carranza and Villa would discredit themselves in the course of the meeting. He also hoped that the convention might result in an alliance of moderates in both camps eager to work together in order to avoid another civil war. He expected that such an alliance would turn to him rather than his rivals for leadership and arbitration. Therefore, Obregón ordered his delegates to play the part of mediators between the Villistas, who insisted on imposing their majority status on the convention, and the Carrancistas, who pointed to the fact that their man was still First Chief. Complicating the task, the twenty-six Zapatista delegates arrived two weeks late on October 26 and aligned with Villa, who, in return, promised to support the Plan of Ayala with its provisions for land redistribution.[32]

For a while, Obregón's scheme worked to his advantage. As the only major factional chief present at Aguascalientes, he cast a statesmanlike image: Zapata had elected to stay in Morelos, and Villa remained with his nearby troops. In a major speech to the convention, Obregón portrayed himself as an honest broker: "I do not betray Carranza ... I do not betray Villa ... I do not betray my fatherland, and I will live my life in its service."[33] When the Carrancistas and Villistas could not come to any agreement, Carranza authorized Obregón to read from a sealed letter offering his resignation and exile if Villa did the same and Zapata renounced his command over his troops. On November 2, 1914, it appeared that Obregón had managed to outmaneuver his rivals, as the convention approved his motion for the resignation of Carranza and Villa and the appointment of a provisional president. As a candidate, he nominated General Eulalio Gutiérrez, a leader with little political clout of his own who had somehow managed to stay above the factional fray. Gutiérrez won the vote, and many delegates believed that they had found a political solution to the factionalism that had threatened to erupt into civil war. The following day, Obregón accompanied a delegation to Mexico City to inform Carranza that he had been deposed as First Chief. [34]

In the end, however, Obregón's plan to use the convention to his own benefit backfired. Villa moved his troops closer to the city of Aguascalientes, which intimidated many delegates who had heard the story of the death threats that Villa had issued to Obregón. The tale increased their fear in a location close to Villista divisions. Moreover, Carranza had second thoughts about the arrangement. When Obregón arrived in Mexico City, he found that the First Chief had left the capital, and on November 8, Carranza asked his delegates to leave the convention. The Convention majority then declared them in contempt, which formally made Villa the chief of the Carrancista armies as well as his own.[35] In addition, Villa's forces encircled Aguascalientes, thereby cutting off all delegates from leaving the city. Therefore, the meeting greatly strengthened Pancho Villa and cost the Obregonistas their independence. In the last days of the convention, delegates embraced Zapata's Plan of Ayala, and they nominated Villa chief of military operations and the real power behind the scenes. These decisions not only handed Villa an outright political victory, but they also bestowed upon him a new aura of legitimacy.[36] Obregón had gambled on the Convention to make him into a crucial arbiter who would benefit from the rift between Carranza and Villa. Instead, he had become a subordinate of the former in what appeared to be a losing cause.

Obregón in the War Between the Factions

Villa's triumph at Aguascalientes forced Obregón's hand. Rather than subordinate himself to a government controlled by Villa, he joined forces with Carranza. Their coalition was henceforth known as the "Constitutionalists," in contrast with the "Conventionists," the alliance between Villistas and Zapatistas which fought to implement the decisions of the convention of Aguascalientes. This name invoked historical continuity from the first Constitutionalist coalition forged under the umbrella of Carranza's Plan of Guadalupe of March 1913, which had included Villa as well as Obregón in the effort to overthrow Huerta. As so many other alliances during the revolution, this was a marriage of convenience. The First Chief never forgave Obregón for seeking his resignation, and Obregón knew that Carranza regarded him merely as an expedient military leader. Moreover, the power relationship was not one of equals. Within the Constitutionalist hierarchy, Obregón remained nominally inferior to Carranza. Even though he counted on a much larger fighting force than any other Constitutionalist commander, this force was dispersed throughout central and northern Mexico, and Carranza retained the title of "First Chief" who had first organized the old anti-Huerta coalition.

Obregón publicly announced his alliance with Carranza on November 19 with the issuance of a "Manifesto to the Nation." In the manifesto, he called Villa a "monster of treason and crime" and lambasted "the perversity of that accursed trinity, [Felipe] Angeles, Villa, and Maytorena." He accused Villa of having "his hands full of dollars" as a result of his corruption, and he compared Mexico to a dying mother who, "before expiring, looks around to see whether all of her children are at her bedside." Obregón expressed his hope that none of the nation's "true children" would abandon their mother in this hour of need, and that they would flock to the Constitutionalist cause despite the privations and hardship that the military campaign against the Villistas would offer.[37]

Despite these denunciations, the war began badly for the Constitutionalists. Their enemies outnumbered them. Villa's biographer, Friedrich Katz, speculated that the "División del Norte was probably the largest revolutionary army that Latin America has ever produced."[38] An estimated 72,000 Conventionists confronted 57,000 Constitutionalists—a faction split into six different geographic areas.[39] In Sonora, Maytorena had taken the offensive long before the Convention of Aguascalientes. Since September, only the small border town of Naco had remained under Calles's and Hill's control. Besieged by Maytorena's forces for over three months, the Constitutionalists held out thanks to their ability to procure food, weapons, and ammunition in Arizona. The situation in the national capital did not look any better, as Carranza fled and relocated his acting government to Veracruz. On December 6, 1914, Villa and Zapata entered Mexico City with 60,000 men.

However, the Conventionists failed to finish off their enemies due to their own lack of unity. Featuring the Conventionist takeover of the capital, the 1952 Hollywood blockbuster "Viva Zapata" pokes fun at Villa and Zapata as they argued over who should occupy the presidential chair. In reality, the two leaders commanded different constituencies, which agreed on little more than a need for land reform and the removal of Carranza. The Conventionists viewed national politics as a way to accomplish their local goals. In the account of a US diplomat, the Villa-Zapata meeting in the National Palace treated national politics as an afterthought; both leaders were satisfied with Gutiérrez as a weak figurehead president.[40] Not surprisingly, Villa's vast alliance was badly fragmented. The general had little in common with his urban-based allies such as the former Porfirian officer Angeles or the intellectual Martín Luis Guzmán, who later wrote a fawning portrait of Villa. His retainers included a number of leaders who often disobeyed their commander and jockeyed for their own positions in the post-revolutionary order. For example, Generals Calixto Contreras, Rodolfo Fierro, and Tomás Urbina all boasted strong regional power bases and armies more loyal to these chiefs than to Villa.

By contrast, Carranza's subordinates displayed disciplined loyalty and saw their (often local and regional) roles in the movement as part of a national vision. As a result, January 1915 brought an early harbinger of success with Obregón's capture of the city of Puebla, east of Mexico City. Once in possession of Puebla, Obregón showed his loyalty to the civilian Carranza—as well as his political shrewdness—by writing a note to the First Chief that expressed his belief that military leaders should be ineligible to run for political office. With reference to Orozco, Huerta, and Villa, he wrote: "… I have come to the conviction that the principal cause of [our nation's misfortunes] is the unbridled ambitions of odious militarism …" He proposed a constitutional amendment stating that any military officer seeking public office needed to resign from the military six months before declaring his candidacy.[41] This initiative not only presented Obregón as an impartial arbiter who put the nation's interests before his own political ambitions, but it also revealed the national perspective of the Constitutionalists. Of course, as the future would show, the six-month rule would not inhibit the aspirations of military leaders, as revolutionary generals would go on to occupy the presidential chair for all but two years of the 1920–1946 period.

Obregón's political future survived, along with that of the Constitutionalists in general, due in large part to their refashioning themselves as advocates of social change. Obregón had gone to Aguascalientes in the belief that the convention might ensure peace by solving the narrow issue of political leadership, only to be confronted with military officers who tapped into deep-seated social grievances. In response, the Constitutionalists formulated a national program that sought to address these grievances, especially as regards labor and the landless campesinos.

Thus, led by Obregón, the Constitutionalists appealed to the poor majority, whether rural or urban. Although Villa and Zapata represented themselves as natural champions of the rural poor, Carranza and Obregón could ill afford to allow their enemies to lay claim to this vast population. A former hacendado of distinguished provenance, Carranza always had trouble relating to campesinos and laborers. Obregón, on the other hand, still recalled his own quest for a respectable living as a youth and young adult. He related to agrarians personally and easily, and his prodigious memory allowed him to remember the names of almost all the people whom he met. In keeping with the distinction between Conventionists and Constitutionalists mentioned above, Obregón saw rural issues as part of a national rather than local panorama. Having witnessed the extensive migration of rural workers to cities and mines, and vice versa, he understood the interconnected nature of rural and urban development, and considered the material improvement of living conditions throughout the countryside an indispensable ingredient in national economic development. Ideally, he would have liked to advocate land reform as a means to achieve a system of privately-owned small-holdings. This perspective differed drastically from that of Zapata, who had demanded the return of all hacienda land alienated from indigenous communities since the fall of Maximilian. But based on his own extensive experience with Mayo and Yaqui troops in his contingents, he realized the political importance of immediate land redistributions. Indeed, campesinos continued to form the backbone of all four major armies during the war between the factions, just as they had in the war against Huerta. As Obregón knew, land remained the major incentive that he could offer those campesinos in exchange for their support. Thus, on January 6, 1915, Carranza promulgated an Agrarian Law suggested by Obregón that promised the restitution of all lands seized illegally since the beginning of the Porfiriato.[42]

Obregón also cultivated ties to the urban poor, especially after his troops reoccupied Mexico City on January 28, 1915. Once in control of the national capital, he found that Carranza's war tactics did not work. Acting on the orders of the First Chief, the general invalidated all paper currency not issued by the Constitutionalists. This move forced the worthless Constitutionalist paper money upon inhabitants who held Conventionist bills. As Obregón witnessed, this decree halted commerce. Women holding fistfuls of Conventionist paper money paraded to his headquarters and begged him to reverse his orders. Struck by these protests, Obregón made himself into a champion of the poor. He organized a Revolutionary Committee for the Relief of the Poor authorized to give away 500,000 pesos in Constitutionalist paper money. The general also ordered all wholesale merchants who sold goods of primary necessity to provide the relief committee with 10 percent of their inventory for distribution to the poor. Foreign merchants were aghast at these measures. Afraid that Obregón would force them to accept Constitutionalist bills, they closed the doors of their stores. In response, Obregón imposed a tax on all capital investments in Mexico City. When a majority of entrepreneurs did not pay this tax, the general had them arrested. The next morning, he ordered those businessmen who still refused to pay to sweep the street in front of the National Palace. Yaqui soldiers looked on at the humiliation of the great *patrones*. While this show of force ostensibly aimed to collect revenue, its main goals were symbolic: to show the world that Obregón and his men fought for common people rather than the entrepreneurs who had played such prominent roles in the Díaz and Huerta regimes.[43]

These gestures worked, as ordinary Mexicans applauded Obregón's tough stance, while the general's measures elicited widespread hatred among foreign residents. One otherwise apolitical German housewife called him the "abominable Obregón" and labeled him "even more dangerous" than Carranza.[44] But Obregón explained that a developmental impulse rather than xenophobia drove his policies toward the foreign business elite:

> We Mexicans do not hate foreigners, but we do envy them for their superior education and business knowledge. We see the foreigners coming into our country, getting good wages, and living in good houses and on the best of the land, while our people live in huts and get barely enough to keep body and soul together. ... All we insist on is a living wage, a decent house to live in, and schools to send the Mexican children to. ... Why should we hate the foreigner upon whom we must depend to teach us modern ways of accomplishing things?[45]

Declarations like this explain why Obregón's six-week occupation of Mexico City broadened the general's popular support. For his part, Carranza displayed a strident nationalism that appealed to the urban middle classes, and he also advocated an eight-hour day for workers alongside other basic social goals.[46]

Obregón also used this opportunity to cement an alliance with the COM. In a formal pact signed by the First Chief, the Casa pledged to support the Constitutionalist cause by means of the formation of "Red Battalions" in the service of the Constitutionalist armies. Beginning in March 1915, up to seven thousand urban workers fought in six battalions on the Constitutionalist side, many of them from the industrial centers of Orizaba and Tampico, cities relatively close to the First Chief's headquarters in Veracruz. In exchange, the Constitutionalists promised to support COM demands for better working conditions and a right to unionize. The pact with the COM drove a wedge between urban and rural workers, with the former waging war on Villa's and Zapata's campesino-based armies. Although the ultimate significance of the Red Battalions to the outcome of the war remains debatable, they bestowed upon the Constitutionalists the much-needed reputation of a friend of organized labor.[47] The alliance with urban labor provided an important boost to Obregón and Carranza.

As the war wore on, the number of fighters ballooned on both sides. As had happened in the fight against both Díaz and Huerta, local caciques took advantage of the chaos in affixing themselves to a faction and anointing themselves military officers, sometimes even giving themselves a general's rank. These officers enjoyed the spoils that came with their military victories, and, in the words of one historian, "they considered their troops their personal property."[48] Everywhere, makeshift armies led by these men sacked haciendas, villages and towns. Women participated in the fighting too, as the numerous accounts of *soldaderas* attest. The Conventionist troops included many women, even though Villa (but not Zapata!) reportedly detested women fighters. According to one historian, Villa in 1916 ordered the machine-gunning of eighty or ninety soldaderas and their children. By contrast, the Carrancistas (under the command of González and others) embraced the support of women. Obregón's views of the soldaderas might have been closer to Villa's. According to one account, Obregón used soldaderas as well as children as human shields by positioning them in front of his troops; however, the existing documentary and photographic evidence of battle scenes does not support that conclusion.[49]

On March 10, 1915, Obregón left the capital to the Conventionists, aware of the cost of defending it and eager to engage Villa on the battlefield. His departure served as the prelude for the ultimate showdown. He knew that Villista troops controlled almost the entire northern two-thirds of the republic. In that light, he drew his enemy into the Bajío, a fertile, grain-producing region in central Mexico eight hundred miles away from Villa's power base. Meanwhile, his allies ensured a steady flow of supplies from Veracruz, the location of Carranza's provisional government. Against Angeles's advice, Villa moved his troops into the Bajío, ready for a frontal assault against Obregón's numerically inferior forces. But Obregón avoided direct engagement with the Villistas while he prepared himself for the inevitable confrontation. He knew that the División del Norte had overextended its supply lines. An avid student of trench warfare in World War One, which had broken out eight months before, he realized the benefits of a strong defensive position, and spent late March laying a trap for Villa's approaching cavalry. [50]

As Obregón and Villa prepared for their epic confrontation, both factions resembled ragtag armies rather than organized fighting forces. Although Obregón enjoyed access to superior material such as machine guns and barbed wire, both armies appeared shoddily clothed, to the extent that an observer could not have seen the difference. For example, one Constitutionalist unit under the command of future War Secretary Joaquín Amaro was known as *los rayados*, or "the striped ones" because they were wearing prison uniforms that they had obtained from nearby jails.[51] The war had also broadened the social base of the Constitutionalist forces. In Sonora, where middle-class *rancheros* had constituted the bulk of the fighting force against the Orozquistas only three years previously, a US military intelligence officer described the composition of the armies as follows: "boys from twelve to seventeen years of age, Mexican peon class, who are in the army for the living it gives them; Yaqui and Mayo Indians, including many half breeds."[52]

On April 6, 1915, the División del Norte confronted Obregón's army in the city of Celaya, Guanajuato. Again ignoring Angeles's stern warnings, Villa went on the offensive against an enemy entrenched behind barbed wire and under the cover of machine guns. After inflicting heavy losses on the attackers, Obregón counterattacked with his cavalry, and his troops decimated the enemy. The battle marked Villa's first major defeat. On April 13, the División del Norte again attacked Celaya. Once again, Obregón's well-positioned forces endured the Villista onslaught, only to mount a devastating counterattack on the flanks of the enemy. Two days later, both sides counted their dead and imprisoned from this second battle of Celaya: Obregón had lost two hundred men, but Villa, nine thousand. This decisive victory over a numerically superior foe turned the tide of the war. Obregón finally went on the offensive and attacked his enemy near León, Guanajuato (see Figure 3.1). On June 5, 1915, the victory of the Constitutionalists in the Bajío was complete with another rout of the Villistas at the hands of Obregón's army.[53]

However, this victory came at great personal cost to Obregón. Two days before this decisive victory, on June 3, 1915, Obregón suffered a loss that changed the way Mexicans thought about him for the rest of the century. Facing another Villista offensive, he had set up his headquarters at the hacienda of Santa Ana de Trinidad, the observation tower from which provided a magnificent vantage point to watch troop movements. At 9 am that day, Obregón observed the rapid approach of enemy artillery toward their position, and he decided to attack immediately. As his troops charged toward the enemy, a grenade knocked several of them to the ground and ripped off his right arm.[54] As an eyewitness reported, Obregón got up and shouted at his troops: "Let's go, guys! Long live

Figure 3.1   Defending León from the División del Norte. Source: FAPEC.

Mexico! Long live the Revolution!"[55] Bleeding profusely and certain of his impending death, the general then took out his pistol and attempted to put a bullet through his heart. Only the fact that the magazine of the pistol was empty kept Obregón alive, allowing his physicians to tend to the wound (see Figure 3.2).[56] With the loss of his arm, he achieved at least part of the martyrdom to which he had alluded in his September 1914 meeting with Villa. Because the Battle of León also signified the ultimate triumph of the Constitutionalists, the lost limb instantly achieved a quasi-religious significance. In the recollection of one of the eyewitnesses of the battle, "the arm … was passed around among Obregón's officers, who looked at it as something sacred, as a relic, as it indeed would be later on in the admiration of the people."[57] Over the next six weeks, Obregón remained on the sidelines while his associates sent the Villistas into full retreat and General González attacked the Zapatistas and rolled them back to their homeland in Morelos. On July 11, González entered Mexico City, and on August 2, Carranza established his government in the National Palace.

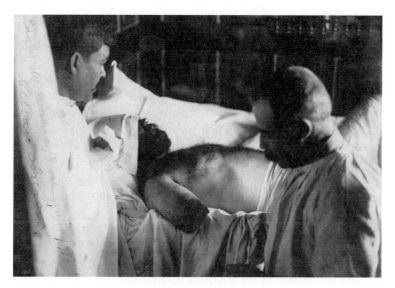

Figure 3.2   Obregón after the loss of his arm, June 3, 1915. Source: FAPEC.

Obregón resisted the temptation to make a public spectacle of his arm as Santa Anna had done with his leg. For Obregón, who considered himself the harbinger of a new and better era, doing so would have invited unwelcome comparisons with one of the most vilified personages in Mexican history. Not surprisingly, Obregón and his aides decided to keep the arm away from the public and use the image of its "sacrifice" in more subtle ways. His physician placed the arm in a formaldehyde solution and kept it in his office in Aguascalientes. The limb remained out of public view, and Obregón never discussed the loss of his arm in his official speeches. Instead, he promoted the idea that he had sacrificed his arm for the good of the nation by means of jokes and allusions. Photographs show him in military uniform, with the right sleeve shortened to draw attention to the missing arm. Without mentioning his arm directly, Obregón repeatedly referred to *sacrificio* as a necessary attribute of a political leader.[58]

Others joined Obregón in making reference to his severed arm. Following a meeting with Obregón five years later, Spanish journalist

Blasco Ibáñez summed up his persona as follows: "All aggressive men have a ... resemblance to birds and animals of prey. ... Obregón, with his short, thick neck, broad shoulders and small, sharp eyes, which on occasion emit fierce glints, reminds of you a wild boar. ... As Obregón has only one arm, and, consequently, cannot devote more than one hand to the care of his person, the 'hero of Celaya' ... is rather slovenly in appearance ..."[59] Of course, the Spaniard missed the fact that Obregón's appearance formed part of his military and political persona, one cultivated to emphasize the connections with ordinary Mexicans who had joined the general in battle. In addition, Ibáñez—a foe of militarism and military leaders in general—exaggerated Obregón's rough-and-tumble features; in fact, the general kept clean, alternating between civilian and military garb as appropriate.

Once Obregón had recovered from his injuries, he and his allies finished off the Conventionists, sending the Villistas into full retreat to their heartland in Chihuahua. On October 19, 1915, President Wilson extended *de facto* recognition to the Carranza government, which allowed it to obtain loans from US banks, as well as to procure weapons in the United States legally rather than by smuggling. Meanwhile, Villa made his last stand in Sonora, sending 17,000 troops to support Maytorena's struggling state government. Even though Carranza had named Calles provisional governor in August, the Constitutionalists only controlled the northeastern corner of the state, including the strategically important border town of Agua Prieta. On November 1, Villa's troops charged the town's well-defended fortifications and experienced another disastrous defeat. Calles took full advantage of US *de facto* recognition to obtain weapons and provisions from north of the border. Arizona authorities even allowed his reinforcements to travel through their state to reach the embattled town. Villa's failure to take Agua Prieta turned Calles into a significant player in the Constitutionalist alliance. Soon after the failed attack, Maytorena fled to Arizona, leaving Calles as the undisputed governor—one of three governors with Sonoran connections in the entire republic, along with Alvarado, imposed by the force of arms in Yucatán, and Diéguez, in his native Jalisco.[60]

Once the Constitutionalists started gaining momentum, their success fed on itself. One indicator of the impending Constitutionalist success lay in their treatment of their troops. With *de facto* US recognition and increasing control over the national territory, a widening gap opened between the standard of living of Carranza's and Obregón's men and that of the Villistas and Zapatistas. As the Conventionists' fortunes declined, their troops failed to receive food or pay with increasing frequency. Soldiers in the Constitutionalist armies, on the other hand, enjoyed the benefits afforded them by their leaders' access to food, clothes, and ammunition in the United States. No longer did the Constitutionalist commanders need to rely upon prison uniforms and similar garb to clothe their soldiers. At the bottom, the pay remained low—one peso, or US $0.50, per month, for privates—but Carranza's and Obregón's officers doled it out regularly. At the top, as of January 1916, the divisional generals earned sixty pesos, or thirty US dollars, per month.[61] In March of that year, the Constitutionalist army included more than 500 generals and 50,000 officers, most of them with self-proclaimed rank, among an army of 200,000. Carranza and Obregón ordered the retirement of 30,000 officers, scaling the army back to 126,000 enlisted troops led by 206 generals, including only eleven *divisionarios*.[62]

With military victory at hand, Carranza believed that the time had come to clip the wings of Obregón and other powerful generals in his coalition. Specifically, he moved to divide political from military responsibility, taking direct aim at governors like Calles who also served as military commanders in their state. Following up on an earlier attempt, in early 1916, Carranza outlawed concurrent service as military governor and military zone commander, or *jefe de operaciones militares*.[63] Of course, this decree could not be enforced in practice. The central government depended on regional strongmen to make its rule respected in the countryside, and many areas remained in the hands of its enemies. In Oaxaca, for example, don Porfirio's nephew Félix Díaz continued to play a significant role and caused trouble for the Carranza administration.

Obregón had emerged from the civil wars of the period 1913–1916 as Mexico's pre-eminent military leader. So far, he had relied on his military successes (and, to a lesser extent, his alliance with urban labor) to build his national stature. In four short years, the colonel who had once commandeered volunteer troops fighting the incursion of Pascual Orozco's troops into Sonora had come a long way. He had helped defeat the usurper government of Victoriano Huerta. And he had led his army to victory against Villa's feared División del Norte. By his count, he had traveled a total of 8,000 kilometers in his three campaigns: 858 kilometers in the war against Orozco, 3,498 kilometers in the campaign against Huerta, and 3,644 kilometers in the recent conflict with Villa, Zapata, and the Convention.[64]

Despite these successes, Obregón knew that his work remained incomplete, and that he had an important role to play in the reconstruction of a ravaged nation. As he expressed in one of his poems:

> I have run after Victory
> And I won her
> But when I found myself beside her
> I felt despair
>
> The glows of her insignia
> Illuminated everything
> The ashes of the dead
> The suffering of the living[65]

Military victory itself was an empty accomplishment, one that begged justification for the many lives lost during the years of violence. Obregón would spend the rest of his years coming to terms with the responsibility of victory, and specifically, the suffering of the living.

4

The Path to Power, 1916–1920

General Obregón ... is about to play the Cincinnatus act. ... He does not consider himself a soldier, but one who has been called from his plow to help free his country, and, having established it, to return to his ... [farm, which] seems to be very much enlarged due to his official position.

US military intelligence report, 1917

Although Obregón felt that he had won the Mexican Revolution, more so than Carranza or González, he knew that the sheen of his military victories would fade over time. The general was also aware that the re-establishment of a tenuous political stability favored the civilian leadership around Carranza. Launching a bid for the presidency—something often imputed to him but not publicly announced until 1919—required asserting a political profile different from that of Carranza while retaining the alliance that had swept their faction into power in the first place. Obregón faced the challenge of remaining independent from Carranza at the same time that he professed loyalty to the First Chief.

Despite Obregón's military triumphs, most Mexicans knew less about him than about the other three major revolutionary leaders, and, specifically, *de facto* President Carranza. As the titular head of the Constitutionalists, Carranza claimed ownership of the program of his

The Last Caudillo: Alvaro Obregón and the Mexican Revolution. Jürgen Buchenau
© 2011 Jürgen Buchenau

faction, and particularly the quest for political legitimacy. Zapata—who still dominated his power base in the state of Morelos—had made a name for himself as the chief defender of indigenous land rights. His 1911 Plan of Ayala remained emblematic for the struggle of indigenous campesinos for the land stolen from them during the Porfiriato by large agricultural estates. Although he had never postulated a plan such as Zapata's, Villa likewise represented poor rural Mexicans; in his case, the hardscrabble *rancheros* of the north who fought to preserve their way of life in the face of modernization. Obregón was the undefeated hero of the military campaigns of the revolution, and his organizational brilliance and entrepreneurial capabilities remained beyond doubt. In addition, he had obtained a reputation as a courageous, reform-minded leader committed to land reform and the improvement in living conditions for rural and urban laborers. However, Obregón's formal political experience consisted of local office in Huatabampo. Branded as a praetorian by Carranza's civilian allies, the general needed a chance to showcase his political ability if he was to set his sights on the presidential chair.

Obregón's Emergence as a Political Leader

Fortunately for Obregón, he soon earned an opportunity to learn the political ropes on the national level. Villa served up a reminder to Carranza that it was premature to think about pushing Obregón and the military aside. Angry at the US government for its support of the Constitutionalists, Villa decided to provoke an international incident that would draw US troops into Mexico. On January 10, 1916, he ordered the murder of sixteen US engineers and technicians in Chihuahua, and on March 9, his troops attacked the town of Columbus, New Mexico and killed seventeen inhabitants. This ploy worked, as President Wilson sent an army into Chihuahua in pursuit of Villa. The attack on Columbus and what came to be known as the Punitive Expedition greatly increased Villa's prestige, as many Mexicans came to regard him as a hero. As Generals John Funston and John J. Pershing (who would lead the American Expeditionary Force in World War One just one year later) chased Villa southward, the Centaur of the North's force grew once again. By the fall of 1916, the Villistas numbered more than ten thousand troops, confronting a government that once again needed to smuggle arms and ammunition across the border because the US government had embargoed weapons exports to Mexico.[1]

The dual menace posed by the Punitive Expedition and the Villista resurgence highlighted Obregón's value at the precise moment when the *de facto* president prepared to centralize power. Only four days after Villa's attack, Carranza named Obregón Secretary of War. As the two leaders agreed, Obregón would defeat Villa as well as caciques throughout the nation who had not yet submitted to the authority of the Constitutionalist government. His new job thrust Obregón into a trial by fire, as he immediately confronted a highly delicate situation that pitted him against the US occupation forces. As might be expected, Mexicans did not receive the military expedition favorably. Instead, the Punitive Expedition heightened xenophobia: in April 1916, civilians in the town of Parral attacked US troops. As a result, Pershing considered the occupation of the entire state of Chihuahua, a step that would definitely have led to war. In response, Carranza attempted to persuade Wilson to withdraw the Punitive Expedition through diplomatic means, while ordering Obregón to negotiate with the leadership of the expedition. For Carranza, Obregón's role offered two favorable scenaria. If the talks succeeded, his government would take the credit for the US withdrawal; and if they failed, the *de facto* president could assign blame to Obregón, whose power he increasingly feared.[2]

The Punitive Expedition ultimately redounded to Obregón's advantage. On May 2, 1916, he met with Generals Pershing and Hugh I. Scott. Obregón promised to root out the remaining Villista forces, a task he had set for himself in any case, and he vowed to prevent incursions (such as Villa's) on US territory in the future. In return, Pershing and Scott agreed to the gradual withdrawal of US troops. It was a significant victory for the Mexican side, reflecting the US commanders' faith in Obregón's leadership. But Carranza sought amendments to the agreement, arguing that the commitment to withdraw remained conditional on circumstances that Obregón could not control. Carranza may have done so because he would not allow Obregón such a significant diplomatic triumph.[3] Carranza's and Obregón's respective attitudes toward the world war also constituted an important factor in the First Chief's torpedoing of the Obregón-Scott agreement. While both leaders favored neutrality for obvious reasons, Carranza sympathized with Germany, and Obregón, with the western allies. Hence, Obregón appeared more willing to trust his US counterparts than did Carranza. In any event, Scott and Obregón continued to negotiate on their own. Their private talks greatly reduced tensions between Mexicans and the expedition forces until Wilson withdrew the Punitive Expedition in February 1917—with war between the United States and Germany in sight.[4]

His office as Secretary of War inaugurated Obregón's shift from a military to a political role. It served Obregón well in beginning a reorganization and professionalization of the revolutionary army, a process that would take two decades under eight different presidents. This professionalization would yield long-lasting dividends, as the armed forces remained loyal to national political authority rather than stage coups d'état like Huerta or the military officers of Cold War-era South America. He also enhanced his position by means of a political party. In the spring of 1916, Obregón, Hill, and several other leaders founded what was to become the Partido Liberal Constitucionalista (Liberal Constitutionalist Party, or PLC). Initially, the party was little more than a booster club for the Constitutionalist leadership, making a vague commitment to the principles of the revolution, and, especially, Maderista liberal democracy. In December 1916, its members assembled at the house of General González, where they chose the party's name. The name reminded Mexicans of the Liberal tradition of the mid-nineteenth century, and, particularly, the legacy of the great Benito Juárez. On that occasion, the PLC nominated Carranza for the presidency. While it might have appeared to others that the PLC organized in support of Carranza, its real goal was to hold the *de facto* president accountable to the people who helped put him in power.[5]

Meanwhile, Obregón found an opportunity to claim a new political space in the constitutional convention held in the city of Querétaro from December 1, 1916 to January 31, 1917. Known as the *constituyente*, this meeting included elected delegates from each state, territory, and the Federal District (Mexico City), at a ratio of one delegate for each sixty thousand inhabitants. In his call for the Constituyente, issued on September 14, 1916, Carranza announced that he would present a draft that would include his most important reforms of the preconstitutional years—the period since Huerta's resignation. Five days later, the First

Chief stipulated that the election of delegates would take place on October 22, 1916, and that political enemies of the Constitutionalists would not be allowed to run. In many districts, a sole candidate carried the vote. Many of the two hundred and twenty delegates were middle-class intellectuals (sixty-two lawyers alone), and eighteen held a senior military rank.[6] With good reason, Carranza expected a "harmonious, one-party gathering."[7]

However, in keeping with the patchwork of regional, social, and political differences that had marked the revolution so far, the convention proved to be far more boisterous and discordant than Carranza had imagined. Along with representatives from the white urban middle classes, it also included mestizos and indigenous delegates, campesinos as well as workers, and even a delegate born in Cuba, a nephew of the great José Martí. People from rural areas formed the majority, and most were young men in their thirties and forties. Of course, there were no women delegates because they lacked the right to vote. While this diversity already presaged difficulties for Carranza in securing swift approval of a new constitution, the draft he presented caused him greater problems. Carranza had long vowed to support a new constitution that would contain elements of socioeconomic reforms, based on decrees such as the Agrarian Law of January 1915 that addressed the needs of the poor majority. But his draft primarily contained political reforms, such as the principle of no re-election and Obregón's provision that would bar military officers from political office. As Carranza saw it, social reform should be left to Congress.[8]

The bland draft gave Obregón an opening to showcase himself as a champion of a more popular-minded, socially oriented perspective, a perspective supported by a majority of the delegates. This majority was aware of the fact that Mexicans had fought not only to remove a dictator and a usurper, but also to achieve a modicum of social justice. Therefore, they wanted safeguards of what one might call "social" as opposed to political rights: work, food, housing, and representation in labor disputes. Delegates from northwestern states loyal to Obregón came to the meeting having already experimented with reform at state and local levels. In Sonora, Obregón's allies Calles and de la Huerta had imposed new taxes on the mighty copper companies, and they had formulated progressive labor codes that provided indemnity payments for workplace injuries and the formation of a Worker's Chamber with direct input into the state legislature. Two other leaders with Sonoran connections had adopted similar measures as governors of Yucatán and Jalisco, respectively. These states served as early "laboratories of the revolution"—states with experiments in reform that would later be applied at the national level.[9]

Obregón took a strong interest in these deliberations. He traveled to Querétaro on various occasions, available to receive visitors who sought his advice. Obregón vociferously opposed the seating of the *renovadores*, Maderista delegates who had served in Congress in February 1913, when the legislature had sanctioned Victoriano Huerta's usurpation of the presidency. Like Carranza, the renovadores viewed the constitution as primarily a political document. The general cheered on the opponents of the renovadores, the so-called "Jacobins," as they promoted articles that would enshrine in the constitution the quest for social justice, economic nationalism, and separation of church and state. A number of these articles made it into the final document, and three deserve particular mention. Article 27 declared both land and the soil underneath it the patrimony of the nation. It not only provided the legal framework under which the government could redistribute land to campesinos, but it also limited the rights of foreigners. Exploitation of subsoil resources could only occur with permission by the government, and foreign companies were required to apply for a government concession. Even though the article permitted private ownership of agricultural land, it barred foreign nationals or corporations from holding great estates. Article 123 stipulated a maximum six-day, forty-eight hour working week, and it gave workers the right to bargain collectively, and even to strike in case they could not come to an agreement with their bosses. More generally, the article made the state into the guarantor of the workers' well-being. Article 3 not only reiterated the separation of church and state, but it also forbade the ministry of foreign–born priests and prevented all clergy from holding political office.[10]

For the first time in world history, a constituent assembly had adopted a basic law that enshrined social rights and economic nationalism. The 1917 Constitution was what political scientist James C. Scott has labeled a "public transcript," or, in other words, "the self portrait of dominant elites as they themselves would be seen."[11] As a public transcript, the constitution gave the revolution its marching orders and a performative script for the future. Henceforth, Obregón and other leaders needed to represent themselves as advocates for the social rights contained in the constitution, and promise their implementation. Ordinary Mexicans could refer to the Constitution when they pressed for land reform, a limited working day for blue-collar workers, or the participation of employees in decisions affecting a corporation. Of course, the actual implementation of these radical provisions was another matter—one that would define the great political debates of the decades that followed. To take effect, each constitutional article required enabling legislation passed by congress. Finally, the Constituyente entailed an important political dimension. It affirmed Carranza as the president of the nation as of May 1, 1917, and thus brought formal closure to four years of factional conflict.

However, this closure remained incomplete. Behind the scenes, the Querétaro convention had already witnessed some jostling about Carranza's successor, to be chosen in national elections in 1920. Both Obregón and González had played significant roles in defeating both Huerta and Villa, and both loomed as favorites. While González's contributions had not been quite as significant as Obregón's, no other Constitutionalist military commander could match his qualifications. Although it was an open secret that Carranza feared the influence of both of these generals, and especially Obregón, accounts differ regarding his own position. According to the memoirs of Adolfo de la Huerta, then provisional governor of Sonora, Carranza asked de la Huerta to persuade Obregón not to declare his candidacy. As de la Huerta put it, Obregón agreed, and Carranza promised, in return, to support the gubernatorial candidacy of the general's older brother, José.[12] Another version, however, posits the existence of a pact between Carranza and Obregón in which the former promised the latter his support during the 1920 elections in exchange for Obregón's loyalty during his administration. Yet another version mentioned a tripartite agreement among Carranza, Obregón, and González, to the effect that the two generals would support Carranza's claim to the presidency in exchange for his support for their respective candidacies in 1920. While Mexican sources remain contradictory, US military intelligence reports indicate that no such agreement with Carranza existed.[13]

Whatever the case, Obregón's role at the Constituyente loomed large in public perception. Although many of the radicals were Carrancistas or independents, the convention president branded them Obregonista Jacobins in reference to their counterparts in the French constitutional assembly of 1791. As one delegate recounted, his influence shook "the atmosphere of the Congress with violence," and there is no doubt that delegates from the northwest as well as those with a military rank looked to him for support.[14] Towards the end of the Constituyente, Obregón made a personal appearance. He closed his remarks with words that reminded his audience of the sacrifice of his arm: "May men mutilate themselves ... for [their] principles, but may they never mutilate ... [their] principles."[15]

In actuality, however, Obregón's influence in Querétaro remained limited to his informal role behind the scenes. As Secretary of War, he was not a delegate and had his hands full with fighting Villistas in northern Mexico. The minutes of the convention do not mention him other than his sole personal appearance, and one single instance of a *Viva Obregón* from the assembly. The available evidence regarding delegates such as Pastor Rouaix, who had drafted most of Articles 27 and 123, do not refer to Obregón's influence. The notion that Obregón manipulated the meeting cheapens their work and discounts their ferocious debates. In addition, it suggests a top-down view of events, as many of the delegates responded to pressure from their constituents rather than mandates from the leadership. But no matter how much influence Obregón actually exerted, the mere perception that he called the shots in Querétaro—as well as the fact that his name became associated with the radical wing of the convention—illustrated an important trend. The delegates knew that Obregón, more so than Carranza, could be counted on to carry out the constitutional reform program, and many of them believed that Obregón was the leader of the future.[16]

Obregón considered Carranza's inauguration as constitutional president an opportune moment to step aside. On May 1, 1917—the same day Carranza took office—he resigned from his post as Secretary of War and returned to Huatabampo. He had personal reasons to return to Sonora as well. By that time, Obregón had a new family. He had married his second wife, María Tapia, in a religious ceremony in the cathedral of Hermosillo on March 2, 1916.[17] The first of seven children had arrived

Figure 4.1   Obregón and his family, c. 1927. Source: FAPEC.

(see Figure 4.1). In addition, Obregón experienced health problems as a long-term result of the loss of his arm (including mood disorders and rapid weight gain) that prompted him to visit hospitals in Cuba and the United States in the only extended international voyage of his life. Obregón never took his eyes from national politics, however, nd it became obvious to everyone that his retirement from politics would not be permanent. As Obregón once reportedly boasted: "I have such good eyesight that I could see the presidency from Huatabampo."[18] Not surprisingly, Carranza knew that Obregón's return to Sonora augured ill for his own government. Having vainly attempted to persuade him to take a diplomatic assignment, he told him: "I will not permit you to go to Sonora."[19] The fact that Obregón did, anyway, indicated that he already figured as the power behind the scenes, planning for a future after Carranza.

94   *The Last Caudillo*

The Cincinnatus of the West (Part One)

Obregón's return to farming therefore reminded observers of the posture of George Washington, a man whom the British poet Lord Byron had dubbed "the Cincinnatus of the West."[20] The quote referred to the ancient Roman aristocrat and political leader who had served as consul and dictator in order to defeat rival tribes, only to return to his farm once the danger had passed. Like Cincinnatus, Washington, and Mexico's own Santa Anna, Obregón claimed that he was just a humble farmer who had only reluctantly given up his profession in order to save his people, and who would henceforth live the rural life that he loved. But few people who knew the general believed this story. After all, Obregón entered his home state as a triumphant hero, having defended Sonora from a series of enemies: the Orozquistas in 1912, the Huerta regime in 1913–1914, and the Villistas in 1915. When he left, Obregón had been the emergent cacique of Huatabampo. He returned as his nation's pre-eminent general, who would bide his time until a political opportunity presented itself.

However, as noted above, Obregón also displayed clear signs of exhaustion and illness. Not only had he resigned from the national government at an opportune time, but he also felt the need to tend to his failing health. The loss of his arm had weakened Obregón physically and emotionally. Only two years after the injury, he looked like he had aged more than a decade. An aide reported that his boss had drawn inward: "he is willing to listen to the importunities of his family and friends, and usually agrees to forego all thought of the presidency …"[21]

One piece of evidence that indicated Obregón's exhaustion was the gubernatorial election held in June 1917, only one month after his return to his native state. This election provided a litmus test for his political strength in Sonora, where he had spent little time since becoming a national military figure in the winter of 1913-1914. As we have seen, Carranza had nominated Calles as military governor in August 1915, a few months after Obregón's victories at Celaya and León. Calles had held both the posts of governor and military commander until May 1916, when his friend de la Huerta replaced him as governor. Calles, however, remained as military commander and worked closely with de la Huerta in pursuing a significant reform program. During his time in office,

Calles had proscribed alcohol, gambling, and prostitution; he had expelled all priests from the state; and he had provided workman's compensation. For his part, de la Huerta had formed the Cámara Obrera, or worker's chamber, essentially a parallel legislature that gave workers input into state politics under the governor's auspices. Carranza and Obregón had considered these measures (and particularly the anti-alcohol and anti-clerical campaigns) too radical. In late 1916, Obregón had deposed Calles as military commander to pave the way for a new pair of leaders that would be more loyal to him. His protégé, General Francisco R. Serrano, became military commander, and Obregón had pegged his brother José to win the governorship in the 1917 elections. However, Calles and de la Huerta prevailed thanks to their extensive political networks. Calles easily defeated José J. Obregón, who in the end received only minimal help from his younger brother, and two years later, de la Huerta won election to a term of his own. These developments demonstrated the limits of Obregón's power in his own state, but also his refusal to waste precious energies on helping his brother to win political office.[22]

Instead, Obregón strengthened his economic position. He had no compunction about using his considerable influence (and particularly the ability to seize lands confiscated from the enemies of the Constitutionalists) to obtain riches. His farm, La Quinta Chilla, grew from 180 to 3,500 hectares, most of them dedicated to the cultivation of chickpeas. By 1919, 1,500 men worked on his estate. Financed in part by US loans, Obregón expanded into new ventures as well, including cattle breeding, meat exports, and investments in mining, and he founded "Alvaro Obregón Importador y Exportador," an export/import agency in the border town of Nogales. In 1918, he spearheaded the formation of the Sociedad Agrícola Cooperativa de Sonora Sinaloa, an affiliation of farmers from the fertile border region between the two states. Also known as the Garbanzo League, this cooperative secured loans in order to finance the seeding, cultivation, and harvest of chickpeas. Through Obregón's agency in Nogales, the league also coordinated the export of chickpeas. Obregón himself took a commission of US $0.50 per bag, which afforded him revenue of over US$50,000 in 1918 alone.[23] Trading on such a large scale yielded unprecedented export opportunities for the farmers, many of whom had so far produced only for the local and regional markets, and it allowed them to raise the price of chickpeas from 7 to 15 US cents per kilo. For example, in Sinaloa, the 1917 chickpea harvest had amounted to five million dollars. The following year, under the auspices of the league, profits multiplied as the value of the harvest soared to over ten million dollars.[24] The formation of the Garbanzo League constituted Obregón's greatest business achievement during those years and showed his commitment to small- and medium-scale capitalist agriculture. A product of his environment, Obregón's vision contrasted both with the Porfirian emphasis on large-scale agribusinesses and the Zapatista demand for the parceling out of small plots of land for subsistence production.

The formation of the Garbanzo League elicited opposition, however. In northern Sinaloa, where the Mayo continued to fight the white settlers who had taken their land, the production of chickpeas got tied up with this ethnic conflict. Indignant citizens accused Obregón of selling food to the United States while inhabitants of that state went hungry. As one citizen remarked in an interesting allusion to the one-armed Obregón:

> You, Obregón, are a traitor to our people … You are to bring three million Yankee dollars with you; why don't you bring some food to your people. This treason will cost you your arm, you snake …[25]

In addition, the cooperative could not remain immune from the world market. The end of World War One in November 1918 brought commodity prices back to earth after four years of wartime boom. The league managed to maintain the garbanzo price for the following harvest, but in 1920, a steep decline of the price left the league in debt. As the league's agent—and in order to avoid political fallout—Obregón personally assumed the debt, but it remained unpaid until his death.[26]

Despite his return to agriculture, Obregón indicated that military and political affairs remained on his mind. For example, just a few months after arriving on his ranch, he expressed the desire to travel to Europe to participate in World War One on the side of the French. It was a foolish idea, of course, but one worthy of the alpha male of the revolution, a war hero who had just vanquished all of his enemies on the battlefield. His friend Aarón Sáenz, a future Secretary of Foreign Relations, persuaded him not to join the bloodbath. As Sáenz wrote, chaos awaited the nation if Obregón should fall victim either to the German submarines on the Atlantic or to their machine guns at the front. Nonetheless, the episode buttressed Obregón's macho image in the minds of his friends.[27] The idea also revealed his strong support for the western Allies, in stark contrast to the pro-German Carranza.

Evidence for this attitude came in the form of Obregón's support for the US blacklist of German and Austrian nationals and companies. Aware that the US government would place the Garbanzo League on this blacklist if it contained even a single person whom it considered an "enemy national," Obregón sent a memorandum to his friends and business associates that urged them not to do business with anyone on the list.[28] Meanwhile, Carranza denounced the list as a violation of Mexican sovereignty. Shrewdly, Obregón had begun to distance himself from Carranza on an important matter of foreign policy, and he had started to cultivate a pro-US image that would prove important in his quest for the presidency and, later on, his efforts to win acceptance from the US government.

The Campaign for the Presidency

By the time World War One ended, elections loomed in July 1920 to choose Carranza's successor. While Obregón gave no outward sign that he was interested in the presidency, he knew that these elections presented him with an excellent opportunity. He had left the Carranza cabinet honorably, and he had remained neutral as the president increasingly alienated the agrarian and labor interests that had once supported him. Obregón's stock was never higher than in those days. Indeed, many Constitutionalist leaders regarded Obregón as Carranza's natural heir. His supporters saw him as the true winner of the revolution and considered him better attuned to the concerns of the poor than Carranza, whose often haughty demeanor had antagonized many erstwhile allies. In addition, his numerous military victories, attained through personal sacrifice as evidenced by the loss of his arm, bestowed upon him a macho aura rivaled only by that of Pancho Villa, who remained at large as an enemy of the government.

As had been evident for some time, Obregón's main rival for the presidency was General González, who had spent most of the past two years combating the Zapatistas in Morelos. In doing so, he acquired political baggage that made him unacceptable to the agrarians in the revolution. In late March, 1919, he sent Colonel Jesús Guajardo on a mission to entrap Zapata. Guajardo offered Zapata his services, along with those of his troops. Suspicious, Zapata asked Guajardo to prove his loyalty by attacking González's forces, and on April 8, Guajardo did so, causing several casualties. Thus convinced, Zapata agreed to meet Guajardo at the hacienda of Chinameca on April 10, 1919. When Zapata entered the hacienda, Guajardo's troops gunned down the popular hero. The cowardly assassination sullied González's name, and, by inference, that of Carranza as well.[29]

At least among the military, Obregón emerged as a clear favorite for the presidency. According to Benjamín Hill's interpretation of the political leanings of the divisional generals in April 1919, at least 86 favored Obregón, and 18 supported González. Another 35 generals leaned toward supporting any Carranza-sponsored candidate, and presumably favored a civilian.[30]

Carranza did not want Obregón to succeed him. In a January 1919 manifesto, the president lambasted political campaigning, highlighting the dangers of "political effervescence" (read: unrest) in the countryside. In a thinly veiled reference to Obregón, he pointed out that "men of certain political prestige" aimed to "extract premature promises before they have had time to reflect sufficiently. ..."[31] He expressed his desire that only candidates run for national political office who enjoyed widespread public support rather than the backing of a few friends. Both of the nation's primary parties pledged their support of Carranza's request so that potential rivals would enjoy more time to build a firm political base. In March, one of Carranza's chief minions, Secretary of Finance Luis Cabrera, went on the attack in support of his *jefe*. In a widely circulated letter, he charged both Obregón and González with peddling influence and favors and tied these charges of corruption to the fact that both candidates were military men. In response, Obregón wrote a scathing letter under a pseudonym. The letter pointed to "public opinion" as an important element in presidential candidacies, and it took Cabrera to task for suggesting that hangers-on took advantage of their clientelist ties to military leaders. It then stated that Cabrera himself would dispense political favors if he were in a position to do so. The letter accused Carranza and Cabrera of trying to stall the political process because Obregón's popularity did not suit their own ends, and it ended with a warning to Carranza not to handpick a candidate whom public opinion would never accept. This exchange of letters brought the conflict out in the open.[32]

Carranza knew that the only way he could prevent Obregón from launching his candidacy was to divide his coalition. In late May 1919, he made just such an effort by appointing Sonora governor Calles to the national cabinet as Secretary of Industry and Commerce. The ploy appeared to make sense, as Calles had numbered among Carranza's most ardent admirers when the First Chief spent the winter of 1914 in Sonora. In addition, Calles had his own reasons to support Carranza rather than place blind trust in Obregón. The latter had amply demonstrated that he considered Calles an expendable asset. In his meetings with Villa in 1914, Obregón had attempted to pawn off Calles in exchange for a joint alliance against Carranza; in 1916, he had undermined his position as governor and military commander; and in 1917, he had pitted his brother against Calles in the gubernatorial elections. However, Calles's misgivings about Carranza trumped any suspicions of Obregón's motives. As governor, he had seen the president overturn the authority of governors and state legislatures even in issues that lay within the states' purview. Therefore, Calles declined to assume his new position until the expiration of his term as governor at the end of August. He used the time to ensure the election of his close friend, Adolfo de la Huerta, as his successor, despite Carranza's efforts to the contrary. Once installed in the cabinet, Calles used his post to help deepen the Sonorans' ties to campesino and labor organizations. Within a few months, he came to resent Carranza's authoritarian leadership style. It was in this appointment to the national government that Calles finally earned Obregón's respect; henceforth, he became an indispensable cog in his political machine.[33]

Upon Calles's appointment, Obregón realized that he should not wait any longer to announce his candidacy. Without the endorsement of any political party, he launched his candidacy on June 1, 1919 in Nogales. He laid out his plans in a lengthy pamphlet entitled (in translation) *Manifesto to the Nation Launched by the Citizen Alvaro Obregón*. Seeking to defuse the president's rhetoric, Obregón indicated that he was no longer a military man, having left the "trappings of a soldier" to live a life of "legitimate well being," an allusion to his return to farming. In true caudillo-like fashion, he feigned reluctance at seeking political office and thereby beginning a period of "anxiety, responsibilities, and danger" in order to do his duty. He also expressed his "absolute independence" from other leaders and interest groups.[34]

The Nogales manifesto divided Mexicans into two great parties, the "conservative" and the "liberal." Obregón used these terms idiosyncratically, with conservatives representing the Old Regime, and liberals, the revolution. According to Obregón, the clergy and hacendados made up the conservative party, with the support of foreign entrepreneurs; on the other side of the spectrum, workers, campesinos, small farmers, and professionals populated the liberal party. Although the liberals far outnumbered the conservatives, the latter party kept control because of fragmentation among liberals (*i.e.*, the revolutionaries). In Obregón's words, many liberal leaders "prostituted their prestige, blinded by their ambition or by the defense of illicit fortunes."[35] These words referred to Carranza and his supporters as former allies led astray by their personal aims. Obregón proceeded to call for the creation of a great liberal party that would unite these disparate tendencies.

In terms of a political program, Obregón emphasized the need to defend national sovereignty, effective suffrage, and the "pacification" of the nation as his primary goals. Like Madero and Carranza before him, he stressed political rather than social and economic goals, indicating that the economy could not prosper while much of the countryside remained at war and self-interested warlords wrestled each other for power and influence. In order to forge a broad national coalition, Obregón did not comment on the new constitution, which had already elicited significant opposition among the clergy, foreign investors, and landowners. Obregón thus employed rhetoric that appealed to the politically moderate middle classes. Throughout the campaign, he portrayed himself as a candidate in search of political equilibrium.

By contrast, Obregón lambasted Carranza for his unmeasured nationalism, particularly in the question of the foreign-owned oil industry. Already in the Nogales manifesto, he had proclaimed his "complete recognition of the legitimately acquired rights ... of foreigners" and announced that he would give foreigners the help they needed in enforcing their rights.[36] Of course, the adverb "legitimately" limited the rights to those in existence after the promulgation of the revolutionary constitution, but the formulation allowed Obregón enough leeway to recognize the government's pre-existing obligations, such as tax exemptions and concessions. This formulation was a good example of appearing to please both sides on an issue. In private, Hill counseled Obregón to go a step further. To gain the "moral and financial" aid of the US government, he argued, it was "necessary to rescind the radical laws ... that threaten the development of trade and the great natural riches of Mexico."[37]

Not surprisingly, Obregón's speeches reflected his faith in capitalism. As he began an extensive campaign tour of the republic that followed the trajectory of his triumphant campaigns against Victoriano Huerta, he emphasized the need to put Mexico on a solid economic footing. He announced in a November 1919 speech in Mazatlán, Sinaloa that the collaboration between entrepreneurs and workers laid the best foundation for the nation's future:

> ... the best ruler will be the one who establishes equilibrium between [labor and capital], so that both may find ... reciprocal advantages. If we do not give guarantees to capital, if we are hostile to it, and if we do not give it what it needs to develop our natural resources ... capital will remain inside the safe deposit box or outside our borders, and then our workers will continue to have to leave the country, in hungry peregrinations, to look for bread in other countries where capital enjoys the sort of guarantees that it cannot find here.

He continued: "we do not gain anything by giving felt hats and shoes to those who wear straw hats and sandals if we take them away from people who own them" if doing so would "set us back one century."[38]

At the same time, during his campaign tours, Obregón actively cultivated the support of the poor in exchange for securing the support of agrarian and labor interests in Congress (see Figure 4.2). He pledged land reform and implementation of Article 27 to the multitudes assembled to greet him, although his speeches were short on specifics on how he would undertake the redistribution of agricultural properties. Obregón then moved to strengthen his connections to urban labor, which dated from

Figure 4.2   Obregón campaigning in the state of Oaxaca. Source: FAPEC.

the pact with the COM during his occupation of Mexico City in 1915. In 1918, the defunct internationalist COM reorganized as the Confederación Regional Obrera Mexicana (CROM, or Mexican Regional Worker's Confederation), a nationalist labor organization under the leadership of Luis N. Morones. On August 6, 1919, Obregón signed a secret pact with Morones under which he pledged to set up a separate labor department, to support the full implementation of Article 123, and to recognize the CROM as the entity that represented the interests of labor. In exchange, Morones pledged his support to Obregón. To give their position political weight, Morones and others formed the Partido Laborista Mexicano (PLM, or Mexican Labor Party) in December 1919. The PLM represented the interests of the CROM in Congress. However, problems soon undermined this pact, as Obregón envisaged the CROM as the voice of urban and industrial labor (a population of no more than 200,000), while Morones coveted the inclusion of the approximately three million rural wage-earning workers. The CROM claimed to speak for all *campesinos* even though the interests of rural food producers often did not mesh with those of urban food consumers, to say nothing of the cultural differences that historian Alan Knight once characterized as those between the "sandal and [the] shoe."[39] The CROM therefore abutted the interests of another pro-Obregón party, the Partido Nacional Agrarista (PNA, or National Agrarian Party). [40]

In addition to the PLM and the PNA, Obregón counted on the backing of two political parties rooted in the middle class: the Partido Liberal Constitucionalista (PLC, or Liberal Constitutionalist Party)—the dominant party in Congress—and the Partido Nacional Cooperatista (PNC, or National Cooperatist Party). As we have seen, the PLC represented the political elite that had reached power with Carranza but that had distanced itself from him due to his authoritarian methods. Founded in 1917 by a young lawyer, Jorge Prieto Laurens, the PNC included many intellectuals loyal to Obregón. The PNC desired greater economic and social justice, favoring the nationalization of land, and more so than the the PLC, the party demanded civilian rule. Of course, at least in theory, Obregón was a civilian even though everyone knew him as "General Obregón," and the PNC supported him just as staunchly as the PLC did.[41]

Obregón worried that his reliance on political parties, and particularly the PLC, would compromise his authority as a candidate, and, eventually, as president. He knew that the PLC could turn on him quickly even though he was one of its founders. As Obregón's "ear" within the national government, Calles agreed. He warned Obregón against relying too much on the PLC leadership. He opined that the party's leaders backed Obregón in the expectation that he would agree to create a true parliamentary democracy in return for their support. In his opinion, the PLC sought open conflict with the Carranza administration and insisted on power-sharing between the executive and the legislative branches at a moment when Mexico was not yet at peace and not all rebels had put down their arms. In criticizing Carranza for his authoritarian practices, Calles believed, the PLC only deepened the president's desire to keep Obregón out of power. Calles asked Obregón to come to the capital in order to encourage Hill to distance himself from the "abominable" PLC strategy lest his campaign end in "disaster."[42] Obregón had already reached similar conclusions. Throughout the fall, Hill and PLC president José Inés Novelo attempted to corral the presidential candidate into drafting their party's electoral platform as a way to obtain his imprimatur for legislative candidates. Obregón steadfastly refused, and his letters to Hill and Novelo took on an increasingly austere and somber tone. He came to regard the PLC leadership—and especially Novelo—as a group of eggheads who did not understand the exigencies of governing a nation that had just emerged from a devastating civil war. He thus did not officially accept PLC support.[43]

As the campaign heated up, Obregón realized the need to downplay his military career. He launched a three-pronged approach to demonstrate that he did not resemble the military caudillos of old. First, aware that he would win any fair and free election, he announced that he would not use military force to win the presidency. "Why," he asked during a rally in Celaya, "would I impose myself by brute force if I have moral force, which is the one that should always reign among humans?"[44] Second, the PLC newspaper *El Monitor Republicano* publicized the fact that Obregón had resigned from the army on May 1, 1917, along with a description of his opposition to militarism. Finally, Obregón advocated reforms that would diminish the size and importance of the military. On December 3, 1919, he proposed to downsize the army to no more than 50,000 troops at peacetime, and to separate political from military authority—an endeavor that Carranza had launched numerous times in his effort to weaken regional strongmen allied with Obregón. At a time when many state governors allied with Obregón simultaneously served as chief of military operations in their area, the latter proposal constituted a significant concession to the Carrancista civilians.[45]

Along with this emphasis on civilian rule, Obregón revisited the loss of his arm in a way that furthered his image as a down-to-earth, popular leader. For example, he made light of the way his men found it on the battlefield. As he told Ibáñez, one of his aides found the arm by holding a gold coin in the air. "At once a sort of bird, with five wings, rose from the ground. It was my missing hand, which had not been able to resist the temptation to fly from its hiding place and seize a gold coin!"[46] Lest this admission of corruptibility might be used against him, however, Obregón only told this joke after telling another. "They have probably told you that I am a bit of a thief," he told Ibáñez. "All of us are thieves, more or less, down here ... The point is, however, I have only one hand, while the others have two. That's why people prefer me. I can't steal so much or so fast!"[47] These jokes illustrates Obregón's strategy of portraying himself as a real human being of flesh and bones, while suggesting that his adversaries were more corrupt than he was. In fact, most revolutionary leaders used their position for financial gain, and Obregón's fortune did not stand out among them as either extraordinary or modest. Although Obregón succeeded in these strategies of broadening his political base, the ultimate prize remained elusive. The more his support grew, the more implacable Carranza became on the subject of the presidential succession—and despite the alleged existence of a pact that promised Obregón the presidency, at least one eyewitness claimed that Carranza believed that Obregón lacked a clear plan of governing, did not understand national problems, and did not possess the "virtues most necessary for governing."[48] In January 1920, Carranza publicly endorsed a Sonoran as his successor: Ignacio Bonillas, the ambassador to the United States. Bonillas had no political personality or faction of his own and appeared entirely dependent on Carranza.[49]

Most likely, the nomination of Bonillas was the single most important reason for the Sonoran rebellion that followed. In early February, Calles resigned from the cabinet and returned to Sonora. Carranza attempted to impose his will by intimidating de la Huerta's state government, which he considered Obregón's primary pillar of support. The president named General Manuel Diéguez chief of military operations in Sonora, Sinaloa, and Baja California. De la Huerta not only considered Diéguez's appointment a slap in the face, but he also argued that the Yaqui would revolt against a leader who had treated them badly in the Constitutionalist campaigns. To make matters worse, Carranza ordered federal troops into Sonora and sent Diéguez to Hermosillo, which he proclaimed to be the headquarters of the military district. When de la Huerta and Calles protested against this show of military force, Carranza proclaimed the dissolution of powers in Sonora, a time-tested method by which he could bring about the fall of a state government. As in 1913, however, the Sonoran authorities would not be bullied by the federal executive. On April 9, 1920, the state legislature proclaimed that it no longer recognized Carranza as the legitimate ruler. Less than two weeks later, 107 military officers—led by Calles—signed the "Plan of Agua Prieta." The plan declared that President Carranza had violated the sovereignty of Sonora; it called for his overthrow; and it announced the creation of a rebel Liberal Constitutionalist Army.[50]

In the meantime, the president had upped the ante by attempting to remove Obregón from the political scene. He first tried to force him into exile in the United States, an action that would have rendered Obregón ineligible to stand for election, and he then brought him to Mexico City on trumped-up conspiracy charges that involved Félix Díaz and other rebel leaders purportedly in contact with him. On April 6, Obregón appeared before a judge in Santiago Tlatelolco prison to answer to these charges, but he convinced the judge that the documents corroborating his conspiracy were forgeries. Nonetheless, he knew that Carranza planned his arrest, and the Plan of Agua Prieta compounded his situation. In Obregón's words, "Adolfo and Plutarco must have good reasons for what they are doing, but we're caught here in a mouse trap."[51]

Followed around by Carranza's agents, Obregón decided to flee the capital. He enlisted the help of the railway workers in a daring plan. He jumped out of his car into a taxi hired by a railway engineer, which took him to the train tracks. The engineer hid Obregón in a box car bound for Iguala, the state capital of Guerrero. There, he secured the support of the nearby Zapatistas, who welcomed the idea of an overthrow of the hated Carranza, as well as General Fortunato Maycotte. Indeed, while Zapata had always loathed Carranza, he had respected Obregón as one who worked the land with his own hands, and his successor, Gildardo Magaña, eagerly embraced the chance to join forces to achieve the president's overthrow. Thus began Obregón's crucial alliance with agrarians from the southern states. His enthusiastic reception in Guerrero showed once again that Obregón—unlike Madero, Huerta, and Carranza—had recognized the support of the rural poor as the single most important social base.[52]

Ultimately, even González got fed up with the president. On April 11, he met with Obregón shortly before the latter's exit from the national capital, and the two generals and presidential candidates agreed that Carranza needed to go. Although González had eschewed the use of violence on that occasion, in late April, he massed his 22,000 troops in the vicinity of the capital, forcing the government out of Mexico City. A procession of trains eight miles long whisked the Carranza entourage toward Veracruz, where the president once again wanted to set up his government, just as he had done in 1914. However, there would be no repeat, as the rebels held up the train and cut the railway line in the state of Puebla. Carranza and his men left the train and headed northward toward the lush sierra, a perfect hiding spot for rebels. After several days, a general who professed loyalty to Carranza offered them shelter in the hamlet of Tlaxcalantongo. There, in the wee hours of May 21, 1920, a group of men attacked the hut where Carranza slept and murdered the president.[53]

Was Obregón responsible for Carranza's death? Some evidence points to his involvement. The murder occurred under the watch of a general who was later found to be in his employ. According to one historian, Obregón privately showed himself to be profoundly satisfied with this turn of events. Publicly, however, he expressed his indignation at the assassination, and he harshly criticized the military men who had accompanied Carranza for not defending the life of their boss.[54] If he masterminded Carranza's murder, Obregón certainly did not want to say so in public, and the evidence remains inconclusive.

When Congress, after some debate, confirmed Adolfo de la Huerta as interim president on May 24, 1920, a new era began. The inhabitants of the capital had seen the Sonorans twice before; once upon the fall of the Huerta regime, and again, during the war between the factions. This time, the strangers had come to stay, and their dominance would last fifteen years. Indeed, the period 1920–1935 has become known as the age of the Sonoran Dynasty. Among the victorious Sonorans, Obregón stood at the apex of a triangle that would account for the next three presidents: aside from de la Huerta, Obregón himself, and Calles. For better or for worse, the new decade would be his to shape. There was no question that Obregón would win the national presidential elections once scheduled, and his influence ranged far and wide, from a majority of the divisional generals through deputies and senators in congress all the way to the exponents of the new popular organizations that the revolution had produced.

However, few people would have predicted in 1920 that the era of the Sonorans would last fifteen years, as de la Huerta inherited a nation ravaged by war, disease, hunger, and international conflict. The violence had devastated infrastructure and agricultural production; and central political authority remained tenuous at best. Moreover, as Mexico City natives beheld the *norteños* entering their city in triumph, Obregón's enemies were already organizing. Among his old foes, Félix Díaz and

Pancho Villa remained in the field, as did several inveterate Carrancista generals. The Catholic Church had not reconciled itself with the anticlerical provisions of the new constitution, and both foreign and domestic entrepreneurs remained opposed to the new order. The Sonorans had an even more significant adversary in the United States government. Ailing after a stroke suffered during the Versailles peace conference the previous year, President Woodrow Wilson refused to award diplomatic recognition to the de la Huerta administration, on the grounds that it had taken power by violent means. Wilson also made it clear that US investors needed assurances that the Mexican government would honor all existing concessions for land and subsoil use. Without diplomatic relations, the Neutrality Laws did not apply to rebels in the United States, who were free to plot against the de la Huerta administration. In addition, the Mexican government could not procure loans from US banks, many of which held millions of dollars in claims against its predecessors. Worse yet was the opposition of Albert B. Fall of New Mexico, the chairman of the Senate Foreign Relations Committee. Enjoying close connections to oil companies and mining interests, Fall demanded the abrogation of Article 27 as a condition of diplomatic recognition.[55]

Despite these problems, interim president de la Huerta laid the groundwork for the gradual reestablishment of political stability that would constitute one of the hallmarks of the Sonoran period. Often treated as a mere footnote in Mexican history, his short tenure proved of great significance, both for the nation and for the building of the Sonoran political machine commandeered by Obregón. A leader whose strengths lay in negotiation, De la Huerta primarily expended his energies on reducing strife and violence throughout the nation. Aided by the advice of Obregón and Calles, then Secretary of War, de la Huerta struck deals with don Porfirio's nephew, Félix Díaz, as well as González and various Carrancista generals. In a climate in which political disagreements had often ended in death—including the murders of Madero, Zapata, and Carranza—the interim president's ability to negotiate with his government's enemies constituted an important step forward.[56]

By far de la Huerta's most famous achievement was his accord with Pancho Villa—an agreement that he accomplished over his allies' most strenuous objections. In July 1920, Villa approached the interim president with an offer to surrender in return for a guarantee for his personal safety. De la Huerta accepted these terms and granted Villa the ranch of Canutillo in his home state of Durango. In addition, Villa received a personal guard of fifty men. Obregón, however, fervently criticized de la Huerta for making a deal with a bandit. In his words, the majority of Villa's past actions had been "condemned by morality, justice, and civilization."[57] Calles made similarly disparaging remarks about this arrangement. Both Obregón and Calles wanted Villa dead or captured. The disagreement marked the first serious sign of discord between Obregón and de la Huerta. De la Huerta's initiative yielded him independent support from factions like the Villistas that had thus far remained hostile to the Sonoran regime. On the other hand, it poisoned his relationship with Obregón, especially in contrast to the stance of Calles. With his generous stance toward Villa, the interim president had therefore raised his own political stature in the nation, albeit at the cost of alienating the two leaders upon whose support he most depended. For Obregón, de la Huerta's position amounted to an open challenge to his authority, one that he would not forget. By contrast, Calles had strengthened his position for an eventual presidential bid of his own.[58]

Even Obregón needed to admit, however, that de la Huerta's accords helped the government orchestrate peaceful elections for president. Although the outcome appeared predetermined, Obregón found a competitor in the engineer Alfredo Robles Domínguez, a man with impeccable revolutionary credentials nominated by an opposition party as well as the Catholic party. Even though Robles's chances of victory were nonexistent, Obregón seized the chance to take on an actual opponent as a reason to embark on an extensive tour of the republic. During this campaign tour, he displayed his talent for connecting with the people whom he met, but he also sent ominous forebodings for the time that lay ahead with him at the helm, once stating that "it has been essentially difficult for [the Mexican] … people to make a proper use of … liberty."[59] On September 5, 1920, Obregón won an overwhelming victory at the polls. Official results awarded him more than 1.1 million votes compared with 47,441 for Robles.[60] On November 30, he was sworn in as president for a term of four years (see Figure 4.3).

Obregón had become the undisputed leader of the nation, and he was swept into office on a genuine wave of enthusiasm. Since his nomination as Secretary of War, he had masterfully played his hand. He had

Figure 4.3   The presidential inauguration, November 30, 1920. Source: FAPEC.

accommodated Carranza when it served his purposes, but distanced himself from the president when he lost popularity. He had adroitly recognized the need to support the inclusion of social and economic goals in the Constitution of 1917, and he had forged alliances with agrarians and workers. Obregón had resigned his position to return to farming in Sonora, but he had kept an eye on Mexico City because he saw himself as Carranza's natural heir as president. In 1919, he had returned to the capital to launch his first political campaign. Because of the wide-ranging coalition that supported Obregón, Carranza's plans to secure the election of a successor hand-picked by him resulted in the president's overthrow and death and the general's ultimate triumph. His followers looked for great things from him as president. But how would he fare with the reins of his nation in his hands?

5

The President, 1920–1924

"What these people need is education, not rifles. A good scrubbing, followed by a few lessons on how we do things in the United States, and you'd see an end to this chaos."
"You're going to civilize them?" the old man asked dryly.
"Precisely."

Carlos Fuentes, *The Old Gringo*

At long last, Obregón had gained unquestioned authority. However, he came to office with far less political experience than most of the other presidents of his generation. When he was sworn in on November 30, 1920, he had held a grand total of three political positions, two of them at the local level: *regidor* and *presidente municipal* of Huatabampo, and Secretary of War. By contrast, Carranza had served as a federal senator and as governor of Coahuila; and de la Huerta had been a federal deputy, ambassador to the United States, and governor of Sonora. Four years later, Calles would boast even greater political experience, having held positions as *regidor*, police chief, governor, Secretary of Labor, Commerce, and Industry, Secretary of War, and Secretary of Gobernación.[1] Even second-tier leaders associated with the Sonoran group in power such as Salvador Alvarado and Manuel Diéguez had more political experience than Obregón, having served as military governors and as members of the Council of Ministers, the national cabinet.

The Last Caudillo: Alvaro Obregón and the Mexican Revolution. Jürgen Buchenau
© 2011 Jürgen Buchenau

Not surprisingly, Obregón's presidency featured, first and foremost, an attempt at political consolidation, an effort that involved the cautious implementation of some of the social and economic provisions of the Constitution of 1917. In these endeavors, the president relied on his extensive connections among the military, Congress, the governors and regional bosses, and on his alliances with popular organizations. Often, these various coalitions pulled Obregón in opposite directions, especially as Obregón and his allies became part of a new entrepreneurial class that resisted the implementation of the Constitution just as the old land and mine owners, the Catholic Church, and foreign corporations did.[2] His presidency deserves a long book of its own; this analysis can only provide a brief summary.

The Construction of Obregón's Political Machine

Obregón faced an enormous task. The beginning of his presidency coincided with the worst period of the worldwide post-World War recession. While Mexican mineral products, and particularly metals, had found high demand during the military conflict, the price of these export commodities now experienced a steep decline. From 1920 to 1921, the value of silver and copper exports decreased from 158 million to 78 million pesos. Moreover, the violence had hit agriculture hard. In areas marked by intense fighting, most proprietors had abandoned their holdings, and the revolutionaries had destroyed the infrastructure, tearing up railroad tracks. Only the performance of the oil industry saved the nation from greater disaster; in 1921, Mexico was the world's leading oil exporter, contributing 26 percent of the world market.[3]

Worse, the toll of the "fiesta of bullets" became fully apparent only in its aftermath. According to recent estimates, Mexico lost at least two million people between 1910 and 1920: a toll attributable to war and the ravages of the flu pandemic of 1918–1920. Caused by a variant of the H1N1 virus, the flu may have claimed between 50 and 100 million lives worldwide, most of them in Asia and the developing world, and it contributed to the postwar recession. According to some estimates, the flu killed some 500,000 Mexicans, and it predominantly hit young to middle-aged adults, the mainstay of the work force. Emigration also contributed to this population loss, as more than three hundred thousand Mexicans moved to California, Texas, Arizona, and other southwestern US states.[4]

To complicate matters, central political authority remained weak even after three years of reconstruction. Governors and local *jefes políticos* defied the federal government to rein in their powers, applying revolutionary-era legislation inconsistently. In some states, such as Chiapas and Oaxaca, the revolution had yet to arrive; in others, such as Tabasco and Yucatán, reforms exceeded federal mandates; and some governors, such as those of Jalisco and Michoacán, retreated from reforms carried out during the 1910s.[5]

Obregón also faced significant international challenges, as neither the British nor the US government tendered diplomatic recognition. A few weeks before his inauguration, Republican candidate Warren G. Harding won the US presidential elections. Harding's victory ushered in the unprecedented influence of the powerful oil lobby and its chief representative, former Senator Albert B. Fall, who took over the post of Secretary of the Interior. The Republicans also enjoyed close ties to the banks that held Mexico's foreign debt, a group that held sway over future Secretary of State Charles Evans Hughes and other cabinet members. Even before Harding's inauguration in March 1921, Fall argued against the re-establishment of diplomatic relations with Mexico, a prerequisite for US loans as well as purchases of weaponry north of the border, even though Obregón—unlike de la Huerta—had been elected at the polls. As Fall argued, the US government should not recognize the Obregón administration unless it agreed to amend Article 27 of the Constitution of 1917, the article that made land and subsoil the property of the nation.[6]

If amending the constitution had solved the problem with the United States without significant domestic repercussions, Obregón might have gladly jettisoned the offending article. However, his most complex problem consisted of the need to address the enormous expectations of his social base. Although most social provisions of the new constitution remained a dead letter, their mere formulation had created hopes for their implementation, and particularly those regarding the situation of workers and campesinos. Obregón's followers believed that they had risked their lives for these ideas. Even more importantly, the constitution created the discursive framework of a populist political culture. The political culture centered on the idea of "the revolution" as a way of bringing redress to a variety of grievances, from the concentration of land in the hands of the wealthy to the Mexicanization of the economy, the absolute separation of church and state, and guarantees for labor. As all politicians, by swearing to uphold it, promised to support its provisions, the question facing the new revolutionary elite was not *whether* to implement social reforms but *when* and *how*. Obregón was known as a pragmatist, not a revolutionary ideologue, but he had no choice but to support legislation that he had no intention of putting into practice.[7] As he had expressed as a candidate:

> True equality—however much we might wish for it ...—cannot be realized in ... the meaning of the word ... In life's struggle, there are men who are more vigorous, more intelligent, better conditioned ... physically and mentally than others; and they, without a doubt, are those who have to gain greater advantages from their efforts... But it is necessary ... that those up high feel more affection for those below; that they do not consider them as mere elements of labor at their service, but as coworkers and collaborators in the struggle for life.[8]

To meet those manifold challenges, Obregón put together a magnificent cabinet (or *consejo de ministros*, as it was then known)—in all likelihood, the strongest supporting cast assembled in the era of the Sonoran Dynasty. The two most glamorous positions went to de la Huerta and Calles, respectively, in deference to their roles as Obregón's most important allies. De la Huerta took over the portfolio of Hacienda, the treasury department, now in charge of reforming the corroded banking system and finding tax and tariff revenue. Calles became Secretary of Gobernación, the powerful ministry of the interior charged with control over the police and the adjudication of state-level electoral disputes, an important job as disputes raged in ten different states in his first nine months in office.[9] The War Department was in the hands of General Benjamín Hill, Obregón's second in command during his campaigns against Huerta and Villa. Finally, the Secretary of Communications and Public Works, General Pascual Ortiz Rubio, had served as governor of Michoacán and had received considerable support for the interim presidency that Congress had ultimately awarded to Adolfo de la Huerta.

However, there was to be no harmony among these strong personalities. Calles and Hill—among the frontrunners to succeed Obregón in 1924—soon found themselves at odds over the role of the ruling PLC in the government, while de la Huerta and Ortiz Rubio squabbled over control over the nation's railroads. As a result, the Obregón presidency saw numerous changes in the cabinet, a pattern that would hold for the remainder of the Sonoran era. Aside from the cabinet, Obregón's power rested on four pillars: congress; the military; agrarian and labor organizations; and regional strongmen, whether formally in power as governor or as strongmen from behind the scenes.[10]

While sympathetic to Obregón, the legislature proved difficult to handle. Throughout the 1920s and early 1930s, congress remained independent of the executive, a far cry from the pliant legislature that marked the days of don Porfirio, and, later on, the heyday of the PRI. Even though a friendly majority in congress helped the president's legislative agenda, the largest party, the Partido Liberal Constitucionalista (PLC), stayed true to its Maderista intellectual roots. Having maintained an independent posture during Obregón's presidential bid of 1919–1920, the PLC insisted on a true democracy and the separation of the three branches of government: the presidency, Congress, and the Supreme Court. Impatient with the democratic process, Obregón and Calles undermined the PLC in favor of the second broad-based party that had supported the Sonorans: the Partido Nacional Cooperatista (PNC), as well as the two parties representing workers and campesinos, respectively: the Partido Laborista Mexicano (PLM) and the Partido Nacional Agrarista (PNA). Together, these parties ousted the PLC majority in the 1922 congressional elections. This weakening of the PLC involved threats and the use of violence. For example, even before Obregón's inauguration, Calles directed harsh words at Hill and PLC President José Inés Novelo. To promote harmony in the government, the new president sponsored a lavish banquet, at the conclusion of which both Hill and Novelo fell seriously ill. While Novelo recovered, Hill died on December 14, 1920, having been attended by Obregón's private physician. Although no evidence was ever discovered, many observers blamed Obregón and Calles for Hill's death.[11] Following so soon after Carranza's murder, Hill's death contributed to a new, darker image of Obregón among the public: one of a power-hungry leader who stopped at nothing—and not even at killing members of his extended family—to achieve his ends. Not for nothing did one long-time German resident of Mexico City label Obregón a "rough-and-ready saber hero."[12]

The president continued to wield significant influence in the military, and in particular, among the divisional generals who had fought in the revolution. Most *divisionarios* appeared firmly in Obregón's corner. Obregón knew that many of the generals believed themselves to be *presidenciables*, or viable candidates for the presidency. It was therefore not surprising that a leader who had risen to the top of the political hierarchy through his military achievements sought to institutionalize the army as a way of thwarting eventual threats to his authority.

Among Obregón's strategies to curb the power of the army leadership, his decision to rotate the zone commanders figured as the most significant. The Department of War had divided the nation into military zones, each with a commander appointed by the secretary. Approximately half of the *divisionarios* served as zone commanders at one point or another. Based on ample precedent, Obregón worried that the commanders would build up independent power bases in their zones—bases from which they could challenge the authority of the federal government. To address this concern, the War Secretariat assigned zone commanders to unfamiliar regions and rotated their command, typically every 2–4 months. Thus a divisional general might serve as zone commander in the Isthmus of Tehuantepec, followed by service in the Northwest and then, an assignment in the national capital. Obregón also resumed the process of reducing the size of the federal army begun by Carranza and continued by Calles when he had served as de la Huerta's War Secretary. The government managed to shrink the army from 100,000 to 60,000 troops, and to reduce its share of the federal budget from an astounding 61 percent in 1921 to a still formidable 36 percent in 1923.[13]

In what emerged as an ominous pattern, another significant strategy against the powerful generals consisted of their physical elimination. As explained above, in December 1920, Hill fell victim to a mysterious illness following a government-sponsored dinner. The following month, Generals Francisco Murguía, Lucio Blanco, and several other Carrancista leaders rebelled against Obregón. With the help of the new War Secretary, General Francisco R. Serrano, Obregón quickly crushed the rebellion, driving Murguía and Blanco into exile in the United States. In June 1922, long after the uprising, Blanco was assassinated by Obregón's men, and later that year, another effort by Murguía to incite a revolt led to his own death. Obregón thought little of his fellow *divisionarios*, whom he considered corrupt: as he once put it, "no general can resist a cannon shot of fifty thousand pesos."[14] When he made that famous comment, he might have had Serrano in mind, who required a payment of eighty thousand pesos to retire a gambling debt. Obregón thought even less of his sole remaining nemesis, Pancho Villa, who lived in retirement on his new ranch in Canutillo, Durango. On July 20, 1923, gunmen assassinated Villa in the town of Parral, Chihuahua. Historians have traced this assassination to the military zone commander, General Joaquín Amaro, as well as Gobernación Secretary and presidential hopeful Calles, who worried that Villa might support de la Huerta in a bid to succeed Obregón in the 1924 elections. With the involvement of both Amaro and Calles, there is little doubt that Obregón at least consented in (and probably masterminded) this murder of a former enemy.[15]

Obregón also cultivated close ties to state governors and other influential regional bosses, many of whom held rank as divisional generals. What set this constituency apart from the others was its strong local base and, in many cases, an inconsistent commitment to the revolution. As in the case of Serrano, relations with these regional bosses showed an opportunistic approach based on mutual benefit, including bribery and graft. As US journalist Ernest Gruening put it:

> Exceptional was the *jefe de operaciones* who did not carry several side lines—usually the exclusive gambling house concession, forbidden by law, the proceeds of a hacienda or two, to which his soldiers would carry the manure of the *jefatura*'s horses, or the lucrative task of "protecting" other *hacendados* from agrarians. The fault, at least in part, was Obregón's.[16]

In the north, Obregón primarily relied on business-oriented governors committed to economic development and reconstruction. Such was the case with a new and very significant ally: the fellow Sonoran Abelardo L. Rodríguez. Born in 1889, Rodríguez was nine years younger than Obregón and twelve years younger than Calles. In August 1920, Obregón sent Rodríguez to Baja California, Mexico's most distant region. His mission was to depose a regional strongman, Esteban Cantú, who had refused to submit to the authority of the federal government. Cantú enjoyed great power thanks to his association with the owners of brothels, canteens, and casinos based in the border towns of Tijuana and Mexicali, towns frequented by US tourists seeking relief from the strictures of the Prohibition era. Rodríguez not only removed Cantú from office, but he also took his place in the regional economy. Over the next decade, he opened new casinos in co-operation with investors from southern California, and particularly the posh Agua Caliente of Tijuana; he modernized the region's fisheries, and he inaugurated the territory's first vineyards. Throughout the 1920s, the Baja California economy boomed in conjunction with that of the neighboring US state, making Rodríguez the most significant of the "junior" Sonoran leaders associated with the Triangle. Notably, beginning in 1923, Obregón allowed Rodríguez to hold both the governor's position and the command of the Baja California military zone, and his ally stayed in both posts until 1929 when he entered national politics as a millionaire.[17] Other pro-business governors ruled over Chihuahua, Coahuila, and Nuevo León, with its state capital in the industrial city of Monterrey.

Farther south, however, Obregón often entered into alliances with agraristas and radical caciques. The four foremost examples number among the most colorful military leaders of the Obregón era: Saturnino Cedillo of San Luis Potosí, Adalberto Tejeda of Veracruz, Tomás Garrido Canabal of Tabasco, and Carrillo Puerto of Yucatán. An agrarista of petit-bourgeois origins, Cedillo allied with Obregón in return for Obregón's patronage. He ran the state through puppet governors and established military-agrarian colonies. By far the most conservative of the four, he repressed the CROM in his state. The other three leaders all served as state governors and carried out land distributions greater than the national average. All three experimented with radical reform: Tejeda and Carrillo Puerto, in the area of worker's mobilization; and Garrido, with his rabid anticlericalism. Significantly, all three governors sought and obtained the support of women's organizations that had formed during the 1910s.[18]

Rebuilding the Nation

Of course, it was not enough for Obregón to assert his control by either repressing or striking deals with regional bosses. Even more importantly, he also needed to address popular concerns by means of social and economic reforms. With good reason, one historian has called Obregón a "great compromiser" who reconciled revolutionary fervor with reactionary opposition, economic nationalism with the nation's position within the global capitalist system, and political centralization with the co-optation of regional leaders who continued to enjoy considerable autonomy.[19]

Obregón demonstrated his talent for opportunistic politics in the area of land reform, perhaps the most important and controversial issue in the revolution. Since Obregón had built much of his political strength through alliances with agrarians, and especially the former Zapatistas, this issue emerged as a paramount topic even before he took office. Within days of Carranza's assassination, the head of the PNA, Antonio Díaz Soto y Gama, had sought Obregón's assurances that he would parcel out land to the campesinos. A former Zapatista delegate to the Convention of Aguascalientes, Soto y Gama emerged as one of the mainstays of *agrarista* support of Obregón. In a speech to Congress in October 1920, Obregón struck a balance between Soto y Gama's demands and the fears of large landowners. He portrayed hacendados as creatures of the past who stood in the way of modern agricultural techniques, but he refused to divide large estates, pointing out that technological innovation could render them more productive and, hence, pay better wages to agricultural laborers. Instead, he desired to leave productive large estates alone and advocated the gradual establishment of one million smallholdings, which would have resulted in a redistribution of six million hectares out of the fifty million hectares under cultivation.[20]

In fact, the achievements of the Obregón regime were even more modest. Days after assuming office, Obregón issued a law that promised the establishment of agricultural collectives, or *ejidos*. However, the devil lay in the detail, as each definitive (as opposed to provisional) assignment of land to an ejido required presidential fiat. Under this law, Obregón redistributed one-fifth of his projected total, or 1.2 million hectares, during his administration. Congress hotly debated issues of land reform, pitting the PNA against the other parties, and local caciques served as the crucial middlemen through whom campesinos and the state negotiated land tenure. Still, Obregón's redistribution amounted to seven times the total achieved under Carranza, and he managed to retain the political support of the PNA.[21] Although this acreage constituted only a small percentage of that demanded by the agraristas, as late as 1923, Soto y Gama called Obregón "the executor of the ideas of Emiliano Zapata."[22] Therefore, land reform under Obregón remained inconsistent and locally contingent. Widespread land distribution only took place in two states. In Zapatista Morelos, many owners had abandoned their haciendas during the destruction of the 1910s. In Yucatán, radical governor Felipe Carrillo Puerto expropriated 20 percent of the land but did not touch the henequen-producing zone that constituted the bedrock of his state's economy. Elsewhere, agrarian reform often followed the whims of caciques. In parts of the state of Puebla, agrarista caciques such as Manuel P. Montes forged an alliance of convenience with the Obregón government. In return for their support, Obregón backed land distribution in the area controlled by Montes. A particularly famous case was that of a US proprietor, Rosalie Evans, the owner of a hacienda located in the area controlled by Montes and his men. Taking advantage of her US passport (as well as her late husband's British nationality), Evans vociferously fought against the redistribution of her land, hoping that two mighty foreign governments would come to her assistance. Obregón turned a deaf ear to foreign pleas on Evans's behalf and expropriated the hacienda by executive decree. The conflict between them escalated until one summer evening in 1924, when Montes's men assassinated Evans and her conductor on her way back to the hacienda. Reflecting on this episode, historian Timothy Henderson trenchantly assessed Obregón as: "a skilled machinator who was prepared to do whatever it might take—from issuing imperious decrees to engaging in the basest subterfuge—to assert some measure of control." As Henderson observed, Obregón's arbitrary use of land reform as an instrument of political power showed the weakness of the state over which he presided.[23] But the Evans episode also had a chilling effect on future expropriations of foreign-owned agricultural property, as the Obregón administration found itself at the center of an international controversy regarding the matter. Of course, this controversy did not help the government in its attempt to secure diplomatic recognition from Great Britain and the United States.

In other regions, land reform paled before other issues related to agricultural production. In Sonora, the Yaqui—a small minority of the state's population—figured as the principal proponents of land redistribution. With the exception of those who had fought on Obregón's side, most Yaqui leaders remained on the margins of state politics, unable to pressure the governor and state legislature on this matter. Access to water elicited far more interest: in the Yaqui Valley, the Compañía Constructora Richardson retained control over water available for irrigation, and the company had not delivered on its promises of improving irrigation in the valley. No stranger to these issues as a prosperous Sonoran landowner, Obregón strove to guarantee water for farmers. As a presidential candidate, he had declared the company's generous Porfirian-era concessions null and void. As president, however, he sought to work with the Richardson Company in provisioning water, and a 1922 agreement essentially reiterated most of the old concessions while binding the company more closely to its promises related to the building of canals and hydraulic plants. This agreement struck a balance between the needs of Mexican farmers and Obregón's desire to showcase himself as a partner of foreign businesses at a time when he was still seeking US diplomatic recognition.[24]

Obregón's policies regarding urban and industrial labor sought to meet basic workers' demands while keeping companies productive and competitive in a capitalist world economy. Whereas Carranza had ignored Article 123, which regulated the rights of workers, Obregón—following a precedent set by de la Huerta—allowed piecemeal implementation of some of its provisions. For example, employees in the larger cities got Sunday off with pay, and Obregón respected the right to strike, subject to government veto. He also allowed Congress to create an institutional framework that imposed increasing fetters on private businesses with regard to their workforce. This framework included boards of arbitration, which regulated labor disputes; indemnity payments to injured workers; and the unionization of employees under the aegis of the CROM, which now enjoyed the cachet of an official labor union. It was a modest beginning, but Obregón's reforms paved the way for the much more comprehensive workers' rights legislation implemented in the 1930s and thereafter. Most significantly, labor gained a permanent voice at the state and national levels during his administration, and Morones got an important position in the national government as the official responsible for munitions. It was not the Industry and Commerce portfolio that the CROM leader had coveted, but it was the first time that a worker—an electrician from the Mexico City suburb of Tlalpan—had received an important political appointment at national level.[25] However, Obregón ultimately disappointed organized labor. He showed impatience at labor activism, especially that which was not authorized by the government. He suppressed strikes organized by any non-CROM unions, and particularly by the railroad workers, who steadfastly refused incorporation into the CROM. For Obregón, these strikes became an issue of authority. Reportedly, he exclaimed in response to the railroad workers' strike: "either the workers rule or I rule!"[26] Unions that operated on the left or right of the CROM—the leftist Confederación Mexicana de Trabajadores (Mexican Workers' Confederation, or CTM) and the sizable Catholic labor unions—could not count on official forbearance, let alone patronage. The president also used the CROM to try to moderate the demands of workers, an effort that further accentuated the ideological demarcation between the CROM as the "official" labor union and more radical labor organizations such as the CTM and the railroad workers' union. He often referred mediation in labor disputes to state governments unwilling to give serious consideration to workers' demands. In addition, Obregón dragged his feet on his secret pact with Morones, which stipulated that he would create an autonomous Labor Secretariat, designate a CROM member as Secretary of Industry and Commerce, and sponsor a comprehensive Labor Law that put into practice the constitutional Article 123.[27] As Obregón's presidency progressed, the president tired of Morones' strong-arm tactics, especially after the assassination of PNC Senator Francisco Field Jurado—a murder widely blamed on Morones. Throughout, Obregón favored the PNA's agraristas over the CROM and its legislative wing, the PLM.[28] By extension, his relationship with other workers movements also cooled, prompting representatives from one regional confederation of unions to complain: "All of our efforts within legal channels have been useless, because neither the state's executive nor the legislative powers will attend to our demands."[29]

This failure to attend to popular demands owed not only to Obregón's entrepreneurial inclinations, which belied official rhetoric, but also to the continuing weakness of the central government. One good example of this weakness—which ironically demonstrated the possibilities for popular movements if they managed to organize independently from the state—was the 1922 renters' strike in Veracruz. The strike began among prostitutes, who protested against the poor and unsanitary conditions of the city's tenements. Organized by the anarchist Herón Proal, a charismatic, one-eyed tailor, the Sindicato Revolucionario de Inquilinos (Revolutionary Renters' Syndicate) helped the strike spread to the rest of the city and the environs. At its height, more than 10,000 renters refused to pay their monthly obligation to their landlords, and Proal became the *de facto* authority in Veracruz, mocking both Governor Tejeda and President Obregón by meting out his own version of revolutionary justice. Tejeda had the strike leader jailed, but Proal escaped and later joined the de la Huerta rebellion. After the defeat of that rebellion, Proal returned to Veracruz to a hero's welcome, while rebels everywhere else in the republic faced imprisonment or death. Obregón never got the situation in Veracruz under his control during his presidency, and many other examples abounded that illustrated the fact that much of provincial Mexico remained in a constant state of upheaval. Well aware of these limitations, Obregón understood the need for political improvisation and allowed Proal relatively free reign, hence displaying much-needed flexibility in dealing with popular movements.[30]

Another good example of flexibility in the face of opposition was the education program of the Obregón administration. Following plans laid down by de la Huerta, Obregón established the new Secretaría de Educación Pública (Secretariat of Public Education, or SEP) under the direction of José Vasconcelos, the head of the National University. A lawyer by training, Vasconcelos was an interesting choice for the job. An ardent Madero supporter, he had spent the Carranza years in exile in the United States, and he remained leery of the direction of the revolution due to his staunch Catholicism. But Vasconcelos agreed with Obregón in the need to spread literacy and basic education throughout the countryside—the primary charge of the SEP in its early years. Most importantly, the SEP sought to alleviate illiteracy, which ran as high as 85 percent of the adult population by the time Obregón took office. Another goal of the education program was to improve hygiene and public health; an objective that had appeared with great urgency in the aftermath of the flu epidemic. Helped by a generous budget, the highest of any federal agency except for the Secretariat of War and the Navy, Vasconcelos ordered the construction of thousands of schools, and he sent graduates of urban teachers' colleges to these new schools. Most of them were in rural areas, but some sought to educate the poor in the small, but growing slums of Mexico City.[31]

The men and women who trekked to the countryside to bring literacy and basic skills in math, reading, writing, social studies, and hygiene to populations that had thus far not enjoyed the chance to pursue a formal education constituted important missionaries of the revolution. As such, they found out that the task was not easy. Quite often, campesino families resisted their teachings, and at other times, the teachers found themselves caught between their mission and the desires of the community to which they were assigned. But most of them considered their job an uplifting task, and the education program constituted an important avenue for the professional advancement of women. Women had just been granted the right to vote in countries such as the United States and Germany but would have to wait three more decades before they gained that same right in Mexican presidential elections.[32] Moreover, the service of teachers in areas far away from their homes enhanced their sense of—and allegiance to—the Mexican nation.

To augment this work, Vasconcelos also invited the production of revolutionary art that might visually educate the public about Mexico's indigenous past and revolutionary present. As the centerpiece of this effort, one of his programs sponsored artists sympathetic to the revolution to create large murals inside public buildings. Several muralists heeded Vasconcelos's call, including Diego Rivera, one of the best-known artists in Mexican history and later, the husband of fellow artist Frida Kahlo. Unlike both Obregón and Vasconcelos, Rivera was a Marxist who viewed class struggle as the dominant issue in history. He began painting inside government buildings in 1922, although he would not create his most famous art until later, beginning in 1929, when his works came to adorn the National Palace and the building of the Secretariat of Public Education. Rivera's murals depict epic struggles between indigenous Mexicans and a series of rapacious invaders, from the Spanish conquistadors to the US invasion army in 1847. They portray the Mexican Revolution as the struggle for redemption of the indigenous population from a vicious alliance of foreigners, capitalists, and caudillos. The fact that Obregón and his successors allowed such politically explicit and radical art inside government buildings testifies to their belief that Mexicans needed to learn the history of their nation in broad outlines. Even more importantly, Rivera refrained from portraying Obregón and the other Sonorans on his murals, leading the viewer to infer that the revolution had brought justice and peace to Mexico at last. Finally, Obregón and Calles knew that their tolerance of radical art bought them the goodwill of intellectuals dissatisfied with the slow pace of reform.[33]

Indeed, government sponsorship of education and the arts contributed to a massive interest in the Mexican Revolution among progressive US and European intellectuals. During the decade of violence, a few intrepid US writers, such as the Marxist John Reed and the aging Civil War-era journalist Ambrose Bierce, had dared to visit Mexico, in a desire to make personal acquaintance with Pancho Villa. Immortalized in Carlos Fuentes's novel, *The Old Gringo*, the latter had disappeared during his quest. Now, with political stability at hand, an astounding number of prominent visitors flocked to Mexico, all in an effort to see a revolution up close. Their ranks included several renowned novelists (D.H. Lawrence and Katherine Anne Porter, to mention just a few), journalists such as Carleton Beals, Gruening and Frank Tannenbaum, and Marxist intellectuals such as Bertram and Ella Goldberg Wolfe. In the words of historian Helen Delpar, the Sonorans had managed to inspire an "enormous vogue of things Mexican."[34] To be exploited by future governments for the purposes of mass tourism, the emerging pride in national culture was one of the major historical processes of the 1920s.

Some of the foreign visitors, including Beals and Gruening, were quite taken with the president's persona. A man who would remain close to the Sonoran rulers for the next decade, Gruening lauded Obregón's simplicity and humor. In turn, Obregón courted Gruening and other North Americans in order to get their help in lobbying for US diplomatic recognition. In so doing, he played to US stereotypes of the Mexicans in order to elicit their sympathy with a nation that was, as he saw it, not at their level. On one occasion, he told Gruening jokingly: "You see, when I left the country and came into the city, the bandits all came in with me. Confidentially, I have some of them in my Cabinet now!"[35]

Contrasting this considerable enthusiasm about revolutionary-era Mexico among left-wing intellectuals and artists, President Obregón encountered significant opposition from the right. This opposition came not only from entrepreneurs and foreign diplomats, but also from the Catholic Church, whose official representative, Archbishop José Mora y del Río, had repudiated the 1917 Constitution from his exile in San Antonio, Texas. In particular, Articles 3 and 130 met with implacable opposition from the Church, which wished to preserve the right to educate Mexican children and to operate freely and without restrictions. Obregón initially attempted to improve his government's relationship with the Vatican; in 1922, for example, he sent a congratulatory telegram to the new Pope, Pius XI. As his conflict with the CROM developed, he appreciated the Church as a crucial counterweight to the anticlericalism of both Calles and Morones. He also knew that a strident position would cost him the support of staunch Catholics such as Vasconcelos or powerful regional strongmen such as Guadalupe Sánchez of Veracruz and Saturnino Cedillo of San Luis Potosí. In 1923, however, Obregón opposed the efforts of the apostolic delegate to consecrate a "Christ the King" shrine on Cubilete Hill in the state of Guanajuato, at the precise geographic center of Mexico. Citing two constitutional articles that outlawed outdoor religious celebrations and permitted the expulsion of foreigners who did not follow Mexican law, respectively, Obregón asked the delegate to leave the country within seventy-two hours. When Archbishop Mora protested, Obregón pointed out that his government pursued similar aims to that of the Catholic Church in that both institutions endeavored to send Mexicans "down the path of virtue, morality, and confraternity," and that acts of provocation such as Filippi's caused needless friction between church and state.[36] Once again, he had steered a middle course between anticlerical radicalism and a return to the Porfirian status quo. This middle course worked in preventing an outbreak of hostilities between revolutionaries and Catholics, but the church-state issue remained a ticking time bomb as long as Catholics did not reconcile themselves with the 1917 constitution, and as long as the state kept Catholics on the political margins.[37]

Finally, in an effort to thwart rebellions that—like those of Blanco and Murguía—originated from US soil, Obregón attempted to repair diplomatic relations with the United States as well as his nation's credit rating. In the summer of 1922, he sent de la Huerta to New York City to negotiate with the International Committee of Bankers under the leadership of Thomas Lamont. Unlike the politicians and oilmen, who impatiently desired the annulment of the nationalist Article 27 of the constitution, the bankers knew that the liquidation of their debts could only be achieved by negotiation. Obregón and de la Huerta hoped that the bankers would exert influence in the Republican Harding administration on behalf of diplomatic recognition, a prerequisite to normal financial relations between Mexico and the United States. They also expected that an agreement with the bankers might enable the Mexican government to apply for new loans. In the resultant agreement, the Obregón administration recognized a debt in the staggering amount of almost 1.5 billion dollars. Although this was a smaller amount than that claimed by the bankers, it constituted a heavy burden on the Mexican government, one alleviated only by the prospect of obtaining the further loans it desperately needed. However, this agreement did not bring about new loans, or a change in President Harding's refusal to recognize the Obregón regime. For the time being, rebels could continue to organize freely in the United States.[38] Fortunately for Obregón, political stability had improved to the point that the government appeared capable of handling minor threats to its authority.

The Violent Breakup of the Sonoran Alliance

However, the Sonoran Triangle proved as much as an alliance of convenience as all other coalitions that Obregón and other revolutionary leaders had forged with each other. In particular, the relationship between Obregón and de la Huerta had never been close. The president cast a stark contrast with the diplomatic, suave Guaymas native, a man with a beautiful singing voice that he had shown off in opera halls but no general's stripes. De la Huerta's status as a civilian was a great disadvantage as far as Obregón was concerned. From his perspective, de la Huerta had served his purpose in easing the transition from Carranza's rule to his own at a time that required his conciliatory abilities. Even more importantly, Obregón considered de la Huerta weak and gullible. He still seethed at the peace agreement with Pancho Villa negotiated by the former interim president, and from his perspective, de la Huerta's failure to secure new loans in New York City was the nail in the coffin of his presidential aspirations.

For his part, de la Huerta had grown disenchanted with Obregón. From his perspective, Obregón demonstrated some of the same strongman tactics that Madero had decried in his 1909 pamphlet inciting the nation to rise against Porfirio Díaz. Even worse, he suspected that his friend Calles participated in these tactics, making full use of his power as Secretary of Gobernación. For example, de la Huerta believed—probably correctly—that either Obregón or Calles had orchestrated the assassination of Pancho Villa in July 1923. Looking toward the upcoming presidential elections, both leaders had harbored fears that Villa would come out of retirement to support de la Huerta. In addition, de la Huerta furiously opposed Obregón's and Calles's interference in a gubernatorial election in the state of San Luis Potosí. Strongman Saturnino Cedillo, one of the president's most important allies, favored an agrarista candidate, Aurelio Manrique, who publicly backed Calles's candidacy for president. His opponent, PNC candidate Jorge Prieto Laurens, supported de la Huerta. On Election Day, violence broke out and forced the early closing of polling sites across the state. Both Manrique and Prieto Laurens declared themselves the winner. To resolve this crisis, Calles—who, as Secretary of Gobernación, enjoyed the right to adjudicate electoral disputes—ordered new elections and established a provisional government friendly to Manrique and, of course, Cedillo.[39]

The conflict that tore apart the Sonoran Triangle broke out in the year leading up to the 1924 presidential election. Formally, the 1917 constitution had reestablished a democratic system of government. However, as early as 1920, Carranza's efforts to impose a president of his liking had made a mockery of the democratic process. Therefore, the election loomed as the test case for a peaceful and constitutional transition of power. Acting under Madero's motto, "effective suffrage, no reelection," the framers of the 1917 constitution had limited elected presidents to a single four-year term. Thus Obregón would need to step aside at the end of November, 1924. As Mexico's most powerful leader, he figured to play the leading role in picking his successor, who would then ride to office with the help of his supporters. This practice would become commonplace under the PRI beginning in 1946, where each outgoing president anointed his successor with the so-called "finger point," or *dedazo*. As the former interim president and Secretary of Hacienda during the present administration, de la Huerta believed to hold a claim to the presidency.

However, Calles staked an equal claim as Secretary of Gobernación, a position that charged him with internal security and federal-state relations. By late 1922, Obregón had manifested his preference for Calles. He viewed Calles as a good candidate because he believed that he could control him. He knew that Calles had earned few laurels as a military leader, and that a brusque and abrasive political persona overshadowed his obvious administrative genius. Obregón also hoped that the *divisionarios* would support Calles because he was one of their own—yet one who could not count on a strong regional base outside Obregón's own state of Sonora. Unfortunately for de la Huerta, Obregón's opinion of who would succeed him mattered more than the nominally democratic process contained within the 1917 Constitution.[40]

And unfortunately for the entire nation, Obregón was wrong in his belief that he could impose Calles as the next president without eliciting significant opposition from de la Huerta and others. Several divisional generals, including Enrique Estrada, Fortunato Maycotte, and Guadalupe Sánchez, resented the imposition of Calles, whom they considered a less accomplished military leader than themselves. At the very least, they demanded an open process for choosing the nation's next leader. In addition, a group of military leaders who had joined the revolution in 1910 expressed their displeasure at Calles, like Obregón someone who had sat out Madero's revolution and only participated in the fighting after its triumph. The ranks of these generals included two influential members of the Sonoran group who had fallen out of favor, former Jalisco governor Manuel Diéguez and former Yucatán governor Salvador Alvarado. Hardly liberal democrats, these two military leaders considered de la Huerta more acceptable than Calles because he—like every member of that group—had publicly supported Madero before his victory.[41]

Despite these developments, de la Huerta would have probably resigned himself to his friend's presidency, as Calles and de la Huerta maintained a strong friendship even as the latter's opinion of Obregón steadily deteriorated. From his vantage point of Secretary of Gobernación, Calles had built a very strong position. The Secretary controlled the federal police force, and he had built strong alliances with radical governors in the east and southeast, including Adalberto Tejeda of Veracruz and Tomás Garrido Canabal of Tabasco. By 1923, these three erstwhile Obregón supporters pledged their primary allegiance to Calles, as did

CROM boss Luis N. Morones. Within the government, Mexicans knew Calles as one of the more reform-minded officials. Despite his many detractors—especially those who had taken a personal dislike to this mysterious and sometimes brooding man—he was in a strong position. He did not owe this position wholly to Obregón's patronage; instead, he had made himself indispensable to the president.[42]

However, Obregón pushed de la Huerta over the edge by adding insult to injury. The president publicly expressed his dissatisfaction (thus far expressed privately) at de la Huerta's failed negotiations with US bankers in the summer of 1922. As he put it, de la Huerta had exceeded his authority in acquiescing to the bankers' demands, and had conducted himself in a less than patriotic fashion. Stung by the criticism, de la Huerta resigned from the Hacienda post in September 1923. Obregón named as successor one of de la Huerta's personal arch-enemies, Alberto Pani. From his new post, Pani accused his predecessor of embezzling public funds, all without any evidence or justification.[43]

Equally galling to de la Huerta was the long-awaited awarding of US diplomatic recognition. By the summer of 1923, conditions for the exchange of ambassadors between the United States and Mexico had improved in the wake of the Teapot Dome scandal. In this affair, Secretary of the Interior Fall—an inveterate opponent of the Mexican Revolution since his days in the Senate—had leased oil fields in the western United States to two oil magnates without competitive bidding. In March 1923, Fall left office after revelations that the two oilmen had provided interest-free loans to him, and later on, he served a prison term. This scandal dealt the oil lobby in the US Congress a severe blow, and Obregón seized this chance to attempt a settlement. In May, negotiators from both nations began to meet in Bucareli Street in Mexico City. They were still meeting in early August when the death of President Harding shook up the US cabinet even further. New President Calvin Coolidge expressed eagerness to award diplomatic recognition if the Obregón administration could provide substantial guarantees to US investors. Obregón did not need to wait long. A few weeks after Harding's death, the Bucareli Agreements laid the groundwork for recognition after more than three years without diplomatic relations. In these agreements, the Obregón government disavowed the retroactive application of Article 27 of the 1917 Constitution as long as foreign companies had undertaken "positive acts" that proved their intent to exploit their property rather than just holding it as an investment. In other words, Obregón's delegates promised that most existing concessions awarded to US investors by the Díaz and Huerta regimes would remain in force. For Obregón, these agreements and the resultant exchange of ambassadors amounted to a significant political victory. For the first time since early 1920, the government could procure loans and ammunition in the United States.[44]

De la Huerta and Mexican nationalists considered these agreements— and particularly the *de facto* exclusion of most foreign economic interests from the threat of expropriation under Article 27—a treasonous sacrifice of national sovereignty. For don Adolfo, the agreements hurt worse because they wounded his personal pride. After perusing the minutes from the meetings, he complained bitterly that Obregón had raked him over the coals one year earlier for promising too much to US negotiators. As de la Huerta saw it, Obregón purchased recognition by means of far greater concessions to US investors than anything that the former Hacienda Secretary had proposed during his meetings in New York City. He charged that Obregón had yielded far-reaching concessions to US imperialism, all in order to strengthen his hand on the eve of the presidential elections scheduled for July 1924. De la Huerta had a valid point, as Obregón's position in the Bucareli Agreements amounted to a stunning about-face after two years of nationalist posturing. However, the accords were not quite as injurious to national sovereignty as de la Huerta believed, as they lacked the force of a binding treaty that would have mandated revisions to the constitution.[45]

De la Huerta's response to the Bucareli Agreements signaled the formal breakup of the Sonoran Triangle. For Obregón, the understanding with the US government arrived just in time. Yet another conflict between brothers in arms lay ahead. For that war, the president needed access to money and ammunition from north of the border. Little did Obregón know that the conflict would inaugurate six years of fratricidal bloodletting among the Sonorans. It was only the first stage in a bloodbath that would not only destroy the Sonoran dynasty that he had created, but also permanently sully his political legacy. Obregón had come to power on the high hopes that he would not only implement revolutionary reforms, but also install a truly democratic system, as he had promised in his 1919 Nogales Manifesto. But the president had ruled through authoritarian means; he had played a role in the assassination of his political enemies, such as Pancho Villa; and had repeated Carranza's mistake in attempting to impose his successor.

On December 7, 1923, de la Huerta pronounced the "Plan of Veracruz." This call to arms against the government listed, as grievances, Obregón's attempt to impose Calles as his successor; his intervention in the affairs of the states; and even the hypothesis that Obregón would seek to return to power following Calles's term. The name of this plan recalled Santa Anna's eponymous call to arms against Emperor Iturbide a century prior. The Plan of Veracruz put into evidence a rift among the Sonorans that, first and foremost, reflected increasing opposition to Obregón's heavy hand in Mexican politics. Thus began the de la Huerta rebellion, the most serious challenge to his rule.[46]

Hundreds of Obregón's former friends and allies found themselves in revolt against the government. Most remarkably, the rebellion divided the larger Sonoran group into two camps. Most of the surviving original Sonoran Maderistas, the aforementioned "generation of 1910" supported the rebellion, as part of a group named "Unión de Militares de Origen Revolucionario 1910–1913" (Association of Military Leaders of Revolutionary Origin 1910–1913). For example, Alvarado and Diéguez both supported the fellow Maderista de la Huerta. Alvarado had been jealous of Obregón since interim governor Pesqueira named the latter the commander of the Sonoran troops during the Huerta dictatorship. Diéguez, as we have seen, had cast his lot with Carranza—and against both de la Huerta and Obregón prior to and during the Plan of Agua Prieta, and he had spent the intervening years in exile before returning to Mexico to join the rebellion. Those who had joined the fighting during the Orozco Rebellion, however, the "generation of 1912," supported Obregón and Calles, fellow late entrants into the revolution. That group included two important generals who enjoyed close personal ties with the outgoing president and his handpicked successor, respectively: Calles ally Arnulfo Gómez and, of course, Obregón's old comrade-in-arms and protégé, Francisco R. Serrano.[47]

The rebellion posed a grave threat to Obregón's rule. One hundred and two generals—one-third of the total on active duty—joined the rebellion. According to a US intelligence report written immediately after the promulgation of the Plan of Veracruz, 47,000 rebels faced off with

Figure 5.1   The human cost of the "headless rebellion." Source: FAPEC.

only 35,000 troops loyal to the government. Other figures put the amount of troops in rebellion at 40 percent, plus 24,000 civilians.[48] Although Obregón had weakened the power of the generals by rotating zones of command and other measures, many of them had developed strong regional support bases. A considerable faction in congress—and particularly Prieto Laurens's PNC—supported de la Huerta, as did several state governors, as well as a large part of the educated bourgeoisie. Not surprisingly, de la Huerta's revolt touched off another major, and intensely violent, civil war (see Figure 5.1).

However, Obregón could count on important allies as well. Of course, Calles and his associates remained loyal to him. With Calles came the firm allegiance of the CROM, and particularly Morones, as rival unions such as that of the railroad workers supported de la Huerta. Perhaps most importantly, however, Obregón found that the agrarian movement provided unshakeable allies. His policy of increasing land distributions paid off even as it had failed to satisfy all demands. According to one estimate, Obregón raised 120,000 new troops from among the agrarian movement alone. The government benefited from the restoration of US-Mexican diplomatic relations, as the US government embargoed the sale of arms to the Delahuertistas. By contrast, the government was able to freely procure loans, weapons, and ammunition north of the border.[49]

Obregón and Calles could also count on the loyalty of the remaining members of their Sonoran coalition. Serrano, Estrada's successor as Secretary of War, coordinated the campaign against the rebels, and Brigadier General Abelardo L. Rodríguez, then military governor of Baja California, provided financial support. The governor remembered the important role Obregón had played in sending him to Baja California and allowing him to build up a business empire and power base. When Obregón, through Calles, asked Rodríguez for help, he responded accordingly. In December 1923, the state government sent $100,000 pesos (approximately $50,000 dollars) to the administration to help defray the costs of recruiting soldiers to combat the de la Huerta rebellion. In the only documented case in which a state government materially aided the Obregón regime during the rebellion, Rodríguez made four additional payments totaling almost $400,000 dollars, and he helped the government purchase two airplanes.[50] Obregón (and Calles after him) richly repaid their friend for his loyalty. The president rescinded a prior order to close the casinos of the Baja California district, and he ensconced Rodríguez in power. While Obregón customarily moved his generals around different military assignments lest they build too much of an independent power base, he and Calles allowed Rodríguez to remain in Baja California as military governor until 1929, by which time he was the nation's longest-serving governor.[51]

As an additional important element in yet another Obregón victory over a formidable foe, the Delahuertistas suffered from utter disorganization. De la Huerta himself did not oversee the revolt. That role fell to a number of generals who did not see eye to eye in their goals. General Enrique Estrada, the foremost commander of the rebellion in Jalisco, desired to oust Obregón and Calles and become president himself, if necessary through another de la Huerta interregnum. Like de la Huerta, Estrada broadly agreed with Obregón's political program, but not with his methods, and his followers believed that they were fighting for Estrada rather than for de la Huerta. On the other hand, General Guadalupe Sánchez, a wealthy landowner and a conservative adversary of the radical agrarista governor of Veracruz, Adalberto Tejeda, rejected the revolutionary program itself. With reason, a contemporary observer dubbed the revolt "*la rebelión sin cabeza*," or the headless rebellion.[52] The rebels had agreed on little other than Obregón's and Calles's elimination.[53] By contrast, the government remained unified. Obregón personally led the charge to defeat the rebels, orchestrating the government victory over General Estrada at Ocotlán, Jalisco, in the decisive battle of the civil war. Obregón would later confess that this battle brought his hardest-fought victory, more difficult still than his campaigns against Villa in the Bajío.[54]

Having prevailed over his enemies, the president pursued them ruthlessly, and he particularly targeted the divisional generals who had deserted him. His old Sonoran allies died on his orders. A firing squad executed Diéguez, on April 21, 1924 after a perfunctory court martial, and on June 9, 1924, Alvarado was shot dead shortly after returning from exile. Thus, the bloodshed added to Obregón's military reputation, but it also dealt a blow to his image as a conciliator and national unifier. Coming on the heels of the violent overthrow of Carranza, his harsh treatment of the rebels contrasted with his promises made in the 1919 Nogales Manifesto to lead a government that would unify the nation's progressive factions.[55]

The defeat of the de la Huerta rebellion offered Obregón a chance to further shrink the top brass of the Mexican military and reduce their influence in national politics. Although the president himself owed much of his influence to his support in the army, he knew the limitless ambitions of many of the divisional generals who—just like himself and Calles—envisioned themselves in the presidential chair. This insight explains his above-mentioned practice of moving military commanders around the republic in order to prevent them from constructing strong regional bases. Of course, Obregón stripped all those officers of their rank who had joined the de la Huerta rebellion, but he also demoted several others who had displayed less than steadfast loyalty to the government. De la Huerta himself went into exile in the United States. Of course, the winners—Calles, Serrano, Rodríguez, and many others, in addition to Obregón—divided the spoils and emerged from the bloodshed stronger, in political and economic terms, than ever before.[56]

In particular, the government's victory over the rebels paved the way for Calles's election to the presidency. With Obregón's support, Calles mounted his nation's first-ever presidential campaign that involved extensive use of the radio. He also undertook an extensive tour of the republic, including a much-publicized appearance at Zapata's grave on the fifth anniversary of the hero's slaying. In July 1924, Calles won an overwhelming victory at the polls over the Sinaloan general Angel Flores, while the same election swept a majority of Obregón's allies into Congress. On November 30, 1924, Calles was inaugurated as president in a new stadium designed by Vasconcelos—the first presidential transition celebrated as a mass event.[57]

Obregón's presidency might be considered in two different ways. On the one hand, he had accomplished a great deal against significant challenges. Obregón had managed to centralize political authority and begin the arduous process of restoring political stability; he had succeeded in restoring diplomatic relations with the United States; and his government had commenced an ambitious educational program. On the other hand, what had begun as an effort to reconcile political adversaries had ended in violence and cynicism. Generals Murguía, Blanco, and Villa died violent deaths even before the de la Huerta rebellion offered Obregón a chance to forever silence his critics among the Sonorenses, men who had entered the revolution earlier than he and favored a decentralized form of government. It cemented the ascendancy of the Sonoran"Generation of 1912"—men who had not fought with Madero in 1910, but who had taken up arms in defense of their own state during the Orozco rebellion sixteen months later.[58]

In the end, Obregón had proven a fanatically pragmatic president—one who consistently sacrificed political ideals and principles for practical solutions. More so than strengthening the state by building its institutions, he resorted to the methods that caudillos knew best—military campaigns, violence, and personal deal-making. In his eyes, the ends justified the means. He distributed land where the local situation required it; he supported the landowners where doing so maximized agricultural productivity; and likewise, he played bosses and workers off against each other with promises and threats. Obregón was a capitalist rancher who allowed Diego Rivera to paint socialist murals in government buildings, and who defended the socially radical provisions of the constitution even as he refused to implement them.

The promotion of Vasconcelos's public education program was probably the one aspect of Obregón's rule that most displayed his own political tendencies and ideas. As a self-taught man, Obregón knew the difficulty of acquiring literacy in the impoverished countryside. Yet there again, he realized the limits of the federal budget and did not fund the program sufficiently to allow its complete success.

By far the most ironic aspect of Obregón's presidency was his imposition of Calles as his successor—an act that contributed decisively to plunging the nation into civil war. While Obregón, unlike Carranza, proved successful despite military resistance, his triumph came at a high cost. Under his leadership, the revolution continued to devour its children, and this time even many of Obregón's erstwhile Sonoran allies. Much like Santa Anna and Díaz, Obregón's political ambitions had rendered him part of the problem, rather than the solution, to many of the ills that continued to plague the nation fourteen years after the beginning of the revolution.

6

The Last Caudillo, 1924–1928

Calles is not the problem. It is Obregón. You cannot imagine the ambition
there is in that man! Don Porfirio was a joke in comparison.
Eulalio Gutiérrez, according to José Vasconcelos

U pon Calles's inauguration on November 30, 1924, Obregón once
again returned to Sonora. This time, he moved to Náinari, his
extensive ranch in the Yaqui Valley and a holding that afforded him new
business opportunities. Even though Náinari yielded the same view of
the presidential chair that he had enjoyed from Huatabampo, the caudillo gave the appearance of living in permanent retirement from
politics. He appeared focused on his thriving agribusiness and none too
eager to return to the spotlight. Obregón apparently did not visit the
capital for the first sixteen months of the Calles presidency.[1] One day, the
Japanese minister, who had just received instructions to return to his
native country, went to Náinari to say goodbye. Seeing him in farmer's
clothes, the minister wondered aloud whether he was wearing a disguise.
Obregón declared: "No, Your Excellency, I am not in disguise. This is my
normal state. You saw the one wearing a disguise in the National Palace."[2]
As president, he had enjoyed the outdoors and spent much time in
Chapultepec Park, an extensive park on the western fringe of the capital
named after the hill atop which the presidential residence, Chapultepec
Castle was located.[3]

The Last Caudillo: Alvaro Obregón and the Mexican Revolution. Jürgen Buchenau
© 2011 Jürgen Buchenau

Yet Obregón could not banish from his mind the national capital and the enormous power that it held. He often received important visitors from Mexico City who sought his advice on political matters, and he frequently sent envoys to President Calles. Beginning in 1926, he visited the capital with increasing frequency, ostensibly to tend to his medical issues, but really as a reminder of his lingering influence. During those visits, Obregón routinely met with the president for an informal chat, and each time, Calles could not help but notice the enormous sway Obregón still held over many members of the national government.

With good reason, many observers considered Obregón the true power in Mexico despite Calles's election. In the absence of a formal political title, Mexicans knew him simply as *el caudillo*. The caudillo still held a commanding position in the army—a position demonstrated in his leadership during the de la Huerta rebellion. Most Mexicans regarded the incoming president as Obregón's creation, the head of an interregnum during which the caudillo's influence would remain unabated. Much like Porfirio Díaz had installed his friend Manuel González in power in 1880 when his first presidential term expired, only to return to serve for twenty-seven additional years, many observers expected Obregón to return to the presidency.[4] In the eyes of most Mexicans, Obregón had imposed Calles with the force of arms, and the new president remained beholden to him. It was no wonder that prior to his inauguration, Calles took an extended trip to Europe. In France and Germany, he bathed in the adulation of labor organizations whose leaders believed that the Mexican Revolution had ushered in a tropical worker's paradise, with Calles as its new exponent. The trip appeared a last respite before the president-elect would find himself submerged in the shadow of his powerful mentor.[5]

Indeed, Obregón had taken steps to ensure that his hold on national politics would remain strong even after Calles's inauguration. With the help of his friends and allies in the military, congress, the national cabinet, and popular organizations, Obregón continued to exert influence from behind the scenes. Calles appeared politically vulnerable and dependent on the caudillo, and Obregonistas enjoyed a solid majority in the new congress. In addition, Obregón's considerable prestige among the remaining generals as well as the agrarian movement meant that no president or governor could rule without his approval. Reportedly,

Obregón and Calles had signed a pact in 1923 that guaranteed the alternation in power of these two men in perpetuity. Historians have never found any evidence for such a pact, but given the caudillo's enormous political power, it is certainly plausible that he pondered a second term even as he finished his first one. In any event, when Obregón had packed his bags to retire to private life in Sonora, few believed that they had seen the last of him as a political leader.

A Troubled Agribusiness

Obregón devoted the bulk of his time in Náinari to furthering his growing agribusiness. For the caudillo, politics and business remained intermingled, as he attempted to expand his business connections in Sonora and Sinaloa with the help of his political allies. Specifically, he sought to involve President Calles and Baja California governor Abelardo L. Rodríguez in joint business ventures with him and Fernando Torreblanca. Obregón's principal partner in these transactions was Rodríguez's private secretary, Ignacio P. Gaxiola. Gaxiola was the fellow owner of the Oficina Comercial de Alvaro Obregón in Nogales, and in 1925, Obregón and Gaxiola founded Alvaro Obregón y Compañía, Sociedad Civil, a holding company devoted to administering the various properties of the caudillo and his allies. In April of that year, Obregón proposed to Torreblanca and Rodríguez the joint purchase of 4,200 hectares in Sinaloa, and he offered Calles his help in buying land in the Yaqui Valley.[6]

At the same time, both Calles and Rodríguez helped Obregón obtain private as well as government loans. In October, Obregón procured a loan of 150,000 pesos from the Calles government.[7] Calles and Torreblanca arranged another 150,000 pesos from the Comisión Nacional Monetaria, and the president proposed to help him secure yet another loan from the soon-to-be established Banco de México, the new unitary bank of issue that constituted one of the cornerstones of Calles's economic project. For his part, Rodríguez sent Obregón the modest amount of six thousand pesos as a personal loan. It appeared obvious to his friends and allies that the caudillo required a lot of cash, but that loans to him proved a sound investment. According to Calles, Obregón's name alone constituted sufficient collateral.[8] In 1926, Obregón obtained a generous loan from the newly established Banco Nacional de Crédito Agrícola (BNCA, or National Bank for Agrarian Credit) and purchased vast tracts of land from the US-owned Compañía Constructora Richardson. In all likelihood, Obregón only got the funds because of his enormous political influence. He also obtained credit from banks in southern California.[9]

Obregón appears to have used these funds for profitable purposes, especially with regard to forging closer commercial ties between Sonora and the United States. With the help of another Banco Nacional loan facilitated by Calles, he invested in a power generator purchased from Fairbanks, Morse & Co. at the cost of US $50,000.[10] The caudillo expanded into new ventures: irrigation; the production of rice, tomato, soap, and jute bags; seafood-packing; and an automobile agency. Floated by loans and profits, Obregón and Gaxiola founded several new enterprises, including a flour mill and a new agricultural company named Obregón y Cía. As part of his involvement in the growing agricultural exports of his state, the caudillo frequently traveled to California, where he portrayed himself as a friend of free trade. In his mind, California and the Mexican northwest constituted "one of the the greatest centers of production in the entire world." As he put it, "the prosperous and great peoples are never those that lock themselves up in their own borders," and if the Mexican government made the mistake "of trying to impose new taxes in order to wage a commercial boxing match, we would commit not only a crime, but also an error that would hurt our own interests."[11] But several months later, he cautioned in a speech to the Pacific Union Club in San Francisco that the nation did not want "filibuster capital" that sought to influence Mexican internal affairs, a shrewd reference to the US filibusters who had sought the annexation of Baja California and Sonora in the 1850s and 1860s.[12]

However, the caudillo confronted adversity in his business dealings, due in large part to his decision to engage in a growing number of financially risky ventures. For example, in October 1926, Obregón's company acquired a majority stake in the Compañía Constructora Richardson, in exchange for assuming most of its financial obligations. Obregón knew that the Richardson Company had steadily lost money since the outbreak of the revolution, but he also realized that the lands close to the Yaqui

River would never reach their full potential as long as irrigation tech-
nologies used in the area remained outdated. The agreement lasted all of
two months, as the directors of the Richardson Company granted control
over the company, including the shares signed over to Obregón, to the
government-run BNCA in December 1926. For the company, this
appeared a worse deal, as the BNCA did not assume its debts. Nonetheless,
Obregón did not fight the government takeover, which was orchestrated
by President Calles and completed in January 1928. The intervention of
the BNCA in Obregón's relationship with the Richardson raises an interesting question. Did President Calles break up Obregón's deal in order
to demonstrate his own authority? Or, as is more likely, did the takeover
represent an effort to save Obregón from a disastrous financial maneuver
that he had only agreed to undertake because he saw no other option?[13]
In the absence of documentary evidence, this question awaits a conclu-
sive answer.

Thus overextended in his endeavor to acquire a commanding position
in the Yaqui Valley, Obregón's business operation faced dangerous cash
shortfalls in the event of natural disasters and price fluctuations. For
example, in June 1926, a severe plague hit his wheat crop, considerably
diminishing its yield. As a result, the caudillo fell behind on some of his
debt service payments. The following year, Rodríguez once again bailed
out Obregón by procuring a loan from his principal partner in the posh
new Agua Caliente casino in Tijuana, a businessman from Southern
California. At the same time, Obregón's agribusiness suffered from
declining demand on the world market for its staples; for instance, in
early 1928, a precipitous fall of the price of rice greatly diminished
revenue.[14]

Perhaps the best evidence of Obregón's economic difficulties at
that time can be found in the documentation regarding his estate preserved in the Calles-Torreblanca archive. For example, as of 1928, the
debt resulting from the 1920 garbanzo harvest remained unpaid, a debt
incurred due to the steep decline of the world market price of chickpeas.
In addition, Obregón himself made reference to his large liabilities in his
last will, composed in March 1927: "all of the assets of our marital union
legally belong to my creditors, and they shall be liquidated in order to
repay their respective loans." He ordered that the remainder be divided
equally among his wife, his eight children, and his three sisters who had

helped educate him when he was a child.[15] Other files on Obregón's testament revealed large debts, both to individuals and to government-backed financial institutions. After the estate paid all debts only his core holdings—"La Quinta Chilla" and the hacienda of Náinari—remained for his heirs.[16]

How had the caudillo gotten himself into such significant financial trouble? Ambitious investment schemes explain a part, but not all of his problems. Instead, the documentary evidence shows that Obregón paid a significant price for maintaining political influence outside the presidency. In particular, he loaned significant sums of money to political allies in return for their support, which gives credence to the hypothesis that national political power drained rather than added to Obregón's resources. As early as 1918, when he geared up for his first presidential campaign, he had given a friend a horse because he wanted him to be successful in finding a mate: as he wrote: "When we men become old … we need a little help to attract the attention of women; either a beautiful mount, an automobile, or a good horse …; I have wanted to send you this horse so that it might help you in your business endeavors."[17] Throughout his stay in Sonora, Obregón used his financial resources as political leverage, hoping that such leverage would translate into political capital and economic success. In the end, as his last will of 1926 demonstrated, he had borrowed too much.

Obregón's financial worries necessitated his continued involvement in politics. The caudillo soon demonstrated that he—just like Santa Anna a century before—missed political power at least as much as he had missed his life as a farmer while in the presidential chair. Once again, "duty" called the Mexican Cincinnatus back into action.

The Cincinnatus of the West (Part Two)

Initially, Obregón's influence in politics remained indirect. He left it to his friends and allies to exert influence on the president, and, in particular, to check the power of Morones, the CROM and its affiliated political party, the PLM. Within the executive branch, the most important among these allies were Secretary of Foreign Relations Aarón Sáenz Garza, an entrepreneur from the northern state of Nuevo León and the first

Protestant to hold national office in Mexico, as well as Secretary of Finance Alberto J. Pani. In congress, the Obregonista majority, led by the vociferous PNA, impeded the PLM from advancing its legislative agenda. In the states, the caudillo could count on numerous staunch supporters, many of them powerful regional strongmen such as Cedillo, Tejeda, and José Guadalupe Zuno Hernández of Jalisco. The latter proved such a thorn in Calles's side that the president attempted to remove him from office. Although Calles succeeded in imposing one of his allies as governor, the Jalisco state congress impeached this puppet governor soon thereafter and installed a Zunista in office.[18] Finally, Obregón enjoyed the support of most of the divisional generals, with the exception of a few Calles loyalists.

Confident in his support network, Obregón stayed out of Calles's way during the first two years of his presidency. At least until 1926, the year before the completion of the last missing railroad link in the western states of Nayarit and Jalisco brought Sonora and the capital closer together, the caudillo's ranch remained remote enough from Mexico City to make frequent personal visits impossible. An examination of Obregón's correspondence during these years also reveals that the caudillo did not occupy his days with political matters. Instead, he tended to his business operations, expressing his opinion only when he believed the national situation warranted it. For example, in April 1925, he sharply criticized the efforts of the staunchly anticlerical Morones to establish a Mexican Apostolic Church—in his opinion, a divisive schismatic maneuver that would only bring the government new enemies.[19]

The caudillo made a smart calculation in staying away from Mexico City, as Calles was intent on proving that he was not going to serve as Obregón's puppet as most observers expected. During 1925 and most of 1926, the president flexed his own political muscle to rid himself from his mentor's overweening shadow. While he had appreciated the support of his predecessor in obtaining the nation's highest office, Calles intended to rule without Obregón's interference. As US Ambassador James R. Sheffield reported one year into Calles's presidency, he decided to be the landlord in his own house.[20]

Even more importantly, Calles had built a regional base on his own in the southeast, where the president enjoyed the support of several important regional strongmen, including governors Tomás Garrido

Canabal of Tabasco and Carlos Vidal of Chiapas. Both Garrido and Vidal represented themselves as firebreathing anticlerical radicals, and as "socialists" determined to bring both secular thinking and social justice to their regions. In Yucatán, Calles, as Secretary of Gobernación, had relied upon Felipe Carrillo Puerto, a radical governor who died at the hands of delahuertista rebels in early 1924. As president, he continued to enjoy the support of Carrillo's party, the Partido Socialista del Sureste (PSS, or Socialist Party of the Southeast).

Other strongmen split their support between the two Sonorans but benefited from a political equilibrium between the two, which benefited Calles in his attempts to gain political weight of his own. General Abelardo L. Rodríguez, the governor of Baja California, constituted an excellent example of this pattern. As we have seen, he participated in the business ventures of both Calles and Obregón. He considered himself their subordinate even though he bankrolled both leaders through his booming enterprises on the border, and despite the fact that Obregón— unlike Calles—did not hold any formal political position at that time. Clearly, Rodríguez remained grateful for the political favors that he had received from his two patrons. In particular, he appreciated Obregón's and Calles's willingness to let him rule Baja California unchallenged at a time when the governorships in almost all other states experienced rapid turnover.[21]

Further countering the caudillo's pervasive influence in his government, Calles benefited from good fortune in that he had obtained the allegiance of two foremost Obregonistas through marriage. The president's second-oldest son, Plutarco, had married the sister of Secretary of Foreign Relations Aarón Sáenz Garza, one of the cabinet members who represented Obregón's influence within the national government. In subsequent years, Plutarco Jr. and the Sáenz family collaborated in a vast sugar enterprise in the Huasteca region near the Gulf Coast. "El Mante" became one of the largest sugar estates of the nation, and a mainstay of Sáenz's considerable fortune. Calles's eldest daughter, Hortensia, was married to Obregón's private secretary, Fernando Torreblanca, who henceforth served both of the Sonoran political giants. At least initially, the president also earned the allegiance of many of the civilians in the government bureaucracy, who saw him as more educated and intelligent than Obregón.[22]

By far the most important ally who allowed Calles to gain significant political space was CROM chief Luis Napoleón Morones, an erstwhile Obregón ally. As we have seen, in 1919, Morones and Obregón had struck an alliance that allowed the CROM to become the principal labor union in the nation. In addition, the CROM's legislative wing, the PLM, held a number of seats in Congress. However, Obregón's relationship with Morones had turned sour during his term as president. While Calles cultivated a special relationship with Morones, the caudillo came to resent the union for its attempted power grab in the countryside. As his influence at national level grew, Morones had begun to argue that the CROM should represent both urban and rural laborers, and in particular, Mexico's millions of campesinos. In so doing, the CROM leader antagonized the agrarian organizations that formed the bedrock of Obregón's support, and particularly the PNA and its Obregonista leader, Antonio Díaz Soto y Gama. Although Calles also paid lip-service to the agrarians, he made clear his preference for Morones, a decision that earned him the unwavering support of the union. Prior to the presidential election of 1924, Calles and Morones had supplanted the 1919 pact with an agreement that more strongly backed the labor union. In 1923, Calles had promised Morones the portfolio of Secretary of Labor, Industry, and Commerce, a cabinet appointment that had eluded him under Obregón. In return, the CROM endorsed Calles as a champion of labor. While this alliance would earn Calles the enmity of Soto y Gama and the PNA, it assured him the support of an organization that endeavored to unite all agricultural and urban laborers under its leadership. If successful, this strategy would have fatally impaired the influence of Obregón's agrarista allies.[23]

Morones especially made his influence felt in the area of oil policy. Protected from the outset by the existence of full diplomatic relations with the United States, the Calles administration backed away from the Bucareli compromise brokered under Obregón. With Calles's support, Morones attacked the Porfirian-era privileges of the oil companies. This move occurred in the context of falling oil production. In 1921, Mexico had produced 193 million barrels, more than any other nation in the world. Over the next three years, however, the oil companies pulled large sums of money out of Mexico and invested them in other countries (such as Venezuela) in which their privileges remained protected. In addition, many of the wells began to manifest signs of depletion. By 1924, production had decreased to 140 million barrels. As Morones saw it, however, the oil companies intentionally decreased production in order to gain political leverage. In December 1925, Calles and Morones authored the Petroleum Law, which levied new taxes on the oil companies and required them, with reference to Article 27 of the Constitution, to apply for confirmatory concessions from the government.[24]

By early 1926, these nationalist policies had allowed Calles and Morones to make significant inroads into Obregón's national power base. Morones made thinly veiled preparations for a run at the presidency, and his CROM had become the largest popular organization in the country. Even more importantly, Calles and Morones gained the support of a majority of the urban population, whether workers or professionals. The government's face-off with the oil companies also earned them the praise of Mexican nationalists. Observers contrasted their defense of subsoil rights with the caudillo's tactical retreat on those issues in order to obtain US recognition in the Bucareli Agreements of 1923.[25]

Calles scored even more significant political capital with a string of developmentalist measures designed to improve the Mexican economy. In 1925, the long-awaited establishment of the Banco de México helped put the financial system on a more solid footing. Within six years, the bank became the nation's only bank of issue. Helped by booming export revenue during the so-called "Roaring Twenties," as well as the introduction of the income tax, Finance Secretary Alberto J. Pani balanced the books of the national treasury after almost two decades of annual deficits. Another tax, this one on the gasoline used by cars, paid for a road building project, and the Calles administration also launched a campaign to improve public health and hygiene. It appeared that Calles had emerged from the caudillo's shadow.[26]

In the summer of 1926, however, a political crisis engendered by Calles's anticlerical policies called Obregón onto the scene. Following statements by the archbishop of Mexico to the effect that the Church had still not reconciled itself to the revolutionary constitution, Calles charged that the Catholic opposition harbored plans to overthrow him. In May 1926, what became known as the "Calles Law" barred priests from teaching activities and required their registration with the government. The law led to the clergy's suspension of religious services throughout the nation, effective July 31, 1926. Although this step at first appeared to validate Calles's hard line, it alienated significant constituencies from the government, which many Catholics viewed as a godless socialist regime.[27]

Obregón soon realized that Calles pursued his anti-Catholic policies with irrational zeal that threatened no less than the political stability of a nation that had just emerged from a series of fratricidal wars. Although Calles was not an effective communicator like Obregón, and although Mexicans already knew him as imperious and authoritarian, the president usually opted for a deliberate approach toward divisive political issues. This time, however, Calles showed an implacable animosity to his enemy. For example, in late August 1926, he held negotiations with two Catholic bishops to resolve the standoff between church and state. During the talks, the bishops identified the mandatory registration of priests as their greatest objection. Aware that the Calles government— like all of its predecessors—applied its laws selectively, they pleaded with the president to show some leniency, even if only in an unofficial manner. Calles, however, appeared offended by the suggestion not to enforce fully the law of the land, offering only the possibility of redress in Congress. Not surprisingly, this religious crisis erupted into open war. On New Years' Day, 1927, campesinos throughout central Mexico, the breadbasket of the nation, took up arms to the cry of "Viva Cristo Rey," or "Long Live Christ the King." Thus began the Cristero War, a devastating conflict that would last two and a half years, kill tens of thousands and contribute to a drop in agricultural production of almost 40 percent.[28]

Although Obregón personally did not participate in the government's campaign against the Cristeros, he felt called upon to give Calles advice on how to deal with the problem, and he got his retainers, including San Luis Potosí strongman Cedillo, to commit troops to the war effort. Having counseled initially in favor of diplomacy, Obregón advised Calles to pursue the war with vigor and resolve. To be sure, the caudillo did not share Calles's fervent anticlerical convictions—for example, he had married his own wife in a religious ceremony, and he had attended the church wedding of Fernando Torreblanca and Hortensia Calles instead of Hortensia's father. He also proved more pragmatic than Calles in his handling of the situation, and in March 1927, he met with representatives of the Church hierarchy in an attempt to find a negotiated end to the war.[29]

The Cristeros, however, did not constitute the only problem of the government, as economic woes hit the nation hard beginning in the second half of 1926. That summer, the price of silver and other export commodities plummeted on the world market. The decline precipitated a serious economic crisis that would not end until well into the early 1930s. In a sense, Mexico entered the Great Depression three years early. National income decreased 4 percent per annum over the next three years. Oil production plummeted from 140 million barrels in 1924 to 50 million barrels in 1928, and export revenue decreased from 192.6 million dollars in 1925 to 172.1 million dollars in 1928. As a result of reduced receipts, government expenditures shrank almost 12 percent between 1926 and 1928, blunting Calles's educational and infrastructure projects. By the end of the Calles presidency, a government that had billed itself as a purveyor of material progress with social justice could no longer deliver either.[30] The crisis and the resultant slower pace of reform therefore indirectly strengthened Obregón's hand.

Finally, Calles faced a growing crisis with the United States. Already in June 1925, US Secretary of State Frank B. Kellogg had declared Mexico to be on "trial before the world" on account of his policies toward the oil companies. The Church-state conflict exacerbated the US stance, as Catholic organizations such as the Knights of Columbus abhorred Calles's heavy-handed measures against the church and enjoined the State Department to out pressure on the Mexican government. To top it off, the Mexican and US governments came to blows over their respective involvement in Nicaragua, where a pro-United States former president, Emiliano Chamorro, had launched a successful coup against a democratically elected government supported by the Calles administration. When the vice president of the deposed administration rose up in arms against Chamorro, he received military assistance from Calles officials. This extraordinary military aid—the only such Mexican involvement in the internal affairs of another nation in the twentieth century—prompted Secretary of State Kellogg to warn the Senate Foreign Relations Committee against the spread of Mexican "Bolshevism" into Central America. Kellogg also leaked a military intelligence report to the press that alleged Soviet influence in the Mexican government. The Bolshevik label cleverly but inaccurately linked the religious, petroleum, and Nicaragua issues in the minds of jingoistic North Americans, and several US newspapers openly speculated about the possibility of an invasion of Mexico. In this war scare, Obregón had found his third and perhaps greatest political opportunity, along with the need to advise the government on the Cristero War and the exigencies of the economic crisis.[31]

This crisis therefore marked Obregón's return to national political involvement. Two issues prompted this involvement: the possibility that Morones might launch a campaign for the presidency, and Obregón's sense that the nation needed him. Much like Santa Anna a century before, the caudillo returned, ostensibly to save the nation—but unlike Santa Anna, Obregón knew that he would be able to work through the existing political structures. Taking advantage of the new direct rail service between Sonora and Mexico City, the caudillo made frequent trips to the capital to advise Calles on a multitude of matters. With good reason, historian Jean Meyer has described the Obregón-Calles political system of the years 1926-1928 as a "diarchy"—the rule of two men.[32] In practice, two presidents jockeyed for influence during those years: one in office, and the other one, his predecessor and (as many already surmised) his successor as well. As in the past, this relationship was not always cordial, governed by a rational understanding of mutual interest rather than genuine friendship. As president, Calles had forged significant political alliances of his own, especially the one with Morones, who had grown bitterly resentful of the caudillo's political ambitions.

For that reason, conflict between Callistas and Obregonistas appeared inevitable, as only a few political leaders—the so-called Obrecallistas— remained close to both. The Obrecallistas included Fomento Secretary Luis L. León and the two loyal Obregonistas with family connections to the Calles clan: Foreign Relations Secretary Aarón Sáenz and Calles's personal secretary, Fernando Torreblanca. It is no coincidence that two of these three men would give the funeral orations for their two mentors: Sáenz, for Obregón in 1928, and León, for Calles in 1945. Torreblanca's wife, Hortensia Elías Calles, did something even more important for the Sonorans' future legacies. For decades, she preserved and organized Torreblanca's and Calles's papers, the main reason why scholars have recently been able to write well-documented biographies of the Sonoran leaders.[33]

From Obregón's vantage point, local affairs got caught up in national events. Most significantly, his investments in the Yaqui Valley brought him firsthand experiences with his state's foremost ethnic conflict: the Yaqui question. Before the de la Huerta rebellion, Obregón and Calles had not seen eye to eye on this issue. The former had counted on Yaqui support for his victories in the revolution, while the latter viewed them as a community that stubbornly refused membership in the Mexican nation. However, as Obregón attempted to expand his holdings, he found implacable opposition among an indigenous community already incensed about the increasing presence of land speculators in their midst. On September 12, 1926, a group of 1,000 Yaqui held up the train in which he was traveling. A day later, Obregón found out that the Yaqui had declared themselves in revolt almost two weeks before, blaming Calles and Obregón personally for the depredations on their land. Even worse, Obregón found out that Adolfo de la Huerta had played a role in the Yaqui revolt, when three letters from de la Huerta to General Luis Matus, a veteran of Obregón's campaign and the leader of the Yaqui resistance, fell into his hands. In these letters, de la Huerta insinuated that Obregón had lied to the Yaqui, whom he had promised full restitution of their lands following the revolution. In de la Huerta's words, "Obregón's purpose was to live like a toad among you, stealing your lands little by little."[34] Obregón was irate at this effort by an exile—and one descended from a Yaqui grandmother, no less—to stir up ethnic conflict in order to cause trouble.

These developments contributed to the caudillo's decision to participate in one last military campaign, which once again took on a group that had supported him in the revolution. Because Obregón did not serve in the army at that point in time, he received a special commission from President Calles as "special representative with the broadest powers" and acted through an intermediary, General Francisco R. Manzo, to convey his orders to the troops and the other commanders. He sent airplanes—including four donated by Abelardo L. Rodríguez—to strafe Yaqui strongholds in the Sierra de Bacatete. With the help of this aerial assault, government forces finally crushed a proud indigenous people that had held out against Spanish-language invaders for four centuries after the conquest of central Mexico. At its height, this final campaign against the Yaqui saw 15,000 troops in the field of battle, or almost one fifth of the Mexican army. Obregón had demonstrated once again that a caudillo did not know friendship or gratitude, but only alliances of convenience. For his part, Calles had reached his stated objective of eliminating the Yaqui as a group existing outside the state's legislative and political purview.[35]

The Yaqui campaign revealed the extent to which the political strategies of Calles and Obregón had merged. Once considered a conciliator, the undefeated caudillo of the Mexican Revolution appeared every bit as ruthless as Calles himself, and Obregón's participation in the war on the Yaqui appeared to justify Calles's own hard line against indigenous Sonorans. Obregón remained in the field until April 1927, proving that he remained indispensable to a weak state that drew its legitimacy from a revolution that his men had won by the force of arms. While the army marched toward their decisive victory and the ultimate surrender of the Yaqui, the caudillo moved to cash in on this newly increased political capital.[36]

The Second Presidential Campaign

It has been commonplace among historians to believe that Obregón always knew that he would seek a second term as president. It is easy to infer, in the spirit of Gutiérrez's epigraph, that the caudillo's enormous ambition constituted an irresistible force that propelled him back toward Chapultepec Castle. The historical evidence, however, suggests that Obregón was ambivalent about a return to the presidency. Even though the caudillo remained hungry for power, his decision to return to political life came only after considerable deliberation.

Among the factors that militated in favor of another presidential bid, Obregón remained hungry for power. In truly "caudillesque" fashion, he considered himself indispensable to the revolution and the nation, especially in the second half of Calles's term. At a moment when the nation once again appeared to be in crisis, besieged by enemies at home and abroad, he projected stability. Calles's radical anticlerical measures had decisively contributed to the outbreak of the devastating Cristero Rebellion. Likewise, while Calles's early showdown with the oil industry and the US State Department had strengthened his political base, the 1927 war scare drew Obregón's supporters to make unfavorable comparisons to Carranza's problems with the United States. To them, the Bucareli agreements appeared in retrospect like an example of a cautious rapprochement rather than the act of a group of sell-outs. At that time, Obregón appeared to his supporters as the only steady hand that could move the nation out of its crisis. Like all other authoritarian leaders, the caudillo held an abiding belief in his political significance. As historian Enrique Krauze has suggested, "the presidential chair attracted him not for the power it would give him—even less so for any programs of social and economic reconstruction he could put into effect—but for the aura of duty and sacrifice surrounding the position."[37] As a secondary consideration, Obregón saw in a return to the presidency a remedy to his evident economic failure. As he knew well, formal political power would allow him to reshape property relations in the Yaqui Valley by government fiat.

However, Obregón saw serious obstacles to seeking a second presidential term. Most importantly, the idea violated the basic principle that commenced the revolution, "effective suffrage, no reelection," and a constitutional provision in Article 82 stating that a president "could not be reelected." To be sure, Obregón held no compunctions, and he insisted that the constitution only forbade immediate reelection, not a subsequent term. As he had once allegedly confided, "Don Porfirio's only sin ... was to grow old."[38] But satisfactory clarification required approval of an amendment by a two-thirds majority in Congress, and an early attempt at such an amendment failed in 1925. Critics alleged that the amendment would allow Obregón and Calles to alternate in power indefinitely, creating a bicephalous version of the Porfirian system. As one congressional deputy from the PNA put it: "On the one hand, we were [Obregón's] personal friends. On the other hand, we did not think he could legally be elected to the presidency again."[39] Of course, the comment betrayed a telling fact: both the Agraristas and the Laboristas in Congress had become part of the governing elite, and they no longer effectively represented their grass roots.

Second, even discounting the unlikely possibility of an electoral triumph of the civilian Morones, other divisional generals readied powerful candidacies of their own. On top of that list was Obregón's protégé, General Francisco Serrano, who had accompanied Obregón from the time of the Orozquista revolt all the way to the national government. Serrano was connected to the caudillo's family by ties of marriage; he had fought at Obregón's side in the battles of the Bajío, and his leadership had played à crucial role in defeating the de la Huerta rebellion. Other generals who prepared their own campaigns included Angel Flores, the runner-up in the 1924 elections who mysteriously died of poisoning in 1926, and the Callista Arnulfo R. Gómez.[40]

Finally, President Calles himself did not favor Obregón's ambitions in the first half of his presidency. Before taking office, he had reportedly promised Obregón his support for a renewed presidential bid in 1928—a promise that was likely a condition for obtaining his backing in 1924. But once Calles found himself in power, this promise carried little weight. Engaged in a power struggle with the Obregonistas in Congress, the military, and among the state governors, Calles had no interest in strengthening the caudillo's hand, especially far in advance of the elections. Although he retained amicable relations with Obregón throughout, and although he knew that the divisional generals would never support a civilian as his successor, he appears to have encouraged Morones to consider a presidential run at the end of his term. Calles correctly identified Morones and the CROM as a power base independent from Obregón—a power base that would continue to support his own influence after he left the presidency. Failing Morones's candidacy, Calles was rumored to favor Serrano or Gómez as his successor.[41]

Ultimately, however, the caudillo vanquished these obstacles. Having publicly disavowed another run as late as April 1926, the caudillo decided to throw his hat into the ring after carefully measuring the political landscape. In October 1926, PNA delegates reintroduced a motion for a constitutional amendment in a climate unfavorable to Calles and Morones. The Agraristas not only checked the Laboristas' agenda of advancing Morones's interests, but they also advertised Obregón as a true advocate of the nation's campesinos. To be sure, Calles had distributed more land in two years than Obregón had done during his four-year term, but after June 1926, the pace of land reform had slowed dramatically. Without much evidence, Soto y Gama and the other Agraristas argued that Obregón would revive this program and take it to a higher level. On November 19, the Senate approved the amendment following a series of stormy debates. The powerful PLM remained opposed to a second Obregón presidency; however, Morones himself recognized the writing on the wall and did not put his own name forward as a candidate. These developments marked the beginning of the decline of Morones's influence. For his part, the embattled Calles decided to support Obregón because he had no other choice.[42]

To coopt the growing number of campesinos and workers dissatisfied with the state of affairs in Mexico, Obregón decided to give his second candidacy a more radical appeal—one that would involve his PNA supporters as well as workers dissatisfied with the monopoly of the CROM. The caudillo remade himself into a critic of capitalism who resolved to help the workers in their disputes with their bosses. This stance resembled that of Calles when he endeavored to distance himself from Obregón during his own campaign four years prior. He insistently referred to himself as a worker of humble origin. Having run in 1919 on a platform that emphasized the importance of the middle class, his rhetoric during the second campaign divided Mexico into two great classes: those who hired and those who worked. The landlord of Náinari represented himself as a proletarian.[43]

This more radical tone became obvious once Obregón formally announced his candidacy. On June 25, 1927, he launched a lengthy manifesto. As he had done in the Nogales Manifesto of 1919, he brought out the Cincinnatus image again by feigning reluctance to return to politics. He indicated that his candidacy destroyed one of his "greatest illusions"— his life as a private citizen interrupted only, as he stated, by brief episodes as a soldier and statesman. He argued that the gravity of the nation's political situation required his involvement. Obregón went on to say that his first term had merely begun the monumental work of the revolution in replacing the Porfirian political and economic system with a fair and just society. He identified the many obstacles and adversaries confronted by his government, including the "Machiavellian" de la Huerta. He then turned to the administration of Calles, whom he labeled a true revolutionary and socialist. The caudillo acknowledged the president's recent difficulties, which he blamed on the work of the "reaction," including foreign investors, the US government, and the clergy as its most "visible head." Making himself and Calles into the exponents of revolutionary progress, Obregón argued that it would not be fair to the Mexican people to withhold his name from consideration if they wanted him to serve another term. He then reminded his readership that his candidacy did not violate the principle of no reelection, since he did not seek consecutive terms.[44]

Turning to his program, the manifesto highlighted the caudillo's previous accomplishments and promised that he would follow up on initiatives stalled during the previous eight years. Obregón pointed out that his administration had handed out twice as much land (in four years) than that of Calles (in 30 months), as well as the scant progress made in that area under his predecessors. That particular boast would prove idle, as Calles ended up redistributing twice as much land as Obregón. In addition, the caudillo showcased his support for labor during his presidency, blaming Congress for the slow pace in ensuring better wages and working conditions. This reference to Congress was a sly move on Obregón's part, because it allowed him to taint both the PLM— as an ineffectual proponent of labor legislation—and the PNC, a formerly mighty party relegated to the sidelines since the de la Huerta rebellion. Of course, the caudillo did not mention the fact that the present Congress featured a majority comprised of his own loyalists who had made life difficult for a president desirous of making his own mark on national politics but not named Obregón. Toward the end, he issued a warning to the same entrepreneurs whom he had courted in 1919 with promises that they did not have to fear the new constitution. "Do not ask or demand anything," he wrote, from a government dedicated to the rule of law and the well-being of all Mexicans. In his opinion, the government had created the conditions to allow them to thrive on their own.[45]

Obregón next confronted the issue of rival candidates. After the death of Flores and a string of legislative defeats for Morones, this list only included two divisional generals: Serrano and Gómez. Serrano believed his time had come, and he claimed that the caudillo had encouraged him to put his name forward. In fact, there is one (possibly apocryphal) piece of evidence for the existence of a pact between Morones and Obregón, signed in February 1926, in which both men agreed to forsake presidential bids in favor of Serrano.[46] For his part, Gómez not only called Obregón "mentally unbalanced" but also predicted: "It is a fight to the death in which one of us must die."[47] In a strange twist, Serrano and Gómez united in opposing Obregón's presidential bid on an antireelectionist platform, yet neither one of them would drop his own candidacy to help that of the other. The fact that the two generals sustained two separate presidential campaigns benefited Obregón, who ridiculed their ambitions and pointed out that the desire of both men to be president trumped their political principles. As he argued, the two campaigns should have united behind one single candidate if Serrano and Gómez harbored serious hopes of political success. "The union of the candidates," he announced on July 3, "results in a hybridism of less significance" than if either one of them ran for president alone.[48]

Obregón's ridicule, however, masked a growing sense of his own political vulnerability. Whereas he had optimistically forged his campaign in 1919, seldom referring to his opponents by name, his speeches made many references to Gómez and Serrano throughout the summer of 1927. These repetitive messages increasingly drowned out his political message. Disturbed by the fact that two other generals had dared to oppose what he had viewed as a triumphant return, Obregón worried with good reason that the joint anti-reelectionist platform of his opponents would gain traction.[49]

In confronting his opponents, Obregón could count on his rivals' own weaknesses. Gómez lacked a national political base, and Serrano suffered from serious character flaws. Many Mexicans knew Serrano as an alcoholic, and he held a well-deserved reputation for violence, as well as notoriety for his pursuit of unmarried women, especially while drunk. Although many among the political elite participated in alcoholic orgies, Serrano's excesses embarrassed his friends as much as did those of Morones, whose character inspired the protagonist in Katherine Anne Porter's noted short story *Flowering Judas*.[50] Obregón, by contrast, painstakingly cultivated an image as a moderate drinker who never consumed so much alcohol that he lost control over his behavior. Calles projected the profile of a former alcoholic who had learned the lessons from his addiction; however, the historical record indicates that he never shook the addiction and drank quite heavily until late in life.[51]

Despite Gómez's and Serrano's shortcomings, the government took their political challenge seriously. When attempts at persuasion did not work in subduing the caudillo's rivals, Calles and Obregón turned to repressive tactics and finally adopted the ultimate solution to political conflicts. On October 3, 1927, Calles ordered the arrest of Gómez and Serrano after he received word that the two generals had designed a coup d'état. Later that day, an army contingent under the direction of General Claudio Fox—a general known for bloodthirsty cruelty— detained Serrano and twelve of his men and machine-gunned them unceremoniously. Thus the caudillo's protégé, a man who had once tended to the caudillo as he lay bleeding from the loss of his arm, died as a result of his mentor's ambitions. Also among the dead was Chiapas governor Carlos Vidal, one of the men who had helped Calles build a power base of his own. A month later, authorities found Gómez hiding in a cave near Coatepec, Veracruz, and executed him a short time afterward. When the smoke had cleared, US intelligence officers estimated that the government had killed more than 500 anti-reelectionists. We will never know precisely what role Obregón played in these killings, but most likely, the caudillo arranged the bloodbath with the help of Calles. Both of these men commanded the unswerving loyalty of General Fox and the other *divisionarios* involved in the carnage. Obregón appears as the probable instigator, as Calles did not stand to gain anything from the deaths of Serrano and Gómez.[52]

The deaths of his opponents left Obregón as the only remaining viable candidate. As a result, he toned down his rhetoric and once again appealed to the middle of the political spectrum in an effort to unify the nation despite the bloodshed. During the first six months of 1928, he toured the country to rally support. He even visited the Bajío and urged the Cristero insurgents operating in that area to exercise patience until he returned to the presidency. His campaign speeches portrayed his candidacy as a continuation of the past eight years. "No more promises," he exclaimed during a campaign rally. "The nation already knows our points of view."[53] Having eliminated his principal opponents, Obregón won an overwhelming victory at the polls in July 1928.

After the bloodbath that resulted in the elimination of Serrano and Gómez, an increasing number of Mexicans realized that Obregón was part of the problem rather than the solution. The general who had run in 1919 with promises of unifying all revolutionaries in a single party had instead perpetuated *caudillismo* and *continuismo*. The lost arm served as a metaphor for the massive blood toll exacted by Obregón, as in one anonymous contemporary saying:

> If with only one hand
> He has assassinated so many
> With two hands he would have left
> The Mexican soil empty[54]

Indeed, the period 1923-1928 had manifested Obregón's dark side: that aspect of his personality that did not spare a life in order to advance the caudillo's ambitions. Without question, the murderous repression of the antireelectionists in 1927 constitutes the greatest stain on Obregón's memory (and Calles's as well). As Mexicans absorbed the chilling reality of the murders of Serrano, Gómez, and their associates, some of them began to believe that Calles and Obregón's bloody hands could only be cleansed by their own deaths.[55]

In the aftermath of the killings, plot attempts against both Sonorans multiplied. In the most serious of these attempts in November 1927, the Catholic engineer Segura Vilchis flung a bomb at Obregón's automobile. Reportedly, the attempt on his life did not faze Obregón, who went on to attend a bullfight as if nothing had happened. The Calles administration responded by executing not only Vilchis, but also Father Miguel Pro, a prominent priest at the forefront of the church-state controversy whom the government falsely implicated in the plot (see Figure 6.1).[56]

Despite his political successes, the Calles presidency had not been a happy time for the caudillo. His business interests had suffered as a result of his ambition, the general economic crisis, and the high cost of maintaining an extensive clientelist network. Politics had become a farce, and Obregón probably felt some remorse at the deaths of his adversaries. He sought to escape by means of an affair with another woman.[57] Once a crucial ingredient in his charm, his humor focused on his own death. As he mocked the increasingly frequent attempts on his life, he felt a sense of foreboding. In an interview, Calles's daughter Hortensia recalled the caudillo as saying "I will live until someone trades his life for mine."[58]

The Death of the Caudillo

Once again, Obregón's instincts proved impeccable. On July 17, 1928, less than two weeks after his victory in the presidential election, a young Catholic named José de León Toral approached his table during a luncheon given in the caudillo's honor by the congressional delegation of the state of Guanajuato. The luncheon took place in "La Bombilla," a restaurant in San Angel, a village close to Mexico City, and those attending were in festive mood (see Figure 6.2). Under the pretense that he was

Figure 6.1   The execution of Father Pro. Source: FAPEC.

Figure 6.2　Obregón's last moments. Source: FAPEC.

drawing portraits of the dinner guests, León Toral drew close to Obregón and shot him in the head five times. The undefeated caudillo of the revolution died instantly. He had proven a mere mortal, a victim—it appeared—of his hubris in believing that he and his friends dictated the political rules. Obregón's opponents considered it a blood toll repaid at long last.[59]

Obregón's assassination touched off one of the wildest waves of rumors and speculation ever experienced in Mexico City. Based on interrogations under torture of Toral and other suspects, President Calles concluded that the crime was the work of Catholic radicals bent on avenging the government's campaign against the Church over the past four years.[60] But the word on the street implicated the government itself in the assassination. Some blamed the death on Morones, who had always been jealous of Obregón's influence over the president. Others accused Calles himself of masterminding the plot, pointing to the fact that the president desired to escape the shadow of his political mentor. Although most historians eventually accepted Calles's version of the story, the circumstances of the assassination have yet to be fully elucidated. In particular, there is some evidence that León de Toral was not the only one shooting at the caudillo during the banquet.[61]

Not surprisingly, the immediate aftermath featured intense speculation over the perpetrators of and the motives for the crime. Was Obregón the victim of religious fanatics opposed to Calles's attack on the Catholic Church, an attack that had led the clergy to suspend almost all religious ceremonies? Had he been murdered because of his own ambition to win election to a second term, an effort that violated the spirit, if not the letter of that same Constitution? Or had he become the target of a sinister plot hatched by Morones and Calles?

Obregón's assassination therefore sparked a crisis that threatened the fragile political system. There was no heir apparent, as the Constituyente of 1917 had abolished the office of Vice President. Even more significantly, the many Obregonistas around the nation did not accept the official story of the killing, but instead blamed Morones, Obregón's main surviving rival for the presidency, if not Calles himself. In particular, Calles faced a severe political problem in the response of the Agraristas to Obregón's death. Since Calles's alliance with Morones, PNA leaders Manrique and Soto y Gama had increasingly resented the president. As ardent Obregonistas, they had played an instrumental role in ensuring the passage of the amendment that allowed the caudillo to run for a second term. Now, they suspected that Calles and Morones had orchestrated Obregón's murder. Indeed, prior to Obregón's death, Soto y Gama had received several letters informing him that Morones planned his assassination as well as that of the caudillo. One of the letters was quite graphic, stating that the murderers intended to mutilate Soto y Gama following Obregón's death, "cutting [his] tongue and each and every part of his body into pieces."[62] Obregón's disappearance also threatened to provoke new revolts by Calles's other political rivals such as de la Huerta or former Education Secretary José Vasconcelos. Under these circumstances, the idea might have occurred to Calles to prolong his time in office. US Ambassador Dwight Morrow, a man who would soon thereafter play a crucial role in ending the Cristero revolt and the church strike, reportedly suggested as much, as did Morones, who knew that his own political star had sunk for good.[63] However, doing so would have confirmed the suspicions of the Obregonistas, and Calles never seriously entertained the possibility.

After a silence of six weeks, Calles used the occasion of his last annual address to Congress to calm the waters. Under no circumstances, he proclaimed, would he serve as president again. Mexico, he stated, had entered the transition from a "country of one man" to a "nation of institutions and laws."[64] With these words, Calles had not only assuaged many of those who had suspected his involvement in the murder, but he had also cleverly distanced himself from the caudillo. In occupying an ambiguous, yet safe political space between the Obregonistas and their enemies, he set the stage for a behind-the-scenes rule as *jefe máximo*.

The caudillo was dead, but despite Calles's words, personalist rule was not. On the ashes of the most brilliant career of the Mexican Revolution—a career that had ended in death due at least in part to the caudillo's over-zealous ambition—Calles and his allies would construct a ruling party that would dominate politics for the rest of the twentieth century. Powerful presidents would continue to rule Mexico from an institutional rather than a caudillo basis. Obregón's assassination therefore marked a decisive turning point in the nation's political history, but it did not end the authoritarian tradition that had produced Mexico's last caudillo.[65]

7

The Unquiet Grave

Obregón was president, general, and rancher ...
And wherever one goes, people weep with sincere sorrow.

Corrido by Guty Cárdenas

With his violent death, Obregón entered the pantheon of national martyrs. After Madero, Zapata, Carranza, and Villa, he was the last of the principal revolutionary leaders to fall victim to an assassination. The murder created two reference points for a hero-cult that emphasized the caudillo's sacrifice: the loss of his arm on June 3, 1915, and the loss of his life on July 17, 1928. Of these two reference points, the first appeared as the more appealing act as the loss of a limb in the course of a fight to the death between the two largest revolutionary factions. As the belated cremation of his arm narrated in the introduction shows, his followers—and the party created to build on his legacy— treated Obregón as a saint even though he had not been a practicing Catholic. Specifically, the arm evolved into a secular relic that embodied the revolution and its sacrifices, and it played a crucial role in making the caudillo's memory into one of the primary building blocks of the postrevolutionary state.[1]

Obregón's post-mortem image played a significant role in facilitating the further consolidation of the central state, particularly in the first twenty years after his assassination. While the immensely popular cults

The Last Caudillo: Alvaro Obregón and the Mexican Revolution. Jürgen Buchenau
© 2011 Jürgen Buchenau

of other revolutionary heroes such as Villa and Zapata celebrated the contributions of the campesinos to the revolution, the image of Obregón highlighted the achievements of the Sonoran leadership, both in the wars of the 1910s and in the era of reconstruction during the 1920s. This image would be less popular than that of Villa and Zapata because the caudillo shared at least part of the responsibility for the failure of the Sonoran revolutionaries to deliver on their promises for democracy, economic development, and social justice.

After the Caudillo

Calles's celebrated address to Congress on September 1, 1928 announced the intention to reinvent a state predicated upon the power of a caudillo who was no longer there. The political realignment that followed purported to replace caudillismo with a ruling party: the Partido Nacional Revolucionario (later called the Partido de la Revolución Mexicana, or PNR, which underwent two name changes and, in 1946, became the Partido Revolucionario Institucional, or PRI). This party promoted a set of ideas that enshrined the protagonists of the Mexican Revolution as fathers of the nation and elided the significant differences among them. First, that the revolution was permanent (*la revolución hecha gobierno*). Second, that the crisis touched off by the assassination required national unity and the forging of a revolutionary family. Third, that the PNR (and later PRI) represented this effort at national unity and permanent revolution (*la revolución hecha partido*). Fourth, that monuments would propagate this official version of the revolution among the population (*la revolución hecha monumento*). The monuments to the fallen heroes of the Revolution thus promoted an official version of Mexican history that held that the Revolution was unitary rather than a heterogeneous process made by conflicting forces. One monument in particular—the Monumento a la Revolución, inaugurated in 1938—served as the official memorial of the revolutionary family, eventually commemorating Madero, Zapata, Villa, Carranza, Calles, and Cárdenas. This monument united Conventionists (Villa and Zapata) with Constitutionalists (Calles and Carranza); and Villa with one of the leaders who had most likely ordered his murder (Calles).[2]

In light of the purpose of this monument, Obregón's omission at first glance appears surprising. As Aarón Sáenz pointed out during a memorial service, he was the "undefeated caudillo of the Revolution," slain only when the bullets of an assassin "did in a few minutes what armies and weapons had not been able to accomplish in many long years of war."[3] Even more eloquent was Ernest Gruening in an article written for *The Nation* two weeks after the assassination:

> In a very definite way Calles and Obregón were complementary to each other. Calles in his four years showed far more material achievement than did Obregón. The Calles regime was the surgical, the operative period of Mexican reconstruction. Obregón's second term would have proved, much as his first term had been, the postoperative, the curative, the healing period. Both periods were and are essential if Mexico is to recover from the multiplicity and complexity of her social and political diseases.[4]

As a major supporter of both Sonoran rulers, Gruening thus summarized Obregón's role as the charismatic caudillo of the Mexican Revolution whose second presidency would have healed a divided nation. Of course, this view glossed over the tremendous human cost of the Obregón and Calles regimes. In particular, it ignored the role of both leaders in killing their political enemies, and particularly Villa, Serrano, and Gómez.

Obregón's remains did not enter the Monumento a la Revolución, however, because his memorialization had already taken a different course. Following his testament, his family had ordered his body to be interred in Huatabampo. Until the 1931 inauguration of a monument in nearby Navojoa, the principal "homenajes" took place there, far from Mexico City.[5] In front of family and close friends, the Sonoran state government used July 17 to remind its inhabitants of the crucial role of their state in the revolution, and to emphasize the theme of national unity. Meanwhile, in the capital, the proposal of a group of university students under the leadership of Obregón's friend Alfonso Romandía Ferreira that a monument be erected on Mexico City's posh Paseo de la Reforma had failed.[6]

As Romandía Ferreira and other Obregonistas soon found out, the national government had grander plans for the caudillo's memory in Mexico City. Years before the inauguration of the Monumento a la Revolución, the symbolism of Obregón's violent and highly public death inspired the construction of a monument at the site of his assassination. This symbolism aided Calles's attempt to achieve an ideological unification of the revolutionary leadership. In 1934, President Abelardo L. Rodríguez—a close ally of both Calles and Obregón and the final member of the Sonoran coalition to become president—commissioned plans for the Monumento al General Alvaro Obregón. Designed by architect Enrique Aragón and sculptor Ignacio Asúnsolo, the monument evoked a blending of Mexico's distant past and present. Inaugurated in 1935, during the first year of the presidency of General Lázaro Cárdenas, it looks like an ancient temple. Outside, two sculpture groups represent triumph and sacrifice respectively. Inside, two fierce twentieth-century guerrillas guard the entrance. Once inside, visitors find a life-size bronze statue of a one-armed Obregón, and the original floor of the "La Bombilla" restaurant including the bullet holes from León de Toral's pistol. This monument remains Mexico's closest approximation of the Invalides in Paris. Each July 17 since 1935, the "Asociación Cívica General Alvaro Obregón," founded to preserve and promote the memory of the slain caudillo, sponsored annual celebrations of his life and death.[7] The national government always sent important representatives to these celebrations: ex-presidents, cabinet members, and highly ranked officers in the military.

The Asociación Cívica was under the leadership of Aarón Sáenz, a man who had gained a prominent economic position in the Mexican northeast as a result of the revolution, and one of the few figures who had remained loyal to both of the principal Sonoran leaders until the caudillo's death. Sáenz's dedication speech at the monument on July 17, 1935 mentioned three key sectors of the PNR—peasants, workers, and soldiers—as mainstays of Obregón's support: "in the place of your sacrifice, the Fatherland consecrates to your memory this reminder made into stone. In it are also figures that represent those who accompanied you in battle: the peasant, the worker, and the soldier."[8] What Sáenz did not mention was that the Obregonistas themselves represented a fourth sector: a new class of landowners and industrial capitalists just like Sáenz, Obregón, Calles, and especially Rodríguez. Their careers recalled Mancur Olson's "roving bandits" who had taken advantage of the opportunities presented by upheaval to reshape property relations in their favor, upon which they became "stationary bandits" who defended the new status quo.[9]

The Monumento Obregón turned what had previously been a relatively low-key ceremony into public ritual on a grand scale. The new monument shifted attention away from Obregón's birthplace on the northern periphery of the nation to the place of his death, and, more importantly, to the center of political power. Two groups shared responsibility for these more public commemorations of Obregón's assassination: the caudillo's family, friends, and comrades-in-arms; and the leadership of the PNR. Had the monument opened during the Maximato, the fact that these two groups shared many members would have made it easy for the organizers to orchestrate an impressive show of national unity.

However, the opening of the monument coincided with an open break between Cárdenas and Jefe Máximo Calles. Following three presidents who had deferred to Calles on significant decisions, Cárdenas decided to reshuffle the political deck. He ditched the state's cooperation with the CROM, and instead allowed a variety of labor unions to organize strikes. He also allied with agrarian interests which had remained marginalized since the Jefe Máximo had decided to end the land redistribution program at the height of the Great Depression. On June 12, 1935, Mexico City newspapers published comments in which Calles criticized the president for his handling of the strikes, and in response, Cárdenas purged the Callistas from his cabinet and congress.[10]

The break complicated the memorial ritual for Obregón, making a sharp distinction between the Obregonistas loyal to Calles and Cárdenas's new PNR leadership. The Callistas agreed on a version of history that saw both Obregón and Calles as leaders who fulfilled the promise of the Revolution. Cardenismo, however, constituted in large part a rejection of the Obregón and Calles years. As Cárdenas redistributed 49 million acres of land to campesinos; as he mobilized peasants and workers in a politics of the masses under his own tutelage; and as he nationalized the foreign-owned oil industry, he became a revolutionary hero in his own right and claimed the mantra of the revolution from Obregón and Calles.[11] In April 1936, Cárdenas ordered Calles deported to the United States, a step that symbolically ended the Sonoran era.

In order to preserve Obregón's role in the revolutionary pantheon during this period of social and economic reform, the Obregonistas needed to claim their fallen hero as a precursor to Cardenismo rather than as the ally and enabler of Calles. The memorial discourses of the years 1935-1940 demonstrate this pattern. Orators at the monument portrayed Obregón as a friend of campesinos and workers who paved the path for Cárdenas. Sáenz's aforementioned dedication speech at the monument proclaimed Obregón a "protector of the working-class movement" and claimed that his friend "laid the groundwork for new justice in the distribution of land."[12] This indirect endorsement of the new order from a significant exponent of the Obregón/Calles years paved the way for the Cárdenas administration to elevate the July 17 event into a show that ultimately included more than one thousand invited guests each year.

The Cárdenas years proved an anomaly, as the political pendulum soon swung back to the right. As early as 1941, only seven months after Cárdenas had handed over power to General Manuel Avila Camacho, the rhetoric of social revolution had given way to a developmentalist agenda that focused on industrialization and material progress. Moreover, Avila Camacho's term coincided with World War Two, which forged an alliance between Mexico and the United States in the struggle against Nazism and fascism in Europe. With the president's acquiescence, if not open support, the Asociación Cívica refashioned the image of the slain caudillo as that of a moderate who rejected both Communism and fascism as totalitarian ideologies.

The most striking evidence of this shift came with the speech of Alfonso Romandía Ferreira, a friend of Obregón's and long-time advocate of the Monumento who used the occasion of his speech on July 17, 1941 to lambast Cardenismo. As the speaker exhorted the audience, "the ceremonies with which nations honor their heroes would not be worth much ... if one did not use the occasion to remember these men's views about the great national issues" of the day. In his view, Cárdenas destroyed national unity by pitting the campesino against his landlord, and the worker against his boss. In clear reference to the Cardenistas, he declared that his nation had "found many destroyers; great distributors of land; great expropriators of private wealth; great thieves of public wealth." Obregón, he believed, organized rather than expropriated agricultural production; educated rather than indoctrinated campesinos; and, most importantly, displayed decorum that Romandía Ferreira found lacking in the Cárdenas regime. "We have left," he announced "the authentic path of the revolution." This speech cited numerous other transgressions against the "true Mexican Revolution" represented by Obregón and Calles.[13]

While no other speaker ever came close to writing another diatribe against the left wing of the Revolution, Romandía Ferreira's speech, which was reprinted in all major Mexico City newspapers, set the tone for the following years. In subsequent years, Mexico's involvement in World War Two as an ally of the United States and the anti-Communist fears provoked by the beginning of the Cold War discredited radicals on the right and left, and led to the government's renewed attempt to achieve national unity.[14] Obregón joined Villa and Zapata as revolutionary leaders who, even in death, represented the new official version of the Revolution, one that rejected all of the "isms" that had given rise to the totalitarian regimes in Germany, Japan, and the Soviet Union. He became the sum of the Revolution's tendencies. Through the cult associated with his memory, the government encouraged its citizens to venerate the other murdered revolutionaries as well.[15]

An Arm and a Revolution on a Stage

It was in this atmosphere of national unity during World War Two—almost three decades after the caudillo's mutilation at the Hacienda de Santa Ana—that Obregón's friends in the Asociación Cívica decided to connect the severed arm with the political culture of their time. On the occasion of the fifteenth anniversary of Obregón's assassination in 1943, the caudillo's private physician, Enrique Osornio, solemnly placed the jar containing the arm into a new, specially designed niche inside the Monumento Obregón. As if to deflect attention from the decomposing arm, the onlookers at the ceremony were then treated to a lecture on "General Obregón and Public Hygiene" by one of Osornio's colleagues.[16] This public display of the arm claimed for the Monumento Obregón the mantle of the principal site of this particular hero cult. It became a tourist attraction as the only place in the nation where a body part of a political leader was on display. Meanwhile, the unpretentious gravesite of Huatabampo where the caudillo's ashes resided (and, by extension, the circle of relatives and acquaintances who lived in Sonora rather than the capital) found itself marginalized in this hero cult. The display of the arm in the Monumento Obregón thus completed the recentering of the caudillo's memory toward the national capital, and away from the periphery where he had lived most of his life. In the words of a public intellectual, the arm also "infused charisma into a bureaucracy that insistently called itself revolutionary" despite the fact that this bureaucracy steadily moved away from revolutionary ideas.[17] To the degree that postrevolutionary reconstruction yielded to the "institutional revolution," the oxymoron enshrined in the new name of the party (Party of the Institutional Revolution), the regime needed this charisma to continue to lay claim to its revolutionary heritage. It was no coincidence that the reappearance of the arm in public led to increased references to Obregón's hands and arms on the part of memorial speakers. For instance, in 1945, the Yucatecan poet Antonio Médiz Bolio, a close friend of the slain caudillo and former diplomat under both Obregón and Calles, referred to these body parts four times in a fifteen-minute speech, thus anthropomorphizing the nation as a body.[18]

In 1946, just as the party's name change occurred, the military generation that had participated in the revolution passed the presidency to one of its university-educated sons: Miguel Alemán Valdés, the son of a prominent Obregonista general. Ironically, Alemán's tenure—the first complete term by a civilian since Sebastián Lerdo de Tejada in the 1870s—witnessed the final steps toward the apotheosis of Obregón as a revolutionary hero. On July 17, 1950, Luis L. León, an Obrecallista who had given the funeral oration at Calles's burial five years before, announced that the "Revolution is a sacred movement... To defame the great revolutionaries is to insult and betray the Revolution." He called upon all revolutionaries "of all the 'isms' to express solidarity with our great movement and to always know how to defend it," and he asked his audience to defend "not only Obregón, but also the triumphs, the greatness, and the accomplishment of all the dead leaders of the Revolution."[19]

Not surprisingly, not everyone within the Asociación Cívica agreed with these sentiments. Notable among the detractors was Humberto Obregón, the eldest son of the fallen caudillo, who resented the fact that entrepreneurs such as Sáenz had seized control of the memorial discourse. In a scathing letter, Obregón asked Sáenz to relinquish his role in an association devoted to the memory of "a caudillo of a revolution of extreme leftist tendencies." He accused Sáenz of having become like the people his father had fought all of his life: a "group of plutocrats" that resembled the inner circle of the Díaz regime.[20] Obviously, Humberto Obregón remembered his father for his military exploits and rhetoric rather than his business practices. He chose to remember only the populist aspects of the caudillo's proclamations rather than his accommodation of capitalists, not to mention his own profitable ventures in Sonoran agriculture.

This document eloquently demonstrates the continuing battle over the legacy of the revolution and of General Alvaro Obregón in particular. For President Calles, Obregón's death had offered an opportunity to forge national unity by fomenting the myth of a single, unified revolution—a myth crucial for establishing the dominance of the ruling party that he had created. For Calles, the fallen caudillo was the most useful symbolic representative of this revolution. By contrast, Cárdenas had posited Obregón as a precursor to his own efforts at social reform. He sought to draw a sharp contrast between the idolized, martyred Obregón, and Calles who seemed to still threaten a return to boss rule from his exile. Romandía Ferreira and Luis L. León resisted the Cardenista reinterpretation, and they reinvented Obregón as a father figure opposed to radical ideologies. Finally, Humberto Obregón's opposition to Sáenz and the other directors of the Asociación Cívica highlights an emerging counter-discourse against the regime's move to the right during World War Two and the Cold War.[21]

Therefore, twenty-five years after Obregón's assassination, the debate about the nature of the revolution and the caudillo's place in it lost some of its currency. For the generation that came of age during the so-called "Mexican miracle" of the 1950s and 1960s, the Revolution was little more than an historical artifact, even as participants in Mexico's great upheaval continued to play important roles in public life. During these years, state-sponsored industrialization yielded promising results: economic growth rates topped 8 percent annually, and the peso entered a 22-year period of stability vis-à-vis the US dollar. By 1960, the revolutionary past seemed a mere prologue to the country's journey toward inclusion among the world's most industrialized nations, an event promised and predicted annually by the PRI's ideologues. Mexico, these politicians proclaimed, was no longer an underdeveloped country, but one *en vías de desarrollo* (in the process of development). In this atmosphere, revolutionary leaders like Obregón were portrayed as father figures who had propelled their nation toward a better future, but who were no longer role models for the country's new civilian and bureaucratic leadership of university graduates. Thus, the annual celebrations of July 17 remained a major event on the PRI calendar, since the party continued to draw its legitimacy from Obregón and the other revolutionaries. But the annual ceremony was marked by boilerplate speeches celebrating the party's achievements rather than a reflection on Obregón's memory.[22]

The lesson was not lost on the public, and press coverage of the event became lackluster, and sometimes overtly critical. For instance, in 1954, an editorial in the newspaper *Novedades* asked: "Obregón, was he a hero? To conquer laurels at the expense of one's brothers is not a triumph, but defeat. … Those who died were those from below, those proletarians of the countryside and the city that now … have become … *braceros* [Mexican workers in the United States.]" Mexicans, the editorial argued, had become tired of both the promises of a perfect revolution, and the assertion that Obregón had helped promote democracy.[23]

A Revolution and a Leader Lose Respect

The year 1968—the fortieth anniversary of Obregón's assassination, and the year the summer Olympics came to Mexico City—marked a major milestone in the memory of Obregón and the other protagonists who had directed the state between 1917 and 1934, principally Carranza and Calles. At the time of the memorial celebration in July, Mexico City found itself in turmoil, as university students joined their counterparts in countries such as France, Germany, and the United States in protesting against the status quo, and particularly the entrenched political elite. On October 2, with the Olympics approaching, thousands of protesters gathered peacefully in Tlatelolco square near the Secretary of Foreign Relations. Shots rang out, and paramilitary forces stationed on the roofs of the buildings surrounding the square began shooting at the crowd. More than four hundred youthful protesters died that fateful day, and the illusion that the Revolution was a process that still continued in Mexico died with it.

When the dust from the Tlatelolco massacre had settled, the disillusionment with the Revolution was general enough that not even the orators attempted to draw an idealized picture of either Obregón or the state that he directed. In 1970, the main speaker at the event conceded: "There are enormous social needs. In the administrative chaos that emerged from the Mexican Revolution, almost twenty years of disorder, turbulence, and misfortunes, we have inherited today a form of political organization determined principally by immutable loyalties to a national caudillo."[24] Before the Tlatelolco massacre, such a stunning critique of the revolution and its legacy at an official commemorative event would have been unthinkable. Now, Cárdenas—the unofficial leader of the Mexican left since the end of his presidential term in 1940—remained the only leader of the 1920s and 1930s with a positive public image. His death on October 18, 1970 added to the soul-searching about what had led the nation astray. At the 1974 commemoration, Senator Alejandro Carrillo labeled Obregón "one of the great constructors of the nation," but admitted that the Revolution, just like any other major social upheaval, had not reached all of its goals.[25]

The arm inside the jar slowly decomposed as the myth of the revolution faded. Imperfectly preserved and damaged by light inside the monument, the arm lost all natural color. It also began to disintegrate, beginning from the point where the grenade explosion had severed it. By the 1970s, the arm had shriveled to the point that a pale white hand seemed to sit on an indistinct mound of pale flesh. Comments by visitors ranged from "not very presentable," in the words of one of the caudillo's sons, to "pretty gross,"[26] as a Chicano visiting Mexico City remarked.

After the debt crisis of 1982 led to a devaluation of the peso that sliced real wages in half—a crisis that brought the shortcomings of the PRI's political and economic strategy into full view—Obregón's decomposing arm once again served as an apt metaphor for the revolution. The PRI's insistence that it represented the ideals of the revolution met with growing cynicism and ridicule among the country's youth; likewise, what was left of the caudillo's arm mocked the idea of preserving the spirit of a revolution in a generation more familiar with Michael Jackson than Emiliano Zapata. Obregón's descendants had long desired to cremate the arm and reunite its ashes with those of the caudillo in Huatabampo, where a large number of family members continued to reside.[27] In deference to the Asociación Cívica and its connection with the government, however, the family never made their wish public. Almost seventy years after the battle of León, they sensed their opportunity.

Nonetheless, some opposed the plan to remove the last physical vestige of the Revolution from the Monumento Obregón. To them, the arm was one of the few remaining symbols of a bygone era. In the minds of many older Mexicans, the romantic appeal of this era lingered in the "lost decade" of the 1980s—a decade marked by sharply declining real wages, the financial devastation of the middle class, and the flight of millions of rural inhabitants to urban shantytowns and across the US border.[28] At a time when neoliberal technocrats such as Carlos Salinas de Gortari (president from 1988 to 1994) sacrificed the PRI's old rhetoric as a part of their attempt to bring Mexico out of its economic doldrums according to the precepts of international lending institutions, the public would have suspected that the burning of the arm was the decision of the government rather than that of the Obregón family. In the Salinas era, removing the arm would therefore draw attention to the fact that the government had given up on its attempt to use the Revolution for political capital. Not surprisingly, the aging caretaker of the monument said in a 1989 interview that the arm had "become a part of history and to take it away would be to change history a little bit."[29]

Meanwhile, regional differences in the remembrance of Obregón added another wrinkle to this debate. The inhabitants of the caudillo's home state had long resented the fact that the Monumento Obregón was not only the principal site at which the state paid homage to the victor of the Revolution, but also the repository of an arm that had been severed from its owner long before that owner met his death at La Bombilla. Along with the Obregón family, many Sonorans wondered why the arm was not cremated alongside and mingled with Obregón's ashes in Huatabampo. As if to emphasize this claim on the whole revolutionary rather than the one-armed martyr, in 1987 authorities in Hermosillo erected a statue of a younger Obregón with both arms . Similarly, a year later, the city government of Ciudad Obregón, located one hour north of the caudillo's birthplace, commissioned a statue of Obregón on horseback with both of his hands firmly on the horse's reins. These most recent Sonoran statues contrast with the earlier representations of the one-armed caudillo, such as the most famous one in the Monumento Obregón.

On July 17, 1989, the Mexico City newspaper *El Universal* published a story about the commemoration of the sixty-first anniversary of the assassination of General Obregón. By then, the occasion was normally given to extended oratory of officials of the ruling PRI to the perfunctory applause of their minions. But that year, as the newspaper reported, there had been a prelude the day before the July 17 celebration. During an "inspiring, but overlong ritual," government officials had cremated the remains of Obregón's badly decomposed arm. As *El Universal* reported, the arm now "inspired pity instead of patriotic sentiments." When the officials cremated the arm and deposited the ashes inside the monument, it appeared, the last severed body part of the revolution was laid to rest.[30] At the precise historical moment when Salinas de Gortari enjoined Mexicans to "reform the Revolution" and let go of old slogans, the cremation and reburial of these ashes seemed like an appropriate political symbol to mark the passage of a long era.

Unfortunately, *El Universal* had jumped the gun on the story, and the frayed lump that was once the caudillo's arm was still—as it had been for forty-six years—in its jar inside the Monumento Obregón. But a dispute among the general's descendants had combined with public outcry over incinerating a piece of the revolution to cancel the ceremony.[31] It was not until November 16, 1989 that Obregón's descendants had the arm cremated and replaced with a marble replica. As they had long desired, the ashes ended up with the rest of the general's remains in his grave in Huatabampo rather than in the Monumento Obregón. In the end, there was no newspaper account of the actual cremation of the arm or the disposition of the ashes. Many Mexicans only learned of these deeds through an article in the *Wall Street Journal*.[32]

An intriguing, though probably baseless rumor highlights the continued fascination with Obregón's arm. When this author visited the Obregón monument in May 2001 as part of his research, a fellow visitor joined him in contemplating the marble replica of the arm. Seeing the tall foreigner taking a photograph, the Mexican asked: "Do you know that a finger of Obregón's arm is still out there, somewhere? Someone cut off a finger before the cremation, so not all of the arm is gone ..."

Hence the story of the caudillo and his arm has come full circle. The story ended in a whimper with the unpublicized cremation of the arm—a cremation about which no details were released to the general public. A public debate over the last mortal relic of the revolution was not in the interest of either the national government or the Obregón clan. The swift action of the Obregón family stole the chance of groups of revolutionary veterans to march upon Mexico City's main square, the Zócalo, and it precluded a national debate on whether the ashes of the arm should repose with the rest of Obregón in Sonora or with the monument in the national capital. A supreme military leader and tactician, Obregón himself would have appreciated the end of his arm's political career.

Obregón's piecemeal transition out of the world of the living into the realm of the dead had created two separate postmortem cults: that of the arm and that of his body. The arm still represents Obregón's victories on the revolutionary battlefield; his masculinity and military prowess. The body, on the other hand, represents one of the most important members of the revolutionary family, a precursor of the institutional revolution and unifier of divergent political tendencies. In terms of symbolism, the assassination of the caudillo in 1928 proved to be more significant than the loss of his arm in 1915. Strikingly, however, the arm was the last physical reminder that connected Obregón to a political culture that had grown increasingly cynical about the "sacrifice" of this particular life—or any human life for that matter—to a cycle of violence that had failed to deliver the change that so many had hoped for.

Notes

Introduction

1 Fideicomiso Archivos Plutarco Elías Calles y Fernando Torreblanca (hereafter FAPEC), Archivo Fernando Torreblanca, Fondo Alvaro Obregón (hereafter FAO), serie 060400, gaveta 33, expediente 2, inventario 5129, "Discurso pronunciado por el Lic. Aarón Sáenz," Monterrey, N.L., July 17, 1929. All translations are mine unless indicated otherwise.

2 "Mexico's Latest Man of the Hour," *The New York Times*, Mar. 14, 1915.

3 FAPEC, Archivo Familia de la Huerta, Nemesio García Naranjo, open letter to the Duke of Alba, "Los verdaderos alteradores de la paz mexicana," Aug. 28, 1928.

4 Given his importance, it is surprising that Linda Hall's classic study of Obregón's emergence as a national leader during the 1910s has remained the only study in English. Linda B. Hall, *Alvaro Obregón: Power and Revolution in Mexico, 1911–1920* (College Station: Texas A&M University Press, 1981). Mexican historian Pedro Castro published an Obregón biography focusing on the 1920s as this volume went to press. Pedro Castro, *Alvaro Obregón: Fuego y cenizas de la Revolución Mexicana* (Mexico City: Ediciones Era, 2009).

5 Judith Butler, *Bodies That Matter: On the Discursive Limits of "Sex"* (London: Routledge, 1993), p. 2.

6 Claudio Lomnitz, *Deep Mexico, Silent Mexico: An Anthropology of Mexican Nationalism* (Minneapolis: University of Minnesota Press, 2001), p. 94.

The Last Caudillo: Alvaro Obregón and the Mexican Revolution. Jürgen Buchenau
© 2011 Jürgen Buchenau

7   Quoted in James I. Robertson, Jr., *Stonewall Jackson: The Man, the Soldier, the Legend* (New York: Macmillan, 1997), p. 746.

8   Hans H. Gerth and C. Wright Mills, eds. and trans., *From Max Weber: Essays in Sociology* (New York: Oxford University Press, 1947), p. 358.

9   Pierre Bourdieu, "Legitimation and structured interest in Weber's sociology of religion," in *Max Weber: Rationality and Modernity*, ed. Scott Lash and Sam Whimster (London: Allen and Unwin, 1987), p. 130.

10 John C. Chasteen, *Heroes on Horseback: A Life and Times of the Last Gaucho Caudillos* (Albuquerque: University of New Mexico Press, 1995), pp. 2–3.

11 John Lynch, *Caudillos in Spanish America, 1800–1850* (Oxford: Clarendon Press, 1992).

12 Chasteen, *Heroes on Horseback*, p. 3.

13 Samuel Brunk, *The Posthumous Career of Emiliano Zapata: Myth, Memory, and Mexico's Twentieth Century* (Austin: University of Texas Press, 2008).

14 Friedrich Katz, *The Life and Times of Pancho Villa* (Stanford: Stanford University Press, 1998).

15 For the distinction between nineteenth-century caudillos and twentieth-century strongmen, see Lynch, *Caudillos*, 425–33. For Obregón's attitude toward the Church, see David C. Bailey, "Alvaro Obregón and Anticlericalism in the 1910 Revolution," *Hispanic American Historical Review* 26.6 (1969): pp. 183–198.

16 For one example of this common usage, see Martín Luis Guzmán, *La sombra del caudillo* (Madrid: Espasa-Calpe, 1930).

17 Plutarco Elías Calles, "El camino hacia la más alta y respetada nación de instituciones y leyes," in *Plutarco Elías Calles: Pensamiento político y social; antología, 1913–1936*, ed. Carlos Macías (Mexico City: Fondo de Cultura Económica, 1988), pp. 240–241.

18 Ramón Eduardo Ruiz, *The Great Rebellion: Mexico, 1905–1924* (New York: W.W. Norton, 1982); Mancur Olson, *Power and Prosperity: Outgrowing Communist and Capitalist Dictatorships* (New York: Basic Books, 2000), pp. 6–10.

19 Roderic Ai Camp, *Entrepreneurs and Politics in Twentieth-Century Mexico* (New York: Oxford University Press, 1989), and *Political Recruitment across Two Centuries: Mexico, 1884–1991* (Austin: University of Texas Press, 1995).

20 Bertolt Brecht, "Fragen des lesenden Arbeiters," in *Poetry and Prose*, ed. Reinhard Grimm (New York: Continuum, 2003), p. 62.

21 Oscar Lewis, *Pedro Martínez: A Mexican Peasant and His Family* (New York: Vintage, 1964).

22 Ruth Behar, *Translated Woman: Crossing the Border with Esperanza's Story*, 2nd ed. (Boston: Beacon Press, 2003).

23   The analysis presented here therefore expands on some of the conclusions from my earlier study of Calles. See Jürgen Buchenau, *Plutarco Elías Calles and the Mexican Revolution* (Lanham, MD: Rowman and Littlefield, 2006). A future book will discuss the Sonoran group more generally.

1   The Background of the Last Caudillo

1   For a good analysis of the governance of colonial Spanish America, see Lyman L. Johnson and Mark Burkholder, *Colonial Latin America*, 7th ed. (Oxford: Oxford University Press, 2009), ch. 3.

2   A good summary of the independence movements and their aftermath appears in John C. Chasteen, *Americanos: Latin America's Struggle for Independence* (Oxford: Oxford University Press, 2008), pp. 123–181.

3   Christon I. Archer, "Death's Patriots—Celebration, Denunciation, and Memories of Mexico's Independence Heroes: Miguel Hidalgo, José María Morelos, and Agustín de Iturbide," in *Death, Dismemberment, and Memory: Body Politics in Latin America*, ed. Lyman L. Johnson (Albuquerque: University of New Mexico Press, 2004), pp. 82–90.

4   Lynch, *Caudillos*, p. 426.

5   Lynch, *Caudillos*, pp. 239–315.

6   Will Fowler, *Santa Anna of Mexico* (Lincoln: University of Nebraska Press, 2007), pp. 3–174.

7   Lesley Byrd Simpson, *Many Mexicos*, 4th rev. ed. (Berkeley: University of California Press, 1967), pp. 242–248.

8   Quoted in Lomnitz, *Deep Mexico*, p. 90.

9   Fowler, *Santa Anna*, p. 308.

10   Mexican politicians often invoke this quote; for example, see cronica.diputados.gob.mx/DDebates/43/2do/CPerma/19570530.html (accessed October 12, 2010).

11   Richard N. Sinkin, *The Mexican Reform: A Study in Liberal Nation-Building* (Austin: University of Texas Press, 1979).

12   Erika Pani, "Dreaming of a Mexican Empire: The Political Projects of the 'Imperialistas,'" *Hispanic American Historical Review* 82,1 (2002): pp. 1–31.

13   Charles Blanchot, *Mémoires: L'Intervention Française au Mexique* (Paris: Librairie Émile Nourry, 1909), 3: 1.

14   Paul Vanderwood, *Disorder and Progress: Bandits, Police, and Mexican Development*, 2nd ed. (Wilmington, DE: Scholarly Resources, 1992), pp. 53–62.   .

15 Lynch, *Caudillos*, pp. 426–428.

16 Paul H. Garner, *Porfirio Díaz* (London: Longman, 2001), pp. 18–68.

17 Víctor Macías-González, "Presidential Ritual in Porfirian Mexico: Curtsying in the Shadow of Dictators," in *Heroes and Hero Cults in Latin America*, eds. Samuel Brunk and Ben Fallaw (Austin: University of Texas Press, 2006), pp. 93–101.

18 Charles Hale, *The Transformation of Liberalism in Late Nineteenth-Century Mexico* (Princeton, N.J.: Princeton University Press, 1989).

19 W. Dirk Raat, *El positivismo durante el porfiriato* (Mexico City: El Colegio de México, 1975).

20 Héctor Aguilar Camín, "The Relevant Tradition: Sonoran Leaders in the Revolution," in *Caudillo and Peasant in the Mexican Revolution*, ed. David A. Brading (Cambridge: Cambridge University Press, 1980), pp. 93–94.

21 Cynthia Radding, *Wandering Peoples: Colonialism, Ethnic Spaces, and Ecological Frontiers in Northwest Mexico, 1700–1850* (Durham, N.C.: Duke University Press, 1997).

22 Héctor Aguilar Camín, *La frontera nómada: Sonora y la revolución mexicana* (Mexico City: Siglo XXI Editores, 1977).

23 On mid-nineteenth Sonora, see Stuart F. Voss, *On the Periphery of Nineteenth-Century Mexico: Sonora and Sinaloa, 1810–1877* (Tucson: University of Arizona Press, 1982). For Porfirian Sonora, see Miguel Tinker Salas, *In the Shadow of the Eagles: Sonora and the Transformation of the Border During the Porfiriato* (Berkeley: University of California Press, 1997).

24 Carlos Macías Richard, *Vida y temperamento: Plutarco Elías Calles, 1877–1920* (Mexico City: Fideicomiso Plutarco Elías Calles y Fernando Torreblanca and Fondo de Cultura Económica, 1995), p. 27.

25 See also Barry Carr, "Las peculiaridades del norte mexicano: Ensayo de interpretación," *Historia Mexicana* 22.3 (Jan. 1973): 320–346.

26 Voss, *On the Periphery*, pp. 64, 96–97, 147–149; Tinker Salas, *Shadow of the Eagles*, pp. 18–22, 38–39.

27 David M. Pletcher, "The Development of Railroads in Sonora," *Inter-American Economic Affairs* 1.4 (March 1948): pp. 3–45; Ramón Eduardo Ruiz, *The People of Sonora and Yankee Capitalists* (Tucson: University of Arizona Press, 1988).

28 Tinker Salas, *Shadow of the Eagles*, pp. 14–16.

29 Tinker Salas, *Shadow of the Eagles*, pp. 57–78.

30 Evelyn Hu-DeHart, *Yaqui Resistance and Survival: The Struggle for Land and Autonomy, 1821–1910* (Madison: University of Wisconsin Press, 1984), pp. 94–154.

31 "Armed Americans at Greene's Mine," *New York Times*, June 3, 1906; John Mason Hart, *Anarchism and the Mexican Working Class* (Austin: University of Texas Press, 1978), pp. 84–93.

32 Aguilar Camín, *La frontera nómada*, pp. 19–69.

2 An Improvised Leader, 1880–1913

1 There is some uncertainty about Obregón's precise date of birth. Some historians list it as February 17, others, as February 19, and his baptismal certificate has not survived.

2 Quoted in Enrique Krauze, *Mexico: Biography of Power*, trans. Hank Heifetz (New York: Harper Collins, 1997), p. 374.

3 E.J. Dillon, *President Obregón: A World Reformer* (Cambridge, MA: Small, Maynard, & Co., 1923).

4 Blasco Ibáñez, *Mexico in Revolution* (New York: E.P. Dutton, 1920), pp. 52–53.

5 Ibid., 53. For the Irish myth, see Richard H. Dillon, "Del rancho a la presidencia," *Historia Mexicana* 6.2 (1956): p. 257. Recent research on Obregón's genealogy is summarized in Ignacio Almada Bay, "Alvaro Obregón Salido: nuevos datos y nuevas interpretaciones," http://www.colson.edu.mx/absolutenm/articlefiles/944-inherm-obregon.pdf (accessed January 22, 2009).

6 Dillon, *Obregón*, pp. 32–33; Aguilar Camín, *La frontera nómada*, p. 296.

7 Dillon, *Obregón*, pp. 33–34.

8 Dillon, *Obregón*, p. 38.

9 Dillon, *Obregón*, pp. 36–44.

10 Dillon, "Del rancho a la presidencia," p. 258.

11 Krauze, *Biography of Power*, p. 375.

12 *Ibid.*, p. 376.

13 Hall, *Obregón*, 20; idem, "Alvaro Obregón and the Agrarian Movement, 1912–1920," in Brading, ed., *Caudillo and Peasant*, p. 129. It is doubtful that Obregón was proficient in this language as he did not interact regularly with the Yaqui until the revolution.

14 Hall, *Obregón*, pp. 22–23.

15 Alvaro Obregón, *Ocho mil kilómetros de campaña* (Mexico City: Fondo de Cultura Económica, [1917] 1959), p. 4.

16 Hall, *Obregón*, 22–23; FAPEC, FAO, serie 060400, exp. 40, leg. 1, inv. 5168 "Homenaje 1968," Alfonso Romandía Ferreira, "Discurso," p. 6.

17 FAPEC, FAO, serie 010200, exp. 24, inv. 30, "Obregón, Alvaro (Poemas de)." All translations are mine unless indicated otherwise.

18 Krauze, *Biography of Power*, pp. 374–403.

19 Almada Bay, "Alvaro Obregón," 13; Esperanza Donjuan Espinoza, *Conflictos electorales durante el porfiriato en Sonora: una revisión de los recursos de impugnación de resultados electorales municipales, 1900–1910* (Hermosillo: Colegio de Sonora, 2006), p. 251.

20 Hall, *Obregón*, 24; Aguilar Camín, "Relevant Tradition," p. 99.

21 Juan de Dios Bojórquez, "El espíritu revolucionario de Obregón," in José Rubén Romero, et al., *Obregón: Aspectos de su vida* (Mexico City: Cultura, 1935), pp. 162–163.

22 John Lear, *Workers, Neighbors, and Citizens: The Revolution in Mexico City* (Lincoln: University of Nebraska Press, 2001), 15–75; Jürgen Buchenau, *Tools of Progress: A German Merchant Family in Mexico City, 1865–Present* (Albuquerque: University of New Mexico Press, 2004), pp. 47–62.

23 For a detailed analysis of the opposition against Díaz and the subsequent Madero revolt, see Alan Knight, *The Mexican Revolution* (Cambridge: Cambridge University Press, 1986), 1: 37–246.

24 Aguilar Camín, *La frontera nómada*, pp. 127–163.

25 Pedro Castro Martínez, *Adolfo de la Huerta y la Revolución Mexicana* (Mexico City: Instituto Nacional de Estudios Históricos de la Revolución Mexicana, 1992), pp. 13–16; Aguilar Camín, *La frontera nómada*, pp. 22–29, 77–86.

26 Aguilar Camín, *La frontera nómada*, pp. 110–123.

27 Aguilar Camín, *La frontera nómada*, p. 298.

28 Obregón, *Ocho mil kilómetros*, p. 5, 12.

29 Ignacio Almada Bay, *La conexión Yocupicio: soberanía estatal y tradición cívica-liberal en Sonora, 1913–1936* (Mexico City: Colegio de México, 2009), pp. 133–152.

30 Knight, *Mexican Revolution*, 1:258.

31 Hall, *Obregón*, p. 25; Antonio G. Rivera, *La revolución en Sonora* (Hermosillo: Gobierno de Sonora, 1981), p. 247; Roberto Esparza Guzmán, *Memorias de don Adolfo de la Huerta, según su propio dictado* (Mexico City: Ediciones Guzmán, 1957), pp. 27–28.

32 Esparza Guzmán, *Adolfo de la Huerta*, pp. 20–21.

33 Héctor Aguilar Camín, *La revolución sonorense, 1910–1914* (Mexico City: Instituto Nacional de Antropología e Historia, 1975), pp. 260–264.

34 Knight, *Mexican Revolution* 1: 257–388.

35 Michael C. Meyer, *Mexican Rebel: Pascual Orozco and the Mexican Revolution, 1910–1915* (Lincoln: University of Nebraska Press, 1967), pp. 52–93.

36 Obregón, *Ocho mil kilómetros*, p. 8.

37 Dillon, *Obregón*, p. 65.

38 Obregón, *Ocho mil kilómetros*, p. 9.
39 Obregón, *Ocho mil kilómetros*, p. 10.
40 Buchenau, *Calles*, p. 35–36.
41 Quoted in Krauze, *Biography of Power*, p. 412; correct translation provided here.
42 Obregón, *Ocho mil kilómetros*, pp. 10–11.
43 Dillon, *Obregón*, pp. 65–66.
44 Obregón, *Ocho mil kilómetros*, pp. 14–18.
45 Obregón, *Ocho mil kilómetros*, p. 21.
46 Hall, "Obregón and the Agrarian Movement," p. 125.
47 Obregón, *Ocho mil kilómetros*, pp. 21–22.
48 Obregón, *Ocho mil kilómetros*, p. 23.
49 Obregón, *Ocho mil kilómetros*, pp. 24–25; Hall, *Obregón*, pp. 31–34.
50 Obregón, *Ocho mil kilómetros*, 25; Hall, *Obregón*, p. 35–36.

3 Chaos and Triumph, 1913–1916

1 "Mexico's Latest Man of the Hour," *The New York Times*, Mar. 14, 1915.
2 Biblioteca Nacional de Antropología e Historia, Mexico City, Archivo Histórico en Micropelícula, 59: Documentos para la historia de Sonora (hereafter DHS), reel 9, José María Maytorena, "Informe del gobernador de Sonora sobre el golpe de estado de febrero de 1913 y hechos posteriores;" National Archives, College Park, MD (hereafter NA), RG 59: General Records of the Department of State, (hereafter DS), 812.00/6434, Hostetter to Secretary of State, Hermosillo, Feb. 22, 1913; William H. Beezley, *Insurgent Governor: Abraham González of Chihuahua* (Lincoln: University of Nebraska Press, 1973), pp. 156–162.
3 Obregón, *Ocho mil kilómetros*, p. 43.
4 Hall, *Obregón*, p. 43.
5 Hall, "Alvaro Obregón," p. 129; Buchenau, *Calles*, p. 42.
6 Douglas Richmond, *Venustiano Carranza's Nationalist Struggle, 1893–1920* (Lincoln: University of Nebraska Press, 1983), 1–44; Katz, *Villa*, pp. 11–206.
7 FAPEC, FAO, serie 010200, exp. 27, inv. 33, "Obregón, Humberto," Alvaro Obregón to Humberto Obregón, en route to Nogales, Sonora, Feb. 27, 1913.
8 NA, DS, 812.00/7760, Sam Bliss, "Border Report," Fort Sam Houston, May 31, 1913.
9 Alfredo Breceda, *México revolucionario, 1913–1917* (Madrid: Tipografía Artística, 1920–1941), 2: 195.

10 Knight, *Mexican Revolution*, 2: 26.

11 Quoted in Richmond, *Carranza's Nationalist Struggle*, p. 55.

12 Martín Luis Guzmán, *Caudillos y otros extremos* (Mexico City: UNAM, 1995), p. 75.

13 Hall, *Obregón*, pp. 50–51.

14 Hall, "Alvaro Obregón," pp. 124–125.

15 For Obregón's offensive against Huerta, see Obregón, *Ocho mil kilómetros*, pp. 86–162; and Hall, *Obregón*, pp. 51–56.

16 Quoted in Jorge Aguilar Mora, *Un día en la vida del general Obregón* (Mexico City: Instituto Nacional de Antropología e Historia, 2008), p. 36.

17 Lear, *Workers, Neighbors, and Citizens*, p. 246.

18 Robert E. Quirk, *The Mexican Revolution, 1914–1915: The Convention of Aguascalientes* (Bloomington: Indiana University Press, 1960), pp. 136–137.

19 Quoted in Quirk, *Convention of Aguascalientes*, p. 136.

20 Knight, *Mexican Revolution*, 2: p. 29.

21 Quoted in William W. Johnson, *Heroic Mexico: The Violent Emergence of a Modern Nation* (New York: Doubleday, 1968), p. 178.

22 Buchenau, *Calles*, pp. 45–46.

23 Katz, *Villa*, p. 360.

24 Buchenau, *Calles*, p. 46–47.

25 Obregón, *Ocho mil kilómetros*, pp. 168–178.

26 Quoted in Katz, *Villa*, p. 368.

27 Obregón, *Ocho mil kilómetros*, p. 203.

28 Quoted in Katz, *Villa*, p. 368.

29 Katz, *Villa*, p. 369.

30 See also Ilene V. O'Malley, *Hero Cults and the Institutionalization of the Mexican State, 1920–1940* (New York: Greenwood, 1986).

31 DHS, José María Maytorena, "Manifiesto," Sep. 23, 1914.

32 Quirk, *Convention of Aguascalientes*, pp. 107–113.

33 Florencia Barrera Fuentes, ed., *Crónicas y debates de la Soberana Convención Revolucionaria* (Mexico City: Talleres Gráficos de la Nación, 1964), pp. 234–235.

34 Hall, *Obregón*, pp. 86–90.

35 Héctor Aguilar Camín and Lorenzo Meyer, *In the Shadow of the Mexican Revolution* (Austin: University of Texas Press, 1993), pp. 48–50.

36 Quirk, *Convention of Aguascalientes*, pp. 122–131. Hall, *Obregón*, 90–95.

37 "Obregón Calls All to Arms," New York Times, Nov. 14, 1914, p. 4; Isidro Fabela, ed., *Documentos de la Revolución Mexicana* (Mexico City: Talleres Gráficos de la Nación, 1960), 1: 396.

38   Katz, *Villa*, p. xiii.

39   Edwin Lieuwen, Mexican Militarism: *The Political Rise and Fall of the Mexican Army, 1910–1940* (Albuquerque: University of New Mexico Press, 1968), p. 32.

40   Quirk, *Convention of Aguascalientes*, pp. 134–141.

41   Cited in Obregón, Ocho kilómetros, pp. 256–257.

42   Hall, "Obregón and Agrarian Reform," pp. 127–130.

43   John Lear, *Workers, Neighbors, and Citizens*, pp. 271–273; National Archives, Kew, England, Foreign Office 371/2396, file 15003, and 371/2398, file 40183, Hohler to Foreign Office, Mexico City, Feb. 25 and 26, 1915.

44   Archivo Boker, S.A. de C.V., Mexico City, Fondo Memorias, Luise Böker to Theodor Pocorny, Feb. 26, 1915.

45   "Mexico's Latest Man of the Hour," *The New York Times*, Mar. 14, 1915.

46   Richmond, *Venustiano Carranza's Nationalist Struggle*, pp. 65–72.

47   Charles Cumberland, *The Mexican Revolution: The Constitutionalist Years* (Austin: University of Texas Press, 1972), pp. 257–261.

48   Lieuwen, *Mexican Militarism*, p. 57.

49   Elizabeth Salas, *Soldaderas in the Mexican Military: Myth and History* (Austin: University of Texas Press, 1990), pp. 38–47.

50   Hall, *Obregón*, pp. 118–122.

51   Martha Beatriz Loyo Camacho, *Joaquín Amaro y el proceso de institucionalización del ejército mexicano, 1917–1931* (Mexico City: UNAM, 2003), p. 34.

52   NA, RG 165: Records of the War Department General and Special Staffs, Military Intelligence Division Correspondence (hereafter cited as MID), box 1942, 8436–119, Capt. F.G. Knabenshue, "Intelligence Report," Sep. 9, 1916.

53   Obregón, *Ocho mil kilómetros*, pp. 299–385.

54   Obregón, *Ocho mil kilómetros*, pp. 370–371.

55   Archivo Histórico General y Licenciado Aarón Sáenz Garza, Mexico City (hereafter AHASG), exp. 183/1641, Elías L. Torres, "Cómo perdió el brazo Obregón."

56   Obregón, *Ocho mil kilómetros*, p. 371.

57   AHASG, exp. 183/1641, "La tragedia de Obregón," *Zócalo*, Aug. 24, 1952.

58   Alvaro Obregón, *Discursos del General Alvaro Obregón* (Mexico City: Talleres Gráficos de la Nación, 1932), 2 vols.

59   Ibáñez, *Mexico in Revolution*, pp. 54–55.

60   Buchenau, *Calles*, pp. 52–54.

61   FAPEC, FAO, serie 010400, exp. 1, inv. 167, "Cuerpo del Ejército del Noroeste."

62   Lieuwen, *Mexican Militarism*, pp. 57–58.

63 Centro de Estudios de la Historia de México, CARSO, Mexico City, Archivo Venustiano Carranza, carpeta 145, leg. 16751, Carranza, "Decreto," n.d. [1916].

64 In total, approximately 4,970 statutory miles. Obregón, *Ocho mil kilómetros*, pp. 484–485.

65 Quoted in José Rubén Romero, "Alvaro Obregón," in *idem, et al.*, *Obregón*, p. 28.

4 The Path to Power, 1916–1920

1 Katz, *Villa*, pp. 545–614.

2 Hall, *Obregón*, pp. 146–148.

3 Hall, *Obregón*, pp. 148–154.

4 *Ibid.*; Friedrich Katz, *The Secret War in Mexico: Europe, the United States, and the Mexican Revolution* (Chicago: University of Chicago Press, 1981), pp. 310–312.

5 Hall, *Obregón*, p. 172.

6 E. Victor Niemeyer, Jr., *Revolution at Querétaro: The Mexican Constitutional Convention of 1916–1917* (Austin: University of Texas Press, 1974), pp. 31–39.

7 *Ibid.*, p. 36.

8 *Ibid.*, pp. 39–42; Richmond, *Carranza's Nationalist Struggle*, p. 108.

9 Based on a quote attributed to President Lázaro Cárdenas with reference to the state of Tabasco, see Carlos R. Martínez Assad, *Laboratorio de la revolución: el Tabasco garridista* (Mexico City: Siglo Veintiuno, 1979). For a discussion of Sonora and Yucatán as laboratories of the revolution prior to the Constituyente, see Jürgen Buchenau and William H. Beezley, *State Governors in the Mexican Revolution, 1910: Portraits in Courage, Conflict, and Corruption* (Lanham, MD: Rowman Littlefield, 2009), chapters 3 and 4.

10 Niemeyer, *Revolution at Querétaro*, pp. 60–210.

11 James C. Scott, *Domination and the Arts of Resistance: Hidden Transcripts* (New Haven, NH: Yale University Press, 1990), p. 18.

12 Guzmán Esparza, *Adolfo de la Huerta*, pp. 79–81.

13 NA, MID, box 1943, 8536-156, Knabenshue, "Weekly Border Report," Jan. 20, 1917.

14 Niemeyer, *Revolution at Querétaro*, p. 224.

15 Speech in Querétaro, Dec. 20, 1916, *Discursos*, 2:466.

16 Niemeyer, *Revolution at Querétaro*, 224. For the view that Obregón held extensive influence, see Hall, *Obregón*, pp. 167–184.

17 These dates are taken from FAPEC, FAO, serie 060400, exp. 40, leg. 1, inv. 5168 "Homenaje 1968," Alfonso Romandía Ferreira, "Discurso," p. 6.

18 Quoted in Romero, "Obregón," 25. On Obregón's health, see NA, MID, box 1943, 8536-156, Knabenshue, "Weekly Border Report," Jan. 20, 1917.

19 NA, MID, box 1943, 8536-238, Knabenshue, "Weekly Border Report," May 12, 1917.

20 Lord Byron, "Ode to Napoleon Bonaparte."

21 NA, MID, box 1943, 8536-149, "Colonel Montano Interview," Nov. 30, 1916.

22 Buchenau, *Calles*, 71–72; Archivo de la Secretaría de la Defensa Nacional, Archivo de Cancelados, XI/III/1-44, vol. 1, 105–107, Calles to Obregón, Empalme, Son., Oct. 21, 1916, and Obregón to Calles, Mexico City, Oct. 24, 1916; NA, MID, box 2163, 9700–42, Commanding General to Chief of Staff, Nogales, AZ, Oct. 30, 1916; box 1943, 8536–156, Knabenshue, "Weekly Border Report," Nogales, Jan. 20, 1917, and 8536-241, Van Schaick, "Weekly Border Report," Nogales, May 19, 1917.

23 Hall, *Obregón*, pp. 200–201.

24 NA, MID, box 1936, 8532-736/1, memo, Col. Harry O. Williard, Apr. 29, 1918.

25 *Ibid.*

26 Hall, *Obregón*, p. 202.

27 FAPEC, FAO, serie 020200, exp. 98, inv. 243, "Sáenz, Aarón," Sáenz to Obregón, Mexico City, Aug. 27, 1917.

28 FAPEC, FAO, serie 020400, exp. 31, inv. 287, "War Trade Board," Obregón, "Decreto sobre relaciones comerciales con el enemigo 'la lista negra,'" Nogales, Jan. 8, 1918.

29 Samuel Brunk, *Emiliano Zapata: Revolution and Betrayal in Mexico* (Albuquerque: University of New Mexico Press, 1995), pp. 217–225.

30 FAPEC, FAO, serie 030100 Exp. H-1/355 Inv. 1425 "Hill, Benjamín G. (Gral.)," leg. 1, Hill to Obregón, Mexico City, Apr. 20, 1919.

31 FAPEC, Archivo Fernando Torreblanca, Fondo Fernando Torreblanca (hereafter FFT), serie 010202, exp. 5B1, 5B2/9, inv. 106 "Obregón, Alvaro (Gral.)"; Carranza, Venustiano, Manifiesto del C. Presidente a la Nación, Jan. 15, 1919.

32 Hall, *Obregón*, pp. 205–208.

33 Buchenau, *Calles*, pp. 86–88.

34 Alvaro Obregón, *Manifiesto a la Nación lanzado por el C. Alvaro Obregón* (Hermosillo: Imprenta Moderna, 1919), pp. 1–5.

35 Obregón, *Manifiesto*, p. 6.

36 Obregón, *Manifiesto*, p. 15.

37 FAPEC, FAO, serie 030100, exp. H-1/355, inv. 1425 "Hill, Benjamín G. (Gral.)," leg. 1, Hill to Obregón, Apr. 20, 1919.

38 Speech in Mazatlán, Sin., Nov. 7, 1919, in *Discursos* 1:70–71.

39 Knight, *Mexican Revolution*, 2:10.

40 Vicente Fuentes Díaz, *Los partidos políticos en México*, 2nd ed. (Mexico City: Editorial Altiplano, 1969), 204–10; Hall, *Obregón*, pp. 199–200.

41 Fuentes Díaz, *Los partidos políticos*, pp. 204–207.

42 FAPEC, FAO, serie 030100, exp. C-1/189, inv. 1158 "Calles, Plutarco Elías (Gral.)," Calles to Obregón, and Calles to Serrano, Querétaro, Oct. 14, 1919.

43 FAPEC, FAO, serie 030100, exp. C-1/189, inv. 1158 "Calles, Plutarco Elías (Gral.)," Obregón to Calles, Oct. 18, 1919.

44 Speech in Celaya, Gto., Jan. 11, 1920, in *Discursos*, 1:111.

45 Hall, *Obregón*, pp. 214–215.

46 Ibáñez, *Mexico in Revolution*, pp. 60–62.

47 Ibáñez, *Mexico in Revolution*, pp. 59–60.

48 Hall, *Obregón*, p. 203.

49 Hall, *Obregón*, pp. 227–228.

50 DHS, reel 10, de la Huerta to Carranza, Hermosillo, Mar. 30 and Apr. 4, 1920, and Carranza to de la Huerta, Mexico City, Apr. 2, 1920, "Al pueblo mexicano," Apr. 9, 1920; FAPEC, AFT, Fondo Plutarco Elías Calles, serie 010100, exp. 6, inv. 6, "Comandante Militar del Estado," de la Huerta to Calles, Apr. 10, 1920.

51 Quoted in Hall, *Obregón*, p. 239.

52 Hall, *Obregón*, pp. 232–241.

53 John W.F. Dulles, *Yesterday in Mexico: A Chronicle of the Revolution, 1919–1936* (Austin: University of Texas Press, 1961), pp. 36–48.

54 Pedro Castro, *La muerte de Carranza: Dudas y certezas*, Boletín 34 (Mexico City: FAPEC, 2000), 13; Dulles, *Yesterday in Mexico*, pp. 57–58.

55 Robert F. Smith, *The United States and Revolutionary Nationalism in Mexico, 1916–1932* (Chicago: University of Chicago Press, 1972), pp. 128–132.

56 Castro, *Adolfo de la Huerta*, 45–107; FAPEC, FAO, serie 030400, exp. C-7 y E-03/104, inv. 2120 "Calles, Plutarco Elías (Gral.)," Calles to Obregón, Mexico City, Jul. 2 and 6, 1920.

57 FAPEC, FAO, serie 030400, exp. 387, inv. 2403, "De la Huerta, Adolfo," Obregón to de la Huerta, Nogales, July 18, 1920.

58 FAPEC, FAO, serie 030400, exp. 387, inv. 2403 "De la Huerta, Adolfo," Obregón to de la Huerta, Nogales, July 17 and 18, 1920, and Culiacán, Sin., July 23, 1920; de la Huerta to Obregón, Mexico City, July 17 and 19, 1920.

59 Quoted in Dillon, *President Obregón*, p. 224.

60 Dulles, *Yesterday in Mexico*, p. 86.

5 The President, 1920–1924

1 Buchenau, *Calles*, pp. 22–110.

2 María del Carmen Collado Herrera, *Empresarios y políticos: Entre la Restauración y la Revolución* (Mexico City: Instituto Nacional de Estudios Históricos de la Revolución Mexicana, 1996).

3 Secretaría de la Economía Nacional, *Anuario Estadístico 1938*, p. 254.

4 Robert McCaa, "Missing Millions: The Demographic Costs of the Mexican Revolution," *Mexican Studies/Estudios Mexicanos* 19.2 (2003): 367–400.

5 Thomas L. Benjamin, "Laboratories of the New State, 1920–1929: Regional Social Reform and Experiments in Mass Politics," in *Provinces of the Revolution: Essays on Regional Mexican History, 1910–1929*," ed. Thomas Benjamin and Mark Wasserman (Albuquerque: University of New Mexico Press, 1990), p. 73.

6 Linda Hall, *Oil, Banks, and Politics: The United States and Postrevolutionary Mexico* (Austin: University of Texas Press, 1995), pp. 36–54.

7 I discuss the idea of the revolution as essentially populist in "Plutarco Elías Calles and Revolution-era Populism in Mexico," in *Populism in Twentieth Century Mexico: The Presidencies of Lázaro Cárdenas and Luis Echeverría*, eds. Amelia Kiddle and María L.O. Muñoz (Tucson: University of Arizona Press, 2010), pp. 38–57.

8 Quoted in Krauze, *Biography of Power*, p. 392.

9 Dulles, *Yesterday in Mexico*, p. 103.

10 Dulles, *Yesterday in Mexico*, p. 102–105.

11 Dulles, *Yesterday in Mexico*, 110; Georgette José Valenzuela, *La campaña presidencial de 1923–1924 en México* (Mexico City: Instituto Nacional de Estudios Históricos de la Revolución Mexicana, 1998), p. 11.

12 Franz Böker to Heinrich Böker, Mexico City, Apr. 20, 1920, AB, Fondo Franz y Luise Boker, folder 1150.

13 Loyo Camacho, *Joaquín Amaro*, 65; Lieuwen, *Mexican Militarism*, pp. 65–66.

14 Quoted in Aguilar Camín and Meyer, *In the Shadow of the Mexican Revolution*, p. 80.

15 Katz, *Pancho Villa*, 765–782; Loyo Camacho, *Joaquín Amaro*, pp. 107–108; Ernest Gruening, *Mexico and Its Heritage* (New York: Century Company, 1928), p. 320.

16 Gruening, *Mexico and Its Heritage*, p. 319.

17 Abelardo L. Rodríguez, *Autobiografía* (Mexico City: n.p., 1962), pp. 101–105; FAPEC, Archivo General Abelardo L. Rodríguez, "Informe que rinde el C. General Abelardo Rodríguez…," Feb. 15, 1922; José Alfredo Gómez

Estrada, *Gobierno y casinos: los orígenes de la riqueza de Abelardo L. Rodríguez* (Mexicali: Universidad Autónoma de Baja California, 2001), pp. 38–63.

18   Dudley Ankerson, *Agrarian Warlord: Saturnino Cedillo and the Mexican Revolution in San Luis Potosí* (DeKalb: Northern Illinois University Press, 1984), pp. 92–102; Gilbert M. Joseph, *Revolution From Without: Yucatán, Mexico, and the United States, 1880–1924*, 2nd ed. (Durham, NC: Duke University Press, 1988), pp. 185–263; Martínez Assad, *Laboratorio de la Revolución*; Andrew G. Wood, "Adalberto Tejeda of Veracruz," in Buchenau and Beezley, *Governors*, ch. 5.

19   David C. Bailey, "Obregón: Mexico's Accommodating President," in *Essays on the Mexican Revolution: Revisionist Views of the Leaders*, ed. George Wolfskill and Douglas W. Richmond (Austin: University of Texas Press, 1979), p. 82.

20   Alvaro Obregón, *The Agrarian Problem: Short-Hand Notes of the Impressions Exchanged Between the President-Elect and a Numerous Group of Congressmen, October 1920* (Mexico City: Imprenta de la Secretaría de Relaciones Exteriores, 1920).

21   Linda B. Hall, "Alvaro Obregón and the Politics of Mexican Land Reform, 1920–1924," *Hispanic American Historical Review* 60.2 (1980): 213–238; Heather Fowler Salamini, *Agrarian Radicalism in Veracruz, 1920–1938* (Lincoln: University of Nebraska Press, 1971), p. 31.

22   Quoted in Brunk, *Posthumous Career*, p. 66.

23   Timothy J. Henderson, *The Worm in the Wheat: Rosalie Evans and Agrarian Struggle in the Puebla-Tlaxcala Valley of Mexico, 1906–1927* (Durham, NC: Duke University Press, 1998), 141–46, 224; FAPEC, Archivo Plutarco Elías Calles, Fondo Presidentes (hereafter FP), serie 0204, inv. 760, Obregón to Calles, Mexico City, Aug. 7, 1924.

24   Atsumi Okada, "El impacto de la Revolución Mexicana: La Compañía Constructora Richardson en el Valle del Yaqui (1905–1928)," *Historia Mexicana* 50.1 (2000): pp. 91–143.

25   Ramón Eduardo Ruiz, *Labor and the Ambivalent Revolutionaries: Mexico, 1911–1923* (Baltimore, Md.: Johns Hopkins University Press, 1976), 74–78; Bailey, "Obregón," p. 87.

26   Quoted in Michael Snodgrass, *Deference and Defiance in Monterrey: Workers, Paternalism, and Revolution in Mexico, 1890–1950* (Cambridge: Cambridge University Press, 2003), p. 49.

27   Viviane Brachet-Marquez, *The Dynamics of Domination: State, Class, and Social Reform in Mexico, 1910–1990* (Pittsburgh: University of Pittsburgh Press, 1994), 59–61; Ruiz, *Labor*, pp. 89–93.

28   See, for example, Obregón's stern letter in FAPEC, FAO, serie 010400, exp. 154, inv. 4690, Obregón to Morones, Celaya, Jan. 25, 1924.

29   Quoted in Snodgrass, *Deference and Defiance*, p. 128.

30   Andrew G. Wood, *Revolution in the Street: Women, Workers and Urban Protest in Veracruz, 1870–1927* (Lanham, MD: SR Books/Rowman and Littlefield, 2001), pp. 51–63.

31   Mary Kay Vaughan, *The State, Education, and Social Class in Mexico, 1880–1924* (DeKalb: Northern Illinois University Press, 1982), pp. 134–140.

32   Vaughan, *State, Education, and Social Class*, pp. 140–148 and pp. 165–189; the long-term consequences of the education program are discussed in Mary Kay Vaughan, *Cultural Politics in Revolution: Teachers, Peasants, and Schools in Mexico, 1930–1940* (Tucson: University of Arizona Press, 1997).

33   Vaughan, *State, Education, and Social Class*, pp. 239–266; Henry C. Schmidt, *The Roots of "Lo Mexicano": Self and Society in Mexican Thought, 1900–1934* (College Station: Texas A&M University Press, 1978), pp. 97–116.

34   Helen Delpar, *The Enormous Vogue of Things Mexican* (Tuscaloosa: University of Alabama Press, 1992).

35   Ernest Gruening, "Alvaro Obregón," *The Nation*, Aug. 1, 1928, p. 106.

36   FAPEC, FFT, serie 010202, exp. 5D/14, inv. 111 "Obregón, Alvaro (Gral.) Discursos, Artículos," file 17/40, Obregón to Mora et al., Mexico City, Jan. 27, 1923.

37   For this tension between anticlericalism and political pragmatism in the revolution, see Ben Fallaw, "Varieties of Mexican Revolutionary Anticlericalism: Radicalism, Iconoclasm, and Otherwise, 1914–1935," *The Americas* 65.4 (2009): pp. 481–509.

38   FAPEC, FFT, serie 010203, exp. 5/6, leg. 2, "Convenio de la Huerta-Lamont," de la Huerta to Obregón, New York, June 13, 1922, and Obregón to de la Huerta, Mexico, June 14, 1922.

39   Ankerson, *Agrarian Warlord*, pp. 105–108.

40   Buchenau, *Calles*, pp. 101–102.

41   Buchenau, *Calles*, 104; Lieuwen, *Mexican Militarism*, p. 75.

42   Buchenau, *Calles*, ch. 4.

43   Castro Martínez, *Adolfo de la Huerta*, 93–95; FAPEC, Archivo Plutarco Elías Calles (hereafter APEC), exp. 56, inv. 1379 "De la Huerta, Adolfo," leg. 8 and 9, de la Huerta to Calles, Mexico City, Sep. 23, 1923, Calles to de la Huerta, Monterrey, Sep. 25, 1923; Obregón to Calles, Mexico City, Sep. 27, 1923.

44   Hall, *Oil, Banks, and Politics*, pp. 131–154.

45   Castro, *Adolfo de la Huerta*, p. 78–84.

46   NA, MID, box 1660, 2657–G–432/38, George Russell, G-2 Report, Mexico City, Dec. 29, 1923; Castro, *de la Huerta*, p. 121.

47   Loyo Camacho, *Joaquín Amaro*, 105–6; Georgette E. J. Valenzuela, *El relevo del caudillo: De cómo y por qué Calles fue candidato presidencial* (Mexico City: El Caballito, 1982).

48   NA, MID, box 1660, 2657–G–432/14, George Russell, G–2 Report, Mexico City, Dec. 8, 1923; Lieuwen, *Mexican Militarism*, p. 76.

49   Hall, "Obregón and the Politics of Mexican Land Reform," 230–31; Brachet-Marquez, *Dynamics of Domination*, pp. 63–65.

50   FAPEC, APEC, gav. 66, exp. 189, inv. 5407, leg. 4/11, Rodríguez to Calles, Mexicali, Dec. 29, 1923; Archivo Particular General Abelardo L. Rodríguez, Universidad Autónoma de Baja California, Tijuana (hereafter cited as APALR), box 3, exp. "Presidencia de la República," Pani to Rodríguez, Mexico City, Jan. 4, 1924, Rodríguez to Lubbert, Mexicali, Jan. 14, 1924, Rodríguez to Obregón, Mexicali, Feb. 3, 1924, Obregón to Rodríguez, Irapuato, Gto., Feb. 5, 1924.

51   Gómez Estrada, *Gobierno y casinos*, p. 146.

52   Alonso Capetillo, *La rebelión sin cabeza: Génesis y desarrollo del movimiento delahuertista* (Mexico City: Botas, 1925).

53   Enrique Plasencia de la Parra, *Escenarios y personajes de la rebelión delahuertista* (Mexico City: Miguel Porrúa, 1998).

54   Fernando Ramírez de Aguilar, *Desde el tren amarillo: crónicas de guerra* (Mexico City: Botas, 1924), pp. 83–86.

55   Mario Alfonso Aldana Rendón, *Manuel M. Diéguez y la revolución mexicana* (Zapopan: Colegio de Jalisco, 2006), pp. 543–545.

56   Castro, *de la Huerta*, 120–25; NA, MID, box 1661, 2657–G–432/60, "Weekly Survey of Mexican Revolutionary Situation, February 1, 1924."

57   Buchenau, *Calles*, pp. 107–113.

58   Almada, *La conexión Yocupicio*, pp. 133–177.

6   The Last Caudillo, 1924–1928

1   Jean Meyer, *Historia de la Revolución Mexicana, 1924–1928: Estado y sociedad con Calles* (Mexico City: Colegio de México, 1977), pp. 126–127.

2   Quoted in Paulina Latapí de Kuhlmann, "La testamentaría de Alvaro Obregón en una época de crisis," in *Estudios de Historia Moderna y Contemporánea de México* 14 (1991): p. 161.

3   Bojórquez, "El espíritu revolucionario," p. 163.

4   NA, MID, box 1661, 2657-G-509, George Russell, G-2 report, July 30, 1924.

5   Georgette José Valenzuela, "El viaje de Plutarco Elías Calles como presidente
      electo por Europa y Estados Unidos," *Revista Mexicana de Sociología* 57.3
      (1995): pp. 191–210; Buchenau, *Calles*, pp. 111–113.

6   José Alfredo Gómez Estrada, "Sonorenses: Historia de una camarilla de la
      élite mexicana, 1913–1932," Ph.D. dissertation, CIESAS-Occidente
      (Guadalajara), 2007, p. 176–179.

7   FAPEC, FFT, serie 010206, exp. 16, inv. 437, "Obregón, Alvaro (Gral.) y
      Fernando Torreblanca," leg. 4/4 Calles to Obregón, Mexico City, Oct. 1, 1925.

8   FAPEC, FFT, serie 010213, exp. 32, inv. 1099, leg. 2, Calles to Torreblanca,
      Durango, July 1, 1925, and Calles to Obregón, July 22, 1925; APALR, box 1,
      exp. "Oficina Comercial de Alvaro Obregón," Rodríguez to Ignacio P.
      Gaxiola, Mexicali, May 30, 1925.

9   APALR, box 1, exp. 5, "Oficina Comercial de Alvaro Obregón," Gaxiola to
      Rodríguez, Navojoa, Dec. 9, 1925.

10   FAPEC, FFT, serie 010213, exp. 32, inv. 1099, leg. 2, Calles to Almada, Aug.
      6, 1925, and Obregón to Torreblanca, Cajeme, Aug. 7, 1925.

11   FAPEC, FFT, serie 010202, exp. 5D/14, inv. 111 "Obregón, Alvaro (Gral.)
      Discursos, Artículos," file 31/40, speech, Nov. 3, 1925.

12   FAPEC, FFT, serie 010202, exp. 5D/14, inv. 111 "Obregón, Alvaro (Gral.)
      Discursos, Artículos," file 32/40, speech published in *Acción* (Navojoa, Son.),
      Mar. 14, 1926.

13   Okada, "Richardson," pp. 132–136.

14   Gómez Estrada, *Gobierno y casinos*, 155; APALR, box 1, exp. "Construcción
      de tanque de guerra," Gaxiola to Rodríguez, June 26, 1926; and exp. "Oficina
      Comercial de Alvaro Obregón," Gaxiola to Rodríguez, Navojoa, Mar. 23,
      1927, and Feb. 14, 1928.

15   FAPEC, FAO, serie 060300, exp. 18, inv. 5118, testament, Mar. 27, 1927.
      A subsequent modification documented in this file converted his sisters'
      share into a small pension of 500 pesos, to be divided equally among
      the sisters.

16   Latapí de Kuhlmann, "Testamentaría de Alvaro Obregón."

17   FAPEC, FAO, serie 020500, exp. 421 "Valenzuela, Blas," Sep. 18, 1918.

18   NA, MID, box 1663, 2657-G-589, Harold Thompson, G-2 report, May 3,
      1927.

19   Obregón to Calles, Navojoa, Apr. 7, 1925, in Carlos Macías, ed., *Plutarco
      Elías Calles: correspondencia personal* (Mexico City: Fondo de Cultura
      Económica, 1991), 1: 151–155.

20   NA, DS, 812.6363, Sheffield to Department of State, Dec. 24, 1925.

21   Gómez Estrada, "Sonorenses," p. 181.

22   Buchenau, *Calles*, pp. 93–94.

23 Camile Nick Buford, "A Biography of Luis N. Morones, Mexican Labor and Political Leader," Ph.D. dissertation, Louisiana State University, 1972, pp. 83–98.

24 Lorenzo Meyer, *Mexico and the United States in the Oil Controversy, 1917–1942*, trans. Lidia Lozano (Austin: University of Texas Press, 1972), pp. 107–114. The Petroleum Law and congressional debate can be found in Archivo General de la Nación, *Boletín del Archivo General de la Nación*, vol. 24/25 *La legislación petrolera en México, 1887–1927* (Mexico City: Archivo General de la Nación, 1983).

25 For one example of Calles's nationalist pronouncements, see FAPEC, Archivo Plutarco Elías Calles, gav. 18 bis, exp. 28, "Declaraciones del general Calles," Calles to Herbert Bayard Swope, Mexico City, June 18, 1925.

26 Buchenau, *Calles*, pp. 119–121.

27 Biblioteca Nacional de Antropología e Historia, Mexico City, Programa de Historia Oral (hereafter PHO) 1/25, Alicia O. de Bonfil and Eugenia Meyer, interview with Rafael F. Muñoz, Mexico City, July 15, 1970; NA, MID, box 1664, 2657-G-616/2, Edward Davis, G-2 Report, Mexico City, Feb. 23, 1926, 2657-G/4, Marion Howze, "Memorandum," July 31, 1926; 2657-G/9, Edward Davis, G-2 Report, Mexico City, Aug. 13, 1926.

28 "Sobre una conversación entre el presidente Calles y los obispos Pascual Díaz y Leopoldo Ruiz," Macías, ed., *Calles*, 1:171–193; Jean Meyer, *The Cristero Rebellion: The Mexican People Between Church and State, 1926–1929*, trans. Richard Southern (Cambridge: Cambridge University Press, 1976), pp. 48–200.

29 Buchenau, *Calles*, p. 93; Bailey, "Obregón and Anticlericalism," p. 193.

30 Nacional Financiera, *Statistics on the Mexican Economy* (Mexico City: Nacional Financiera, 1977), p. 385.

31 Jürgen Buchenau, *In the Shadow of the Giant: The Making of Mexico's Central America Policy, 1876–1930* (Tuscaloosa: University of Alabama Press, 1996), pp. 163–177.

32 Meyer, *Estado y sociedad con Calles*, p. 57.

33 On Hortensia's efforts, see Adriana Eller Williams, *Hortensia Elías Calles de Torreblanca: Homenaje en el centenario de su nacimiento*, Boletín No. 48 (Mexico City: Fideicomiso Archivos Plutarco Elías Calles y Fernando Torreblanca, 2005).

34 FAPEC, FFT, 010202 exp. 5A16/33 inv. 130 "Yaqui, Tribu," de la Huerta to Matus, San Antonio, June 24, 1926.

35 Loyo, *Joaquín Amaro*, pp. 150–152.

36 FAPEC, FP, serie 0204, Obregón to Calles, Náinari, Apr. 15, 1927.

37 Krauze, *Biography of Power*, p. 399.

38   Quoted in Krauze, *Biography of Power*, p. 392.

39   PHO/1/20, Daniel Cazes, interview with Luis Sánchez Pontón, Mexico City, Apr. 1961.

40   Pedro Castro, *A la sombra de un caudillo: Vida y muerte del general Francisco R. Serrano* (Mexico City: Plaza Janés, 2005), pp. 69–88, 127–148.

41   NA, MID, box 1665, 2657–G–622/2 and 6, Edward Davis, G-2 reports, Mexico City, Apr. 23 and Oct. 29, 1926. For a (likely overstated) assessment of Morones's political strength, see NA, RG 59, 711.12/856, Sheffield to Kellogg, Mexico City, Jan. 5, 1927.

42   Rafael Loyola Díaz, *La crisis Obregón-Calles y el estado mexicano*, 3rd ed. (Mexico City: Siglo Veintiuno Editores, 1987), pp. 20–22; Meyer, *Estado y sociedad con Calles*, pp. 123–150; Gonzalo N. Santos, *Memorias* (Mexico City: Grijalbo, 1984), pp. 310–315; NA, MID, box 1665, 2657–G–622/2, Edward Davis, G–2 report, Mexico City, Apr. 23, 1926; box 1665, 2657–G–657/1, Lt. Col. H.A. Parker, Nogales, AZ, May 9, 1928, to Assistant Chief of Staff.

43   Speech in Guadalajara, July 16, 1927, in *Discursos*, 2: 129.

44   Speech in Mexico City, June 25, 1927, in *Discursos*, 2: 49–68.

45   Speech in Mexico City, June 25, 1927, in *Discursos*, 2: 68–83.

46   FAPEC, APEC (Anexo), exp. 672 "Alexander Weddell, cónsul general americano en México, Abril 1926 (Reporte)," "Acuerdo privado provisional entre el General de División Alvaro Obregón, por sus propios derechos, y el señor Arturo de Saracho como representante del Sr. Luis N. Morones, Cajeme, Son., Feb. 10, 1926," pp. 55–56.

47   Quoted in Krauze, *Biography of Power*, p. 401.

48   Speech in Nogales, July 2, 1927, in *Discursos*, 2: 97.

49   For example, speech in Saltillo, Coahuila, *Discursos*, 2:271.

50   Katherine Anne Porter, *Flowering Judas and Other Stories* (New York: Harcourt, Brace, and Co., 1935), 139–60; Castro, *Serrano*, p. 28.

51   Buchenau, *Calles*, p. 162.

52   NA, MID, box 1665, 2657–G–622/22, Harold Thompson, G-2 report, Mexico City, Oct. 5, 1927; Castro, *Serrano*, pp. 173–228.

53   Speech in Orizaba, Veracruz, Apr. 20, 1928, in Obregón, *Discursos*, 2: 382.

54   Quoted in "La mano de Obregón perdió su última batalla," *Proceso* 663 (17 July 1989): p. 47.

55   Ignacio Almada Bay, "Las dos mitades de Plutarco Elías Calles," *Historia Mexicana* 58.3 (2009): p. 1162.

56   Dulles, *Yesterday in Mexico*, pp. 313–315.

57   FAPEC, FAO, serie 050100, exp. 32, inv. 4828, "León, Luis L.," León to Obregón, no date.

58   Quoted in Krauze, *Biography of Power*, p. 402.
59   Almada, "Las dos mitades," pp. 1162–1163.
60   FAPEC, FAO, serie 060100, exp. 2, inv. 5046, Plutarco Elías Calles, "A la nación."
61   See Krauze, *Alvaro Obregón*, 205; idem, *Plutarco Elías Calles*, 136. Even Calles opponent José Vasconcelos later concurred, albeit not without elevating León de Toral to hero status. José Vasconcelos, *El proconsulado* (Mexico City: Ediciones Botas, 1939), pp. 22–23.
62   FAPEC, FFT, serie 010207, exp. "234"/182, inv. 633, "Obregón, Alvaro (Gral.)," Manuel Ramos to Soto y Gama, May 18, 1928; anonymous to Soto y Gama, no date (probably June 27, 1928).
63   FAPEC, Fondo Plutarco Elías Calles (hereafter cited as FPEC), serie 011400, exp. 20 "Homenajes 1964," eulogy by Luis L. León, Oct. 19, 1964.
64   Plutarco Elías Calles, "El camino hacia la más alta y respetada nación de instituciones y leyes," in *Plutarco Elías Calles: Pensamiento político y social; antología, 1913–1936*, ed. Carlos Macías (Mexico City: Fondo de Cultura Económica, 1988), pp. 240–241.
65   Arnaldo Córdova, *La Revolución en crisis: La aventura del maximato* (Mexico City: Cal y Arena, 1995), p. 23.

7   The Unquiet Grave

1   An earlier version of this chapter was published as "The Arm and Body of a Revolution: Remembering Mexico's Last Caudillo, Alvaro Obregón," in *Death, Dismemberment, and Memory: The Politics of the Body in Latin America*, ed. Lyman Johnson (Albuquerque: University of New Mexico Press, 2004), pp. 179–206.
2   Córdova, *La Revolución en crisis*, p. 31 and passim; Thomas Benjamin, *La Revolución: Mexico's Great Revolution as Memory, Myth, and History* (Austin: University of Texas Press, 2000), especially p. 131.
3   FAPEC, FAO, serie 060400, exp., inventario 5129, "Discurso pronunciado por el Lic. Aarón Sáenz," Monterrey, N.L., July 17, 1929.
4   Gruening, "Alvaro Obregón, *The Nation*, Aug. 1, 1928,
5   FAPEC, FAO, serie 060400, exp. 2, inv. 5129.
6   "Un monumento al General Alvaro Obregón en el Paseo de la Reforma," *El Universal*, July 26, 1928.
7   FAPEC, FAO, serie 060400, exp. 7, inv. 5134, Departamento del Distrito Federal, *Monumento al General Alvaro Obregón: Homenaje nacional en el lugar de su sacrificio; prospecto.*

8   FAPEC, FAO, serie 060400, exp. 8, inv. 5135, Aarón Sáenz, "Discurso pronunciado en la solemne inauguración del monumento erigido a la memoria del señor General Alvaro Obregón, 17 de julio de 1935."

9   Mancur Olson, *Power and Prosperity: Outgrowing Communist and Capitalist Dictatorships* (New York: Basic Books, 2000).

10 "Sensacionales declaraciones del General Calles," *El Universal*, June 12, 1935; Dulles, *Yesterday in Mexico*, pp. 640–646.

11 Arnaldo Córdova, *La política de masas del cardenismo* (Mexico City: Ediciones Era, 1974).

12 FAPEC, FAO, serie 060400, exp. 8, inv. 5135, Aarón Sáenz, "Discurso pronunciado en la solemne inauguración del monumento erigido a la memoria del señor General Alvaro Obregón, 17 de julio de 1935."

13 FAPEC, FAO, serie 060400, exp. 13, inv. 5140, Alfonso Romandía Ferreira, "Discurso," 18 [sic] July 1941.

14 Steve Niblo, *Mexico in the 1940s: Modernity, Politics, and Corruption* (Wilmington, DE: Scholarly Resources, 1999), pp. 1–74.

15 Cf. O'Malley, *Myth of the Revolution*, pp. 114—132, which overlooks the Obregón cult as a unifying force.

16 FAPEC, FAO, serie 060400, exp. 15, inv. 5142.

17 Claudio Lomnitz, "Elusive Property: The Personification of Mexican National Sovereignty," in *The Empire of Things: Regimes of Value and Material Culture*, ed. Fred R. Myers (Santa Fe, NM: School of American Research Press, 2001), p. 128.

18 FAPEC, FAO, serie 060400, exp. 17, inv. 5144, "Discurso pronunciado por el Lic. Antonio Médiz Bolio."

19 FAPEC, FAO, serie 060400, exp. 22, inv. 5149, "Discurso pronunciado por el Sr. Ing. Luis L. León...," pp. 12–13.

20 FAPEC, FAO, serie 060400, gav. 33, exp. 22, inv. 5149, Humberto Obregón to Aarón Sáenz, Mexico City, June 7, 1950.

21 On the post-revolutionary state and the cultural project of the PRI state, see Arthur Schmidt, "Making It Real Compared to What? Reconceptualizing Mexican History Since 1940," in *Fragments of a Golden Age: The Politics of Culture in Mexico Since 1940*, eds. Gilbert Joseph, Anne Rubenstein, and Eric Zolov (Durham, NC: Duke University Press, 2001), pp. 25–33.

22 FAPEC, FAO, serie 060400, exp. 22–37, inv. 5149–5161.

23 "¿Cada año, el 17 de julio, hay cátedra de obregonismo?" *Novedades*, July 23, 1954.

24 FAPEC, FAO, serie 060400, exp. 42, inv. 5169 "Homenaje 1968."

25 "Ninguna Revolución en el Mundo Ha Alcanzado Todas sus Metas: la Mexicana no es Excepción," *El Nacional*, July 18, 1974.

26 "Some Still See Decaying Display as Piece of Revolutionary History Farewell to Arm?" *Los Angeles Times*, Sep. 11, 1989.

27 *Ibid.*

28 Nora Lustig, *Mexico: The Remaking of an Economy*, 2nd rev. ed. (Washington, D.C.: Brookings Institution, 1998), ch. 3; Alma Guillermoprieto, *The Heart That Bleeds: Latin America Now* (New York: Vintage Books, 1995), especially pp. 47–67 and pp. 237–258.

29 "Some Still See Decaying Display."

30 *El Universal*, July 17, 1989.

31 *Proceso*, July 24, 1989.

32 "If Only the General Could Have Ruled On the Fate of His Arm: Revolutionary Hero Lost Limb In Battle, and It Surfaces As Issue," *Wall Street Journal*, Nov. 28, 1989.

Bibliography

Sources Cited

Archives

Mexico
Archivo Boker, S.A. de C.V., Mexico City.
Archivo Histórico General y Licenciado Aarón Sáenz Garza, Mexico City.
Archivo Particular General Abelardo L. Rodríguez, Universidad Autónoma de
Baja California, Tijuana.
Biblioteca Nacional de Antropología e Historia, Mexico City.
Archivo Histórico en Micropelícula.
Documentos para la Historia de Sonora.
Programa de Historia Oral.
Centro de Estudios de la Historia de México CARSO, Mexico City.
Archivo Venustiano Carranza.
Fideicomiso Archivos Plutarco Elías Calles y Fernando Torreblanca, Mexico
City.

United States
National Archives, Washington, D.C. and College Park, Md.
RG 59: General Records of the Department of State.
RG 165: Records of the Army General and Special Staffs. Military Intelligence
Division.

Yale University Library.
James R. Sheffield Papers.

Great Britain
National Archives, Kew.
Foreign Office.

Newspapers

Excelsior, Mexico City.
El Nacional, Mexico City.
El Universal, Mexico City.
Los Angeles Times, Los Angeles.
Novedades, Mexico City.
New York Times, New York.
Proceso, Mexico City.
Wall Street Journal, New York City.

Published Primary Sources

Aguilar Mora, Jorge. *Un día en la vida del general Obregón*. Mexico City: Instituto Nacional de Antropología e Historia, 2008.

Archivo General de la Nación. *Boletín del Archivo General de la Nación*. Mexico City: Archivo General de la Nación, 1977.

Barrera Fuentes, Florencia, ed. *Crónicas y debates de la Soberana Convención Revolucionaria*. Mexico City: Talleres Gráficos de la Nación, 1964.

Blanchot, Charles. *Mémoires: L'Intervention Française au Mexique*. 3 vols. Paris: Librairie Émile Nourry, 1909.

Bojórquez, Juan de Dios. "El espíritu revolucionario de Obregón." In José Rubén Romero, et al., *Obregón: Aspectos de su vida*. Mexico City: Cultura, 1935, 147–174.

Breceda, Alfredo. *México revolucionario, 1913–1917*. Madrid: Tipografía Artística, 1920–1941.

Dillon, E.J. *President Obregón: A World Reformer*. Cambridge, MA: Small, Maynard, & Co., 1923.

Elías Calles, Plutarco. *Pensamiento político y social: Antología, 1913–1936*. Ed. Carlos Macías Richard. Mexico City: FAPEC and Fondo de Cultura Económica, 1988.

Elías Calles, Plutarco. *Correspondencia personal, 1919–1945*. Ed. Carlos Macías Richard. 2 vols. Mexico City: FAPEC and Fondo de Cultura Económica, 1991–1993.

Fabela, Isidro, ed. *Documentos de la Revolución Mexicana*. Mexico City: Talleres Gráficos de la Nación, 1960.

Gruening, Ernest. *Mexico and Its Heritage*. New York: Century Company, 1928.

Guzmán, Martín Luis. *La sombra del caudillo*. Madrid: Espasa-Calpe, 1930.

Guzmán, Martín Luis. *Caudillos y otros extremos*. Mexico City: UNAM, 1995.

Guzmán Esparza, Roberto. *Memorias de don Adolfo de la Huerta, según su propio dictado*. Mexico City: Ediciones Guzmán, 1957.

Ibáñez, Blasco. *Mexico in Revolution*. New York: E.P. Dutton, 1920.

Nacional Financiera. *Statistics on the Mexican Economy*. Mexico City: Nacional Financiera, 1977.

Obregón, Alvaro. *Manifiesto a la Nación lanzado por el C. Alvaro Obregón*. Hermosillo: Imprenta Moderna, 1919.

Obregón, Alvaro. *The Agrarian Problem: Short-Hand Notes of the Impressions Exchanged Between the President-Elect and a Numerous Group of Congressmen, October 1920*. Mexico City: Imprenta de la Secretaría de Relaciones Exteriores, 1920.

Obregón, Alvaro. *Discursos del General Alvaro Obregón*. 2 vols. Mexico City: Dirección General de Educación Militar, 1932.

Obregón, Alvaro. *Ocho mil kilómetros en campaña*. 2nd ed. Mexico City: Fondo de Cultura Económica, 1959.

Porter, Katherine Anne. *Flowering Judas and Other Stories*. New York: Harcourt, Brace, and Co., 1935.

Ramírez de Aguilar, Fernando. *Desde el tren amarillo: crónicas de guerra*. Mexico City: Botas, 1924.

Rodríguez, Abelardo L. *Autobiografía*. Mexico City: n.p., 1962.

Romero, José Rubén. "Alvaro Obregón." In *idem, et al., Obregón: Aspectos de su vida*. Mexico City: Cultura, 1935, 5–36.

Santos, Gonzalo N. *Memorias*. 4th ed. Mexico City: Grijalbo, 1984.

Vasconcelos, José. *El proconsulado*. Mexico City: Ediciones Botas, 1939.

Secondary Literature

Aguilar Camín, Héctor. *La revolución sonorense, 1910–1914*. Mexico City: Instituto Nacional de Antropología e Historia, 1975.

Aguilar Camín, Héctor. *La frontera nómada: Sonora y la Revolución Mexicana*. Mexico City: Siglo Veintiuno Editores, 1977.

Aguilar Camín, Héctor. "The Relevant Tradition: Sonoran Leaders in the Revolution." In *Caudillo and Peasant in the Mexican Revolution*, ed. D. A. Brading. Cambridge: Cambridge University Press, 1980, 92–123.

Aguilar Camín, Héctor and Lorenzo Meyer. *In the Shadow of the Mexican Revolution*. Austin: University of Texas Press, 1993.

Aldana Rendón, Mario Alfonso. *Manuel M. Diéguez y la revolución mexicana*. Zapopan: Colegio de Jalisco, 2006.

Almada Bay, Ignacio. *La conexión Yocupicio: Soberanía estatal y tradición cívico-liberal en Sonora, 1913–1939*. Mexico City: Colegio de México, 2009.

Almada Bay, Ignacio. "Las dos mitades de Plutarco Elías Calles." *Historia Mexicana* 58.3 (2009):1155–1169.

Ankerson, Dudley. *Agrarian Warlord: Saturnino Cedillo and the Mexican Revolution in San Luis Potosí*. DeKalb: Northern Illinois University Press, 1984.

Archer, Christon I. "Death's Patriots—Celebration, Denunciation, and Memories of Mexico's Independence Heroes: Miguel Hidalgo, José María Morelos, and Agustín de Iturbide." In *Death, Dismemberment, and Memory: Body Politics in Latin America*, ed. Lyman L. Johnson. Albuquerque: University of New Mexico Press, 2004, 63–104.

Bailey, David C. "Alvaro Obregón and Anticlericalism in the 1910 Revolution." *Hispanic American Historical Review* 26.6 (1969): 183–198.

Bailey, David C. "Obregón: Mexico's Accommodating President." In *Essays on the Mexican Revolution: Revisionist Views of the Leaders*, ed. George Wolfskill and Douglas W. Richmond. Austin: University of Texas Press, 1979, 81–99.

Beezley, William H. *Insurgent Governor: Abraham González of Chihuahua*. Lincoln: University of Nebraska Press, 1973.

Behar, Ruth. *Translated Woman: Crossing the Border with Esperanza's Story*. 2nd ed. Boston: Beacon Press, 2003.

Benjamin, Thomas L. "Laboratories of the New State, 1920–1929: Regional Social Reform and Experiments in Mass Politics." In *Provinces of the Revolution: Essays on Regional Mexican History, 1910–1929*," ed. Thomas Benjamin and Mark Wasserman. Albuquerque: University of New Mexico Press, 1990.

Benjamin, Thomas L. *La Revolución: Mexico's Great Revolution as Memory, Myth, and History*. Austin: University of Texas Press, 2000.

Bourdieu, Pierre. "Legitimation and structured interest in Weber's sociology of religion." In *Max Weber: Rationality and Modernity*, ed. Scott Lash and Sam Whimster. London: Allen and Unwin, 1987, 119–136.

Brachet-Marquez, Viviane. *The Dynamics of Domination: State, Class, and Social Reform in Mexico, 1910–1990*. Pittsburgh: University of Pittsburgh Press, 1994.

Brecht, Bertolt. "Fragen des lesenden Arbeiters." In *Poetry and Prose*, ed. Reinhard Grimm. New York: Continuum, 2003, 62.

Brunk, Samuel. *Emiliano Zapata: Revolution and Betrayal in Mexico*. Albuquerque: University of New Mexico Press, 1995.

Buchenau, Jürgen. *In the Shadow of the Giant: The Making of Mexico's Central America Policy, 1876–1930*. Tuscaloosa: University of Alabama Press, 1996.

Buchenau, Jürgen. *Tools of Progress: A German Merchant Family in Mexico City, 1865–Present*. Albuquerque: University of New Mexico Press, 2004.

Buchenau, Jürgen. "The Arm and Body of a Revolution: Remembering Mexico's Last Caudillo, Alvaro Obregón." In *Death, Dismemberment, and Memory: The Politics of the Body in Latin America*, ed. Lyman Johnson. Albuquerque: University of New Mexico Press, 2004, 179–206.

Buchenau, Jürgen. *Plutarco Elías Calles and the Mexican Revolution*. Lanham, MD: Rowman Littlefield, 2006.

Buchenau, Jürgen. "Plutarco Elías Calles and Revolution-era Populism in Mexico." In *Populism in Twentieth Century Mexico: The Presidencies of Lázaro Cárdenas and Luis Echeverría*, eds. Amelia Kiddle and María L. O. Muñoz. Tucson: University of Arizona Press, 2010, 38–57.

Buchenau, Jürgen and William H. Beezley, eds. *State Governors in the Mexican Revolution, 1910: Portraits in Courage, Conflict, and Corruption*. Lanham, MD: Rowman Littlefield, 2009.

Buford, Camile Nick. "A Biography of Luis N. Morones, Mexican Labor and Political Leader." Ph.D. dissertation, Louisiana State University, 1972.

Butler, Judith. *Bodies That Matter: On the Discursive Limits of "Sex."* London: Routledge, 1993.

Camp, Roderic A. *Entrepreneurs and Politics in Twentieth-Century Mexico*. New York: Oxford University Press, 1989.

Camp, Roderic A. *Political Recruitment across Two Centuries: Mexico, 1884–1991*. Austin: University of Texas Press, 1995.

Capetillo, Alonso. *La rebelión sin cabeza: Génesis y desarrollo del movimiento delahuertista*. Mexico City: Botas, 1925.

Carr, Barry. "Las peculiaridades del norte mexicano: Ensayo de interpretación." *Historia Mexicana* 22.3 (Jan. 1973): 320–346.

Castro Martínez, Pedro. *Adolfo de la Huerta y la Revolución Mexicana*. Mexico City: Instituto Nacional de Estudios Históricos de la Revolución Mexicana, 1992.

Castro Martínez, Pedro. *La muerte de Carranza: Dudas y certezas*. Boletín 34. Mexico City: FAPEC, 2000.

Castro Martínez, Pedro. *A la sombra de un caudillo: Vida y muerte del general Francisco R. Serrano*. Mexico City: Plaza y Janés, 2005.

Castro Martínez, Pedro. *Alvaro Obregón: Fuego y cenizas de la Revolución Mexicana*. Mexico City: Ediciones Era, 2009.

Chasteen, John C. *Heroes on Horseback: A Life and Times of the Last Gaucho Caudillos.* Albuquerque: University of New Mexico Press, 1995.

Chasteen, John C. *Americanos: Latin America's Struggle for Independence.* Oxford: Oxford University Press, 2008.

Collado Herrera, María del Carmen. *Empresarios y políticos: entre la restauración y la revolución.* Mexico City: Instituto Nacional de Estudios Históricos de la Revolución Mexicana, 1996.

Córdova, Arnaldo. *La Revolución en crisis: La aventura del maximato.* Mexico City: Cal y Arena, 1995.

Córdova, Arnaldo. *La política de masas del cardenismo.* Mexico City: Ediciones Era, 1974.

Cumberland, Charles. *The Mexican Revolution: The Constitutionalist Years.* Austin: University of Texas Press, 1972.

Delpar, Helen. *The Enormous Vogue of Things Mexican.* Tuscaloosa: University of Alabama Press, 1992.

Dillon, Richard H. "Del rancho a la presidencia," *Historia Mexicana* 6.2 (1956): 257.

Dulles, John W.F. *Yesterday in Mexico: A Chronicle of the Revolution, 1919–1936.* Austin: University of Texas Press, 1961.

Eller Williams, Adriana. *Hortensia Elías Calles de Torreblanca: Homenaje en el centenario de su nacimiento.* Boletín No. 48. Mexico City: Fideicomiso Archivos Plutarco Elías Calles y Fernando Torreblanca, 2005.

Fallaw, Ben. "Varieties of Mexican Revolutionary Anticlericalism: Radicalism, Iconoclasm, and Otherwise, 1914–1935." *The Americas* 65.4 (2009): 481–509.

Fowler, Will. *Santa Anna of Mexico.* Lincoln: University of Nebraska Press, 2007.

Fowler-Salamini, Heather. *Agrarian Radicalism in Veracruz, 1920–1938.* Lincoln: University of Nebraska Press, 1971.

Fuentes Díaz, Vicente. *Los partidos políticos en México,* 2nd ed. Mexico City: Editorial Altiplano, 1969.

Garner, Paul H. *Porfirio Díaz.* London: Longman, 2001.

Garrido, Luis Javier. *El partido de la revolución institucionalizada: La formación del nuevo estado en México (1928–1945).* Mexico City: Siglo Veintiuno Editores, 1982.

Gerth, Hans H. and C. Wright Mills, eds. and trans. *From Max Weber: Essays in Sociology.* New York: Oxford University Press, 1947.

Gómez Estrada, José Alfredo. *Gobierno y casinos: El origen de la riqueza de Abelardo L. Rodríguez.* Mexicali: Universidad Autónoma de Baja California, 2002.

Gómez Estrada, José Alfredo. "Sonorenses: Historia de una camarilla de la élite mexicana, 1913–1932," Ph.D. dissertation, CIESAS-Occidente (Guadalajara), 2007

Bibliography

Guillermoprieto, Alma. *The Heart That Bleeds: Latin America Now*. New York: Vintage Books, 1995.

Hale, Charles A. *The Transformation of Mexican Liberalism in the Late Nineteenth Century*. Princeton: University of Princeton Press, 1989.

Hall, Linda B. "Alvaro Obregón and the Agrarian Movement, 1912–1920." In *Caudillo and Peasant in the Mexican Revolution*, ed. D. A. Brading. Cambridge: Cambridge University Press, 1980, 124–139.

Hall, Linda B. "Alvaro Obregón and the Politics of Mexican Land Reform, 1920–1924," *Hispanic American Historical Review* 60.2 (1980): 213–238.

Hall, Linda B. *Alvaro Obregón: Power and Revolution in Mexico, 1911–1920*. College Station: Texas A&M University Press, 1981.

Hall, Linda B. *Oil, Banks, and Politics: The United States and Postrevolutionary Mexico*. Austin: University of Texas Press, 1995.

Hart, John Mason. *Anarchism and the Mexican Working Class*. Austin: University of Texas Press, 1978.

Henderson, Timothy J. *The Worm in the Wheat: Rosalie Evans and Agrarian Struggle in the Puebla-Tlaxcala Valley of Mexico, 1906–1927*. Durham, NC: Duke University Press, 1998.

Hu-DeHart, Evelyn. *Yaqui Resistance and Survival: The Struggle for Land and Autonomy, 1821–1910*. Madison: University of Wisconsin Press, 1984.

Johnson, Lyman L. and Mark Burkholder. *Colonial Latin America*. 7th ed. Oxford: Oxford University Press, 2009.

Johnson, William W. *Heroic Mexico: The Violent Emergence of a Modern Nation*. New York: Doubleday, 1968.

José Valenzuela, Georgette. *El relevo del caudillo: De cómo y por qué Calles fue candidato presidencial*. Mexico City: El Caballito, 1982.

José Valenzuela, Georgette. "El viaje de Plutarco Elías Calles como presidente electo por Europa y Estados Unidos." *Revista Mexicana de Sociología* 57.3 (1995): 191–210.

José Valenzuela, Georgette. *La campaña presidencial de 1923–1924 en México*. Mexico City: Instituto Nacional de Estudios Históricos de la Revolución Mexicana, 1998.

Joseph, Gilbert M. *Revolution From Without: Yucatán, Mexico, and the United States, 1880–1924*. 2nd ed. Durham, NC: Duke University Press, 1988.

Katz, Friedrich. *The Secret War in Mexico: Europe, the United States, and the Mexican Revolution*. Chicago: University of Chicago Press, 1981.

Katz, Friedrich. *The Life and Times of Pancho Villa*. Stanford, CA: Stanford University Press, 1998.

Knight, Alan. *The Mexican Revolution*. 2 vols. Cambridge: Cambridge University Press, 1986.

Krauze, Enrique. *Mexico: Biography of Power*. Trans. Hank Heifetz. New York: Harper Collins, 1997.

Latapí de Kuhlmann, Paulina. "La testamentaría de Alvaro Obregón en una época de crisis." *Estudios de Historia Moderna y Contemporánea de México* 14 (1991): 161.

Lear, John. *Workers, Neighbors, and Citizens: The Revolution in Mexico City*. Lincoln: University of Nebraska Press, 2001.

Lewis, Oscar. *Pedro Martínez: A Mexican Peasant and His Family*. New York: Vintage, 1964.

Lieuwen, Edwin. *Mexican Militarism: The Political Rise and Fall of the Revolutionary Army, 1910–1940*. Albuquerque: University of New Mexico Press, 1968.

Lomnitz-Adler, Claudio. *Deep Mexico, Silent Mexico: An Anthropology of Nationalism*. Minneapolis: University of Minnesota Press, 2001.

Lomnitz-Adler, Claudio. "Elusive Property: The Personification of Mexican National Sovereignty." In *The Empire of Things: Regimes of Value and Material Culture*, ed. Fred R. Myers. Santa Fe, NM: School of American Research Press, 2001.

Loyo, Martha Beatriz. *Joaquín Amaro y el proceso de institucionalización del ejército mexicano, 1917–1931*. Mexico City: UNAM, 2003.

Loyola Díaz, Rafael. *La crisis Obregón-Calles y el estado mexicano*. 3rd ed. Mexico City: Siglo Veintiuno Editores, 1987.

Lustig, Nora. *Mexico: The Remaking of an Economy*. 2nd rev. ed. Washington, D.C.: Brookings Institution, 1998.

Lynch, John. *Caudillos in Spanish America, 1800–1850*. Oxford: Clarendon Press, 1992.

Macías-González, Víctor. "Presidential Ritual in Porfirian Mexico: Curtsying in the Shadow of Dictators." In *Heroes and Hero Cults in Latin America*, eds. Samuel Brunk and Ben Fallaw. Austin: University of Texas Press, 2006, 93–101.

Macías Richard, Carlos. *Vida y temperamento: Plutarco Elías Calles, 1877–1920*. Mexico City: FAPEC and Fondo de Cultura Económica, 1995.

Martínez Assad, Carlos R. *Laboratorio de la revolución: el Tabasco garridista*. Mexico City: Siglo Veintiuno, 1979.

McCaa, Robert. "Missing Millions: The Demographic Costs of the Mexican Revolution." *Mexican Studies/Estudios Mexicanos* 19.2 (2003): 367–400.

Meyer, Jean. *The Cristero Rebellion: The Mexican People Between Church and State, 1926–1929*, trans. Richard Southern. Cambridge: Cambridge University Press, 1976.

Meyer, Jean, Enrique Krauze, and Cayetano Reyes. *Historia de la Revolución Mexicana, 1924–1928: Estado y sociedad con Calles*. Mexico City: El Colegio de México, 1977.

Meyer, Lorenzo. *Mexico and the United States in the Oil Controversy, 1917–1942.* Trans. Lidia Lozano. Austin: University of Texas Press, 1972.

Meyer, Michael C. *Mexican Rebel: Pascual Orozco and the Mexican Revolution, 1910–1915.* Lincoln: University of Nebraska Press, 1967.

Niblo, Steve. *Mexico in the 1940s: Modernity, Politics, and Corruption.* Wilmington, DE: Scholarly Resources, 1999.

Niemeyer, E. Victor, Jr. *Revolution at Querétaro: The Mexican Constitutional Convention of 1916–1917.* Austin: The University of Texas Press, 1974.

O'Malley, Ilene V. *The Myth of the Revolution: Hero Cults and the Institutionalization of the Mexican State, 1920–1940.* New York: Greenwood Press, 1979.

Okada, Atsumi. "El impacto de la Revolución Mexicana: La Compañía Constructora Richardson en el Valle del Yaqui (1905–1928)." *Historia Mexicana* 50.1 (2000): 91143.

Olson, Mancur. *Power and Prosperity: Outgrowing Communist and Capitalist Dictatorships.* New York: Basic Books, 2000.

Pani, Erika. "Dreaming of a Mexican Empire: The Political Projects of the 'Imperialistas.'" *Hispanic American Historical Review* 82.1 (2002): 1–31.

Plasencia de la Parra, Enrique. *Escenarios y personajes de la rebelión delahuertista.* Mexico City: Miguel Porrúa, 1998.

Pletcher, David M. "The Development of Railroads in Sonora." *Inter-American Economic Affairs* 1.4 (March 1948): 3–45.

Quirk, Robert E. *The Mexican Revolution, 1914–1915: The Convention of Aguascalientes.* Bloomington: Indiana University Press, 1960.

Raat, W. Dirk. "Ideas and Society in Don Porfirio's Mexico." *The Americas* 30 (1973), 32–53.

Raat, W. Dirk. *El positivismo durante el porfiriato.* Mexico City: El Colegio de México, 1975.

Radding, Cynthia. *Wandering Peoples: Colonialism, Ethnic Spaces, and Ecological Frontiers in Northwest Mexico, 1700–1850.* Durham, N.C.: Duke University Press, 1997.

Richmond, Douglas. *Venustiano Carranza's Nationalist Struggle, 1893–1920.* Lincoln: University of Nebraska Press, 1983.

Rivera, Antonio G. *La Revolución en Sonora.* Hermosillo: Gobierno de Sonora, 1981.

Robertson, James I., Jr. *Stonewall Jackson: The Man, the Soldier, the Legend.* New York: Macmillan, 1997.

Ruiz, Ramón Eduardo. *Labor and the Ambivalent Revolutionaries: Mexico, 1911–1923.* Baltimore, MD: Johns Hopkins University Press, 1976.

Ruiz, Ramón Eduardo. *The People of Sonora and Yankee Capitalists.* Tucson: University of Arizona Press, 1988.

Salas, Elizabeth. *Soldaderas in the Mexican Military: Myth and History.* Austin: University of Texas Press, 1990.

Scott, James C. *Domination and the Arts of Resistance: Hidden Transcripts.* (New Haven, NH: Yale University Press, 1990).

Schmidt, Arthur. "Making It Real Compared to What? Reconceptualizing Mexican History Since 1940." In *Fragments of a Golden Age: The Politics of Culture in Mexico Since 1940*, eds. Gilbert Joseph, Anne Rubenstein, and Eric Zolov. Durham, NC: Duke University Press, 2001, 25–33.

Schmidt, Henry C. *The Roots of "Lo Mexicano": Self and Society in Mexican Thought, 1900–1934.* College Station: Texas A&M University Press, 1978.

Sinkin, Richard N. *The Mexican Reform: A Study in Liberal Nation-Building.* Austin: University of Texas Press, 1979.

Simpson, Lesley B. *Many Mexicos.* 4th rev. ed. Berkeley: University of California Press, 1967.

Smith, Robert F. *The United States and Revolutionary Nationalism in Mexico, 1916–1932.* Chicago: University of Chicago Press, 1972.

Snodgrass, Michael. *Deference and Defiance in Monterrey: Workers, Paternalism, and Revolution in Mexico, 1890–1950.* Cambridge: Cambridge University Press, 2003.

Tinker Salas, Miguel. *In the Shadow of the Eagles: Sonora and the Transformation of the Border During the Porfiriato.* Berkeley: University of California Press, 1997.

Vanderwood, Paul. *Disorder and Progress: Bandits, Police, and Mexican Development.* 2nd ed. Wilmington, DE: Scholarly Resources, 1992.

Vaughan, Mary Kay. *The State, Education, and Social Class in Mexico, 1880–1924.* DeKalb: Northern Illinois University Press, 1982.

Vaughan, Mary Kay. *Cultural Politics in Revolution: Teachers, Peasants, and Schools in Mexico, 1930–1940.* Tucson: University of Arizona Press, 1997.

Voss, Stuart F. *On the Periphery of Nineteenth-Century Mexico: Sonora and Sinaloa, 1810–1877.* Tucson: University of Arizona Press, 1982.

Womack, John. *Zapata and the Mexican Revolution.* New York: Knopf, 1968.

Wood, Andrew G. *Revolution in the Street: Women, Workers, and Urban Protest in Veracruz, 1870–1927.* Wilmington, DE: Scholarly Resources, 2001.

Wood, Andrew G. "Adalberto Tejeda of Veracruz." In *State Governors in the Mexican Revolution, 1910: Portraits in Courage, Conflict, and Corruption*, ed. Jürgen Buchenau and William H. Beezley. Lanham, MD: Rowman Littlefield, 2009.

Sources on the World Wide Web

Almada Bay, Ignacio. "Alvaro Obregón Salido: Nuevos datos y nuevas interpretaciones." http://www.colson.edu.mx/historia/ialmada/inherm-obreg%F3n.pdf (accessed Nov. 21, 2005).

Index

Illustrations and maps are indexed separately, thus: 133*ill.*, 26*m*. Relatives of Obregón are indicated as, for example: Salido, Cenobia (mother of AO).

The Last Caudillo: Alvaro Obregón and the Mexican Revolution. Jürgen Buchenau
© 2011 Jürgen Buchenau

France, influence on Mexican politics, 16, 18, 20–1
Fronteras, 55–6
Fuegos fatuos (poem), 36

Gadsden Purchase (1853), 15
Gándara, Manuel María, 23–4
Garbanzo League, 95–6
Garrido Canabal, Tomás, 118
Garrido, Tomás, 144–5
Gaxiola, Ignacio P., 140, 141
Gómez, Arnulfo, 132, 156–7, 158
González, Abrahám, 48, 59
González Garza, Pablo, 60, 63, 64, 80, 88, 98, 106
González Salas, José, 48
Gruening, Ernest, 117, 125, 166
Guadalupe, Plan of, 60–1
Guajardo, Jesús, 98
Gutiérrez, Eulalio, 72, 74
Guzmán, Martín Luis, 62–3

Hall, Linda, 63
Harding, Warren G., 113, 127
Headless Rebellion, 131–6
Henderson, Timothy, 120
Hermosillo, 42–3
Hernández, José Guadalupe Zuno, 144
heroes (popular idols), 3–4, 165–6
Hill, Benjamín G. (nephew of AO), 42, 59, 61, 67, 68, 103–4, 114
  death, 115
history
  colonial period, 11–12, 22–3, 32–3
  Revolution *see* Mexican Revolution
  US-Mexican War (1846–1848), 15
  Wars of Independence (1810–1821), 12, 13, 14
honor, 69–70
House of the World's Worker *see* Casa del Obrero Mundial (COM)
Huatabampo, 31, 37–9, 44–6
Huerta, Adolfo de la, 42, 105, 151
  political career, 94–5, 99, 107, 108–9, 114, 115, 126–8

relationship with Obregón, 44–5, 109, 127–8, 129–30, 131
Huerta, Victoriano, 2, 52–3, 54, 58–9, 64

Ibáñez, Blasco, 32, 82, 104
Iguala, Plan de, 14
indigenous peoples, 16, 17, 23–4, 28, 151–2
  elections of 1911, 44, 46
  and land reform, 75–6, 120–1
  military service, 49, 60
  industrial action (strikes), 28–9, 123
  workers' rights, 90–1, 121, 122
infrastructure, 18, 24, 25, 27, 19*m.*, 26*m.*
intellectuals, support for revolution, 103, 124–5
International Committee of Bankers, 126–7, 130–1
irrigation, 38, 121, 142
Iturbide, Agustín de, 12–13
Izábal, Rafael, 27

Juárez, Benito, 16, 17, 18

Katz, Friedrich, 67, 73
Kellogg, Frank B., 149
Kloss, Maximiliano, 54, 55
Knight, Alan, 62, 102
Krauze, Enrique, 36, 153

labor organizations, 65, 77, 101–3, 121–2, 146
land reform, 47, 75–6, 119–21, 133, 151–2, 154, 156
land tenure, 2, 25
leadership styles, 3, 46, 63, 108
  caudillos *see* caudillos
  definition, 5–6
  dictatorships, 17–18
  emperors, 16–17
  European influence on, 16–17, 18, 20–1
  and honor, 69–70
  separation of powers, 74–5, 83–4, 104
León, Battle of (1915), 79–80, 80*ill.*
León, Luis L., 150, 171